The Conscientious Objector's Wife

Also published by Handheld Press

HANDHELD CLASSICS
1 *What Might Have Been: The Story of a Social War* by Ernest Bramah
2 *The Runagates Club* by John Buchan
3 *Desire* by Una L Silberrad
4 *Vocations* by Gerald O'Donovan

HANDHELD RESEARCH
1 *The Akeing Heart: Letters between Sylvia Townsend Warner, Valentine Ackland and Elizabeth Wade White* by Peter Haring Judd

The Conscientious Objector's Wife

Letters between Frank & Lucy Sunderland,
1916–1919

Edited by Kate Macdonald

Handheld Press

Handheld Research 2

First published in the UK in 2018 by Handheld Press Ltd.
72 Warminster Road, Bath BA2 6RU
www.handheldpress.co.uk

Copyright of the Notes and Introduction © Kate Macdonald
Copyright of the Letters © The Descendants of Frank and Lucy Sunderland

All rights reserved. No part of this publication may be reproduced, stored in or introduced into a retrieval system, or transmitted, in any form, or by any means (electronic, mechanical, photocopying, recording or otherwise) without the prior written permission of the publisher.

The moral rights of the authors have been asserted.

ISBN 978-1-9998813-6-8

1 2 3 4 5 6 7 8 9

Series design by Nadja Guggi and typeset in Open Sans.

Printed and bound in Great Britain by TJ International, Padstow.

Front cover: Chrissie, Dora, Morris and Lucy Sunderland, with Morris in 'the Motor', June 1917.
© The Descendants of Frank and Lucy Sunderland

Contents

Acknowledgements	vi
List of Figures	vii
Introduction	ix
Further Reading	xxvi
1. From Letchworth to Wandsworth Prison, November 1916 to February 1917	1
2. In Wandsworth Prison and Bedford Prison, April to August 1917	42
3. 'I never wanted your presence more than now', August 1917 to March 1918	75
4. 'The countryside is glorious', April to August 1918	136
5. 'These last days are the most trying', August 1918 to April 1919	200
Index	305

Acknowledgements

The editor is grateful to Elizabeth and Tom Heydeman, Julia Prescott, Robert Sunderland, and the other descendants of Frank and Lucy Sunderland, for their work in retyping their grandparents' letters, for their assistance in identifying individuals and places, and for permission to publish the edited letters. She is also grateful for Rebecca Wynter's useful suggestions, and Tanya Izzard's list of corrections discovered while making the index.

List of Figures

1. Dora and Chrissie Sunderland, March 1918.
2. Lucy and Morris Sunderland, March 1918.
3. Frank in the uniform of the City of London Volunteers.
4. Frank and Lucy's wedding photograph, 1904.
5. Letter-writing instructions, Wandsworth prison.
6. Lucy's message on the 1917 family photo to Frank.
7. Chrissie, Dora, Morris and Lucy, June 1917.
8. Noel Palmer, Katie, Morris, Dora, Frank, Chrissie and Lucy, Letchworth 1919.

Kate Macdonald is a literary historian, and has published widely on British publishing and print history of the First World War. After teaching English literature at Ghent University and at the University of Reading, she returned to her former career of publishing to establish Handheld Press. She researches the business relationships between twentieth-century authors and their publishers.

Introduction

BY KATE MACDONALD

Background

Traditional histories of the First World War tend to exclude women writers in favour of male-authored literature from the trenches, which helps to restrict public understanding of the war to the soldier's perspective. The literary historian Margaret Higonnet notes that 'An emphasis on the firing line, which distinguishes the masculine battlefront from the feminine home front, has diverted attention from the history of women's experience of war'.[1] This edited collection of First World War letters fits into this reframing of the literature of war, and will, I hope, encourage a more complete understanding of the effects of war on the family unit, and on the burdens shouldered by women left to bring up their families alone.

Frank and Lucy Sunderland were English pacifists and fervent believers in Labour politics and the Garden City movement. They had moved to Letchworth from London for their children's health,[2] and were enthusiastic supporters of this community, which was designed for social and environmental harmony. After Frank was imprisoned for his conscientious objection to military service, Lucy worked to support their family of three children by collecting insurance premiums and taking in sewing. The predominantly pacifist and Quaker community in Letchworth supported them during their ordeal, in contrast to the attitudes of their families in London, who viewed Frank's stance as unpatriotic. Frank and Lucy wrote to each other as often as the law permitted, from his first arrest in November 1916 until his release in April 1919. Lucy's letters are rare surviving evidence of a working-class woman's wartime experience in her own words.

As well as testifying to their love and loyalty to each other, the letters show how their shared beliefs upheld the couple through two and a half years of separation, thinking through how a better future for all in a more equal society could be achieved. The letters record their daily lives,

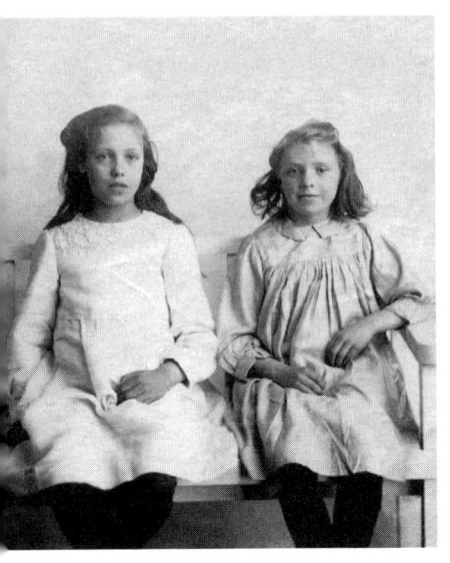

1. Dora and Chrissie Sunderland, March 1918.
2. Lucy and her son Morris Sunderland, March 1918

the increasing hardships of war on the Home Front, how Lucy began to involve herself more in politics during the war, and contemporary events. Lucy's nascent feminism was inspired by attending adult education classes and public talks by Sylvia Pankhurst and other feminist campaigners. She gained self-confidence by finding herself able to support her husband and family financially and emotionally, though the strains were hard. Her increasing involvement in civic and local organisation helped her cope with the stress of separation, and strengthened the networks that supported her during the frightening outbreak of scarlet fever in their family, and her mother's sudden death. Frank maintained his psychological equilibrium by enlarging his political and theological knowledge through extensive reading and cell discussions.

Frank was an example of the 'worthy' conscientious objector (CO), an older man of tested principles who was respected by the authorities for his beliefs.[3] The Military Service Act of 2 January 1916 came into force on 2 March, introducing conscription for unmarried men aged between 18 and 41 (there were some exemptions). A second Act in May 1916 extended conscription to all married men. A 'conscience clause' was included in the original Act, after lobbying by the Quakers and the No Conscription Fellowship. The legal historian Lois Bibbings notes that:

> those with a conscientious objection to military service could be granted various forms of exemption from conscription by (successfully) applying to a tribunal system [...] The most limited form of exemption allowed for recognised objectors to be enlisted into the military but provided that they were only required to undertake non-combatant work in the Non-Combatant Corps (partial exemption) [...] Alternative service exempted men from the military on the condition that they undertake or continue to be employed in work that was deemed to be acceptable and of national importance (conditional exemption).[4]

Frank had left school at the minimum age but continued to read voraciously, educating himself in the classic fashion of an autodidact for the period. He and Lucy married in 1904. He served in the City of London Volunteers as a young man and was listed in the 1911 Census as an iron machinist for the Midland Railway. He later became a cabinet maker and, after the war, a picture framer and smallholder.[5] His granddaughter Julia Prescott recalls that Frank was a passionate man, and an idealist, but his sense of humour was not always understood by Lucy. His daughter Dora spoke of him as being great fun and how he enjoyed the company of young people. It is clear in the letters that Letchworth people liked him. But he also had a volatile character, swinging up and down.[6] Frank's grandson Robert Sunderland describes Frank as a 'driven, self-taught man who was never afraid to voice his opinion [... and was later in life] the only socialist in a Tory village'.[7]

When war broke out in 1914, Frank had evolved his politics, and his stance on fighting as a means to end conflict, in line with his Christian faith. He had been a Presbyterian, but he asked for a Quaker chaplain on entering prison, and occasionally mentions preaching himself, an extension of the ad hoc lectures that he would deliver

3. Frank in the uniform of the City of London Volunteers.
4. Frank and Lucy's wedding photograph, 1904.

to his cell-mates.[8] Frank believed in a universal brotherhood of men and women, which gave him the strength of purpose to resist incorporation into the British armed services. From evidence in the letters it is likely that he was an adherent to, if not a member of, the No Conscription Fellowship. This British organisation had been founded in November 1914 when there was no sign that the war would end soon or by negotiation. The philosopher Bertrand Russell and the Labour politician Fenner Brockway were among its leaders, and both are mentioned in the Sunderlands' letters, since Frank and Lucy kept themselves informed about the treatment of other pacifists by the authorities. Frank became an 'absolutist' conscientious objector, refusing even to undertake work that would free another man for the army. However, he did not receive 'absolute exemption' at any of the military tribunals to which he appealed.[9]

The letters are remarkable for the almost complete absence of any discussion of the war itself, of its battles or its notable events. This may have been due to Frank and Lucy's awareness of the Censor (passing on information likely to demoralise the armed forces or the population in general was restricted closely by the Defence of the Realm Acts, enforced throughout the war), and the likelihood of their letters being monitored as they went into and out of the prison system.[10] Discussion of national events, for instance the elections, only becomes detailed towards the end of the war.

Some impressions of the strains of the war can be discerned. Lucy's letter of 9 October 1918, about a man of 50 due to appear before the military tribunal, reminds us that the younger men had already gone, and that the male population of Britain was involved in the war to such an extent that the reserves of the older generations were now being tapped. This would have increased social pressure on those men opposed to serving at all. Some of the other Hertfordshire men that Frank and Lucy were in touch with shared Frank's absolutist stance, but many took up the offers of alternative service from the authorities.

Letchworth was probably the best community in Britain in which to be a conscientious objector. It is likely that living there, in a community mostly sympathetic to pacifist beliefs, made Lucy's life much easier than it would have been had she lived elsewhere. Letchworth was the first of the Garden Cities in Britain, 'a link between the nineteenth century's search for the improvement of social conditions and the twentieth century's political hope of "a new collective consciousness" in a new space [...] the garden city was meant to be as much a social as a moral experiment, one which not only catered better for the physical needs of society but also promoted "a step forward on the moral, the intellectual and, let us hope, on the spiritual plane"'.[11]

Planning for the Garden Cities began at the very end of the nineteenth century, when Ebenezer Howard and his colleagues, several of them Quakers, set up the Garden City Association, and a Company to issue shares to help fund its development. Letchworth was designed as a model town built on former agricultural land in Hertfordshire, the county due north of London. 'The main object of the Company will be to attract manufacturers and their workpeople from crowded centres': many of these manufacturers would later take on war work, a variation from Letchworth's largely pacifist community.[12] W H Smith had a large printing and bookbinding works there, 'the greatest centre of the Firm's activities outside London'. One local inhabitant reported

xiii

in 1908 that 'a few years ago it was the fashion to laugh at Letchworth, and to describe the few inhabitants as "cranks", but a place that has grown from 400 to nearly 6000 inhabitants in a little over three years shows that if the organisers are "cranks" the "cranks" are excellent men of business'.[13]

The Sunderland family participated in the many clubs and societies in Letchworth during the war years, following Independent Labour Party (ILP) politics, organising and participating in adult education classes (the 'Adult School', held at the Skittles temperance inn), and supporting the expansion of the Garden City movement, hoping to buy shares in the venture and participate fully as cooperative members. Frank began learning Esperanto while in prison, and Lucy tried to follow Dora's Esperanto lessons from school; both expecting that this newly created universal language would enable them to travel abroad after the war.

Lucy's descriptions of her Letchworth social circle show that all the men are COs or in reserved occupations. There is hardly a serviceman in the Sunderlands' extended network of friends, and the letters make no mention of the war wounded or of service families, except when Lucy is looking for a house after the war. This sense of enclosure, or separation, indicates the solidity of the network of Quakers and other Christian and politically active friends who supported Lucy during her struggle to maintain a normal life for her children, and to keep their home ready for Frank's return. The sheer number of public meetings and talks that Lucy attended on the themes of socialism, pacifism and the anti-war movement reflect what a nexus Letchworth was for this strand of activism.

One of the very few records of Letchworth's pacifist community in popular culture is in John Buchan's third Richard Hannay novel, *Mr Standfast* (1919), written when Buchan was the British government's Director of Information. He depicted 'Biggleswick' as one of a series of settings for German spy activity during the war, but of which the Garden City inhabitants are innocent. His depiction respected the 'cranks', who held firmly to their own views, and had something to teach the rather over-confident Hannay in how to argue an unpopular position. Frank's confidence in engaging with his cellmates in discussion, on any subjects, and Lucy's increasing interest in attending political meetings, and recounting their themes to Frank in her letters, indicate the Letchworth atmosphere of learning and debate that Buchan tried to satirise.

Frank's ordeal

On 4 November 1916, Frank, then aged 37, travelled by train with some Letchworth constables to Hitchin police station, where he was arrested for not accepting military service under the Military Service Act 1916. He was court-martialled as an absentee on 13 November, classed as an 'absolutist' conscientious objector, and on 15 November was sentenced to six months hard labour, commuted to two months' imprisonment at Wormwood Scrubs.[14] His sentence was extended by further court martials: at Northampton on 31 January 1917 (one year's hard labour at Wormwood Scrubs), and at Bedford on 13 August (two years hard labour).[15]

Quaker historian Rebecca Wynter notes that 'Frank could have taken up alternative service not associated with the military or munitions in the Friends' Ambulance Unit's General Service Section. He could have joined the Home Office Scheme to remove himself from prison (being diverted to a work camp, such as that at Princetown)'.[16] Refusing these options indicate the strength of Frank's beliefs, and his courage in making an absolutist stand.

The family was not well off. Frank earned most of the family income by collecting insurance premiums, and Lucy, who had run her own dress-making business with her sister Katie before her marriage, had been taking in sewing as work she could do with young children at home.[17] Dora was then aged nine, Chrissie was seven and Morris was five. Frank's family did not support his position, though they were not unfriendly, but Lucy's father was unsympathetic. Frank was anxious for Lucy to take on his insurance collection accounts to keep the Letchworth agency of Britannia Insurance open. His manager Mr Hancox, though not in agreement with Frank's stance, was very willing to help Lucy set herself up as a new employee. Within three days of Frank's arrest Lucy was writing saucily: 'Got on all right with work, Lloyds and everyone. Made out sheet and sent to Hancox. Shall quite cut you out yet.'[18] But taking over her husband's familiar routines could be unexpectedly heart-rending: 'I made up the Britannia sheet all right, I hope, but [...] I could not remember at all how you made the little slips out and I felt bad while doing it. The memory of you doing it every Wed, for so long, was too much for me'.[19]

Lucy's endurance

Despite Frank's prolonged absence Lucy stoutly maintained her usual routines, and most of her community in Letchworth were generous. They offered Lucy sewing work, and made sure she and the children were supported. Her faith in the rightness of Frank's actions sustained her, and she was assiduous in sending Frank food parcels for his vegetarian diet, books, candles and clean clothes when she could, although prison meals meant that he soon reverted to eating meat. She kept hens, which added significantly to the family's diet, and their income. From her letters we can see that local egg prices rose in the war from under 2½d to 7d each before being controlled at 5½d and eventually falling to 3d.[20] In March 1919, for example, Lucy reports that she had sold over 28/- of eggs (twenty-eight shillings) in three months, about £60 in 2017 terms, which could have paid for new shoes and clothes for the children.

Her normal activities centred around attending the evening classes at the Letchworth Adult School, and by the end of 1917 she was running its committee. She kept herself and Frank informed about the planning for the next New Town to be built on rationalist principles, which would become Welwyn Garden City after the war. She was irritated by the pro-war teachings in their Church of England parish, and attended Letchworth Quaker Meeting with the children.

But Lucy's health was undermined by the strain of running her home alone, and keeping up Frank's spirits as well as her own. She and the children caught illnesses in rotation, and after six months of solo parenting she was exhausted. By the summer of 1917 Chrissie was suffering from skin infections, Morris had a recurring cough, and Lucy's teeth were troubling her. Scarlet fever broke out, but due to restrictions on how often COs could receive and write letters Frank did not know about the hospitalisation of his children, and was not able to write to Lucy, until September.

Lucy was very conscious of her own family's safety in London during the bombing raids. The bombs that hit London from Zeppelins and Gotha aircraft in October 1917 were heard in Letchworth, though the children slept through the noise. Lucy's sister Katie came to stay for some respite later that month, and four months later their mother came, driven out of London by the terrible air-raids of February 1918. Mrs Clifton stayed with Lucy for a month, and died there unexpectedly on a Saturday afternoon, from complications from bronchitis.

Her mother's death was a terrible event in Lucy's life, and her letters show her in a stunned state, forcing herself to keep going as there was no-one to relieve her. Her account of the relentless grind of looking after herself and her children, enduring her bereavement, and all the time hoping for Frank's release, would have been gruelling enough in its cumulative details, without wartime conditions and shortages as well. The fear of the air-raids, only sixty miles away over London, and their perpetual ill health, persuaded Lucy to decide that she and the children must leave Letchworth, if only for a few months. In April she arranged to sublet the bungalow, and took the children to Bedford prison to see Frank before their departure for Barnstaple in Devon, where she had taken rooms.

Lucy was fortunate to leave Letchworth when she did: in June she wrote to Frank that the Spanish influenza epidemic had affected six hundred people in the town. Given their low resistance to infection, all four could have succumbed to the virus, had they stayed in Letchworth. She reported later that her cousin Marie had died in the epidemic, after battling to care for her children in the absence of her soldier husband.

The Devon countryside and the plentiful food had a powerful restorative effect on them all. Lucy began to write to Frank about her surroundings, rather than the worries of work and the children's health. Her letters become lyrical, responding to the natural beauty around her, and the joy of seeing her children healthy and happy. She began to take an interest in agricultural conditions, and enjoyed reading Thoreau's classic work *Walden*, on simple living in natural surroundings. Her letters spoke hopefully of when Frank would be free, when the war would be over, and how the new future could be created at last, following modern principles of cooperation and equality. Women's roles in this future were much on her mind, as she spent time thinking how daily life could be made easier for women and mothers.

By mid-August 1918 Lucy and the children had returned to Letchworth, and their friend Noel Palmer had become their lodger, with his goat. She was plunged back into housekeeping and making ends meet with her insurance collecting. Her letters are full of Labour Party and trade union news, with Letchworth's evening meetings full of agitation. She had reluctantly taken in a new lodger who had nowhere to live, a Belgian girl working locally in munitions, showing that the need for a women's hostel for war workers was becoming acute. Serbs were rumoured to be arriving for a new shells factory, but by 3 November Lucy was writing confidently that peace was expected daily. Peace was declared on 11 November, and on 14 November the Peace celebrations were still going on. Lucy wrote of her grief at all the death, the loss, the sorrow while the rest of the country was rejoicing, and reported being asked continually when Frank would be coming home. They would have to wait for five more months.

With the end of the war, everybody expected normality to return immediately. Lucy was realising that the much hoped-for new Garden City would be some time in the making, so she was looking for a bigger house to rent, as well as making plans to move to Normandy, a village near Guildford, where Noel Palmer had offered Frank work on a new fruit farm. Food was still scarce, and not very good quality, and Lucy's neuralgia, rheumatism and sciatica all returned together in the cold weather. The local results in the 1918 general election disappointed her further, since Labour and ILP candidates did not do as well as she had hoped. She was worried about rumours that COs would be sent to France to work on reconstruction for four years. She and the girls were ill again, fuel was expensive and scarce, and she was frustrated by being unable to rent a house, wondering if being a CO's wife had affected her chances. For the first time her letters to Frank became exasperated.

Vigour had returned to Lucy by March 1919, as she was swept up in the excitement of new elections and meetings to remonstrate about the suffering in countries overseas. She wrote excitedly to Frank about international Labour politics and the success of local and London candidates. The mood of their letters in the early post-war years is hopeful, that the new world might truly be around the corner, and that all that they had both suffered during Frank's imprisonment could be forgotten when they were reunited, to work for a reconstructed society.

Letters as history

The subject of these letters switches continually between the personal, the political, and the international. Frank and Lucy saw themselves as part of a national community with international responsibilities, and the letters show Lucy growing increasingly confident as she explored her own contribution, and her own opinions for the reconstruction and development of society. This collection echoes what Margaret Higonnet says about the importance of variety in studying the evidence of wartime experience: that 'if we do not examine women's roles in the mobilization for war, resistance to war, and demobilization and recovery, we will understand the processes involved in war itself incompletely'.[22] Lucy Sunderland was part of a small community—largely women—resisting militarism on the Home Front, while the male pacifists were imprisoned or assigned to non-military service, and is a valuable witness to their motivations and aspirations.

Women's lives are notoriously under-recorded in history, especially from periods and class strata where literacy, and letter-writing, are irrelevant to the business of running a home and a family and earning a living. If the war had not happened, we would never have heard of the Sunderlands. They were a working-class family with slightly unusual social and political preferences, though in line with the English tradition of working-class radicalism. They had no other reason to be recorded in history, had the war not happened. Frank was principled enough and stubbornly resolute enough to resist social pressure about 'doing his bit' by not joining the army (in his case, rejoining, since he had served in the London Volunteers for some years in his youth). He withstood this for two years, before making his act of public resistance in giving himself up to the police and the military authorities, and served years in prison for refusing to fight and kill men he did not know but whom he regarded as brothers.

Lucy's predicament was planned, since she and Frank had agreed that he would take this step, but she clearly did not expect him to be in prison for so long — how could anyone know how long the war would last? The letters show her first responding to the shock of being a single parent, a lone mother without her husband and best friend on whom she had depended since their marriage, and then settling down for the long term. Her sturdy resilience turned, of necessity, to endurance, as the strains of running the home, earning enough for the four of them to eat, maintaining her social networks, and trying to improve her understanding of ideas and current events, began to wear her down.

When read in terms of a continuous record of Home Front morale, Lucy's letters are instantly recognisable in their daily details, but also profoundly valuable as a record of daily life in wartime conditions: when food shortages began, when rationing began to bite, what it was like to hear the air raids over London, how her locally-generated prejudice against Belgian refugees in general turned to concern and solidarity when she was presented with a vulnerable factory worker without digs. Food historians will find much primary evidence in the letters for vegetarian shopping, cooking and dietary awareness during the war. Quaker historians will find material about Letchworth life as a Quaker and pacifist community. War historians, more generally, will find these letters important as a record of the rich detail of civilian life, which is, ultimately, their main appeal. The Sunderlands lived very familiar lives, making this extract from their lives a human story of value to us all.

Afterword

After his last letter from prison, 7 April 1919, Frank was released, and worked for a time in Noel Palmer's fruit farm in Normandy, Surrey, as part of his recovery. Morris Sunderland's son Robert, who was brought up by his grandparents due to his mother's ill-health, recalls Frank telling him that:

> he was funded by the likes of the Webbs and George Bernard Shaw[23] to set up a picture-framing business in The Wynd, Letchworth [...] Ironically, the picture-framing business did quite

well as there was considerable demand for elaborate framed photographs of loved ones lost in the War.[24]

Frank and Lucy bought a plot of land in Cashio Lane, Letchworth and he physically built their new house 'Applegarth'. Sydney Palmer and family were now living in Langholme around the corner in Croft Lane. The gardens joined and the children mingled. In 1925 Dora became engaged to Sydney's son William; they married in 1927. In the later 1920s the Sunderlands could no longer make ends meet despite taking in lodgers. The house, no longer affordable, was let for a time. They later sold Applegarth, moving to Preston, a village seven miles south-west of Letchworth, in 1934. There they lived in an early eighteenth-century cottage called The Wilderness with about three acres. There they grew fruit and vegetables and kept goats and hens, and Lucy created a beautiful flower garden. Their grandchildren were welcomed on visits and enjoyed playing there. Frank died in 1956, aged 77, and was cremated. Lucy survived him by five years, dying at the age of 83, and is buried in the churchyard at St Martin's in Preston.

Frank and Lucy kept their wartime letters, and occasionally, while their grandson Robert was living with them, he was allowed to read them. After Lucy's death the letters were stored by Morris and his second wife, Barbara. Later most were passed to Dora Palmer, whose husband, William, gave photocopies to their daughters. Dora's daughter Julia Prescott, son-in-law Tom Heydeman and granddaughter Lucy Heydeman typed and collated the letters. They were hard to read, closely written, and with fading writing on poor quality paper. This went on for many years as a family project, with the intention of publication should any opportunity for this arise.

I became friends with the Heydemans through our Quaker connections, and as I had published some research on the First World War, they asked me if I would like to read the letters. Naturally I was delighted to do so: the opportunity to work on a large and unstudied collection of letters from a historically significant period is a rare occurrence in a scholar's life. I saw immediately that with some careful editing they would make a fascinating book. Other publishers agreed with me, but they wanted me to extend the project, perhaps to write a book on the history of all the wives of conscientious objectors during the war, or on the histories of all the Hertfordshire COs. These suggestions did not give Frank and Lucy's letters the centrality they deserved, as a continuous, cumulative narrative. The power of their letters is in the richness of their social and historical detail, and the texture of daily life that is so often missing from histories of the war.

After several years of looking for a publisher who would agree with me on the best way to publish the letters, I had by then returned to my earlier, pre-academic profession of publishing myself, and had set up Handheld Press. *The Conscientious Objector's Wife* was high on my list of books that I wanted to publish, and I was warmly encouraged by the family to do so.

Note on this edition

For this edition of the letters, around 93,000 words were edited out from the originals, so that this text constitutes a little over half of the complete set (an edition of the complete letters has been published for the family's private use). The omissions mainly consist of the serial stories Frank invented and wrote in his letters to the children, local news of neighbours, abbreviated remarks on their wider family, Frank's written 'lectures' to Lucy from 19 November 1917 relating to his reading programme and her questions, most of the letters between the children and Frank, and most of Lucy's verbatim reports of lectures that she had attended.

Punctuation and spelling have been silently corrected. Text in [square brackets] signifies a clarification, such as [*Labour Leader*] where the original had 'L L'; or suggesting a word that makes sense in the context but was omitted, where this is needed to clarify meaning. Square brackets enclosing an ellipsis [...] indicate where text has been cut from the original letter, to distinguish this from an ordinary ellipsis in the original.

Deciding whether to present the explanatory notes as footnotes or endnotes was a problem. Footnotes are undeniably intrusive to the layout of the page, especially when they carry a lot of necessary information. But the notes would look even worse interpolated within the text of the letters, and would be much less useful as endnotes, at the end of the book. Accordingly, the notes for this Introduction have been set as endnotes whereas the notes for the letters have been given as footnotes to the pages holding the points they explain. I hope that their usefulness will compensate for some occasional awkwardness in page layout.

Most of the personal names in the letters have been identified where they are known, but readers are asked to assume that the unexplained names were the Sunderlands' many friends and neighbours.

Endnotes

1. Margaret R Higonnet, *Lines of Fire: Women Writers of World War I* (Plume 1999), xx.

2. Information from Tom and Elizabeth Heydeman to KM, October 2017, and Julia Prescott to KM, 25 February 2018.

3. Lois Bibbings, *Telling Tales About Men. Conceptions of Conscientious Objectors to Military Service During the First World War* (Manchester University Press 2009), 176.

4. Bibbings 2009, 28–29.

5. Information from Julia Prescott to KM, 25 February 2018.

6. Information from Julia Prescott to KM, 25 February 2018.

7. Information from Robert Sunderland to KM, 29 January 2018.

8. Information from Julia Prescott to KM, 25 February 2018.

9. 'Absolute exemption completely absolved men from the terms of the legislation. However, some tribunals were reluctant to grant any exemption or more than partial exemption and a number disputed whether conditional exemption or absolute exemption was available in cases of conscience.' Bibbings 2009, 29.

10   The Defence of the Realm Acts were first passed in August 1914, and updated throughout the war to maintain government control of the media and censorship (see Lucy's letter of 16 November 1917, for example).

11   Christoph Ehland, 'The spy-scattered landscape of modernity in John Buchan's *Mr Standfast*', in *John Buchan and the Idea of Modernity*, eds Kate Macdonald and Nathan Waddell (Pickering & Chatto 2013), 111–123, 116–17; citing Ebenezer Howard, 'Our First Garden City', *Saint George. A National Review Dealing With Literature, Art, and Social Questions in a Broad and Progressive Sp*irit 7:27 (July 1904), 170–88, 177.

12   Howard 1904, 173–75.

13   Anon, 'The Letchworth Picnic', *The Newsbasket (The WHS Monthly Journal) A Miscellany of News and Progress Items and Matters of Interest to the Staff of W H Smith & Son* 6:1 (June 1908), 22–25, 22.

14   Wormwood Scrubs was a men's prison in west London, though Frank does not describe having done any work that could be described as hard labour.

15   Information from Cyril Pearce, *Pearce Register of British World War One Conscientious Objectors*, hosted by the Imperial War Museum at http://blog.livesofthefirstworldwar.org/conscientious-objectors-in-the-first-world-war accessed 7 February 2018.

16   Information from Rebecca Wynter to KM, 2 April 2018. The Home Office Scheme was designed to relieve prisons of conscientious objectors by offering work of 'national importance' to those convicted COs deemed to be genuine, instead of military service. Such work was carried out at Dyce in Aberdeenshire, and at Dartmoor Prison, Princetown, Devon, and was similar to that performed by convicted criminals. Some men died at both sites from ill-health and overwork, yet others, presumably young and fit, found the work almost congenial: the work ranged from hard labour to sewing mail bags. For those who refused to support the war in any way, such work was a way of allowing another man to join up, and was a de facto military service in its own right.

17 Information from Robert Sunderland to KM, 29 January 2018.

18 LS to FS, 8 November 1916.

19 LS to FS, 9 November 1916.

20 Pre-metric British coinage was in pounds, shillings and pence, often referred to as LSD, from their abbreviations of l (pounds, derived from the Latin for pound, libra), s (shillings) and d (the pennies, the d apparently derived from the Roman denarius). Six shillings and fivepence, for example, was written: 6/5.

21 Jerry White, *Zeppelin Nights. London in the First World War* (Vintage 2015), 218–19.

22 Higonnet 1999, xxi.

23 Sydney and Beatrice Webb were leading socialists, founders of the Fabian Society, and social reformers. The playwright and contrarian George Bernard Shaw, also a socialist and Fabian, made a point of helping individuals of whose actions he approved.

24 Information from Robert Sunderland to KM, 29 January 2018.

25 Philip Wray, *A History of Preston in Hertfordshire*, http://www.prestonherts.co.uk/page45.html accessed 7 April 2018.

26 Information from Julia Prescott and Robert Sunderland, 8 and 12 April 2018

27 Information from Robert Sunderland to KM, 26 January 2018.

Further Reading

All works cited in the Introduction and notes are listed here. Some but not all of the books that Frank and Lucy reported reading are also given here.

Anon, 'The Letchworth Picnic', *The Newsbasket* (*The WHS Monthly Journal*) *A Miscellany of News and Progress Items and Matters of Interest to the Staff of W H Smith & Son* 6:1 (June 1908), 22–25.

Lois Bibbings, *Telling Tales About Men. Conceptions of Conscientious Objectors to Military Service During the First World War* (Manchester University Press 2009).

Christoph Ehland, 'The spy-scattered landscape of modernity in John Buchan's Mr Standfast', in *John Buchan and the Idea of Modernity*, eds Kate Macdonald and Nathan Waddell (Pickering & Chatto 2013), 111–23.

Margaret R Higonnet, *Lines of Fire: Women Writers of World War I* (Plume 1999).

Richard Hoare ed., *John Hoare. A Pacifist's Progress. Papers from the First World War* (Sessions Book Trust 1998).

Victor Horsley and Mary D Sturge, *Alcohol and the Human Body* (Macmillian 1909).

Ebenezer Howard, 'Our First Garden City', *Saint George. A National Review Dealing With Literature, Art, and Social Questions in a Broad and Progressive Spirit* 7:27 (July 1904), 170–88.

Jack London's *The Valley of the Moon* (1913, Thomas Nelson & Son 1917).

Rodney Lowe, 'The failure of consensus in Britain: The National Industrial Conference, 1919–1921', *The Historical Journal* 21 (1978), 649–675.

Ramsay MacDonald, *Margaret Ethel MacDonald* (Hodder and Stoughton 1913).

Cyril Pearce, *Pearce Register of British World War One Conscientious Objectors*, hosted by the Imperial War Museum at http://blog.livesofthefirstworldwar.org/conscientious-objectors-in-the-first-world-war

Frances Swiney, *The Awakening of Women* (William Reeves 1905, 2nd edition).

Jerry White, *Zeppelin Nights. London in the First World War* (Vintage 2015).

Richard Whiteing, *No 5 John Street* (J M Dent & Son 1899)

Philip Wray, *A History of Preston in Hertfordshire*, http://www.prestonherts.co.uk/page45.html accessed 7 April 2018.

1. From Letchworth to Wandsworth Prison, November 1916 to February 1917

Barrack Room, Bedford
November 4th 1916

Dear Wifey

I'm again in the Barrack room and have to see the Colonel in the morning then back to him for decision. Until then I am making the best of things. Cheer up darling and try and feel that I am doing the best I can. I feel unable to write a long letter so you must put up with a short one.

Lots of love and kisses for the kiddies.

Yours ever
Frank

Bedford Barracks
November 5th 1916

Dearest Wife

Am sitting down to write you a graphic account of my doings for the last 24 hours. I had a pleasant hour at Letchworth Police station talking to the constables and Mr Warren and then we caught the 10.19 to Hitchin. Mrs Harding was at the station and gave me a cheery word as a send-off. Randolph was also there and he travelled to Hitchin with us.[1] At Hitchin Mrs Taylor (a Friend)[2] met us and Mrs Price introduced her. She is a cousin I think of Rowntree Gillett[3] and she told me her husband had been to Devonshire House where a gathering of COs on furlough was held. He said it was a most inspiring meeting and R Gillett was there.

We arrived at Hitchin where I was duly searched etc and then I was allowed to take exercise in a yard about 10 yards by 6 surrounded by four walls 14 ft high. A few dead leaves scattered about gave it a human touch so to speak and I ate an apple and the nuts[4] you gave me and felt refreshed. At twelve o'clock I was taken into the Superintendent's office and charged with being an absentee.[5] They were all awfully kind to me and the Magistrate refused to fine me because I was so reasonable … I was handed over to a military escort and taken to the recruiting office. The Sergeant was a decent fellow and we had a chat together. The Colonel also had a long chat with me but of course I failed to convince him that our attitude is the right one. However, we parted friends and I came to Bedford by the 2.48.

Mrs Price and Mr and Mrs Taylor met me at the station and I went and had some coffee with them. I also met Mr Clarke (another of our COs)

1   Letchworth is four miles from Hitchin; Hitchin is seventeen miles from Bedford. These are small towns in Hertfordshire, north of London.

2   Where 'Friend' is capitalised, this denotes a Quaker, a member of the Religious Society of Friends, who were numerous as a community in Letchworth.

3   Joseph Rowntree Gillett (1874–1940), a prominent Quaker prison visitor.

4   Frank and Lucy were vegetarian, a lifestyle choice that had been popularly associated with 'cranks' and free-thinkers before the war (see H G Wells' 1909 novel *Ann Veronica* for an example of this). Wartime food shortages, then rationing, and rising prices made vegetarianism more mainstream. But Frank had to revert to meat-eating while in prison to ensure that he had enough to eat.

5   Frank was deemed by law to be already in military service.

1. FROM LETCHWORTH TO WANDSWORTH PRISON

on the station and had a chat. Mrs Price bought me a book and Taylors bought some papers so I am stocked for a little while.

I posted your card before entering the barracks. On reaching the barracks I was taken, with some other fellows to the orderly room and given 2/7 which I refused.[6] Then before the doctor I was asked to undress and I refused. The Ser[geant] Major told me of the seriousness of the offence and took me to the Colonel. He also told me of the trouble I should get into and I told him I quite understood. He had a chat with me and told me I could have until Monday to think it over. So I am not yet in the guard room. The fellows here call it prison and it is nearly so. They are not allowed out in plain clothes. But I, when it was dark, squared the guard and went out. I went round to Hancox[7] and spent the evening there.

[...] I slept in a bed and had four blankets and a pillow like a bullet for hardness but slept very well. Up at 6 o'clock just fancy and had breakfast at 7.20. Bacon and tomatoes which I did not touch and mar[garine] and bread. Being hungry I made a good breakfast with m and b an apple and tomatoes, the remainder of those given me by Mrs Price. After breakfast a clean up and then a Sergeant told us that those who had not been examined could not be missed and were to draw 2/7 a day and find their own food. Too late to get it today, we are to have it tomorrow, so I shall draw mine as I think that they ought to keep me on it.

The Sergeant major had a talk with me and advised me to be examined by the doctor as I should then know how I stood and it would not prevent me from refusing to serve. They are getting used to having COs here and have learned how to treat them. He told me that two COs have been Court Martialled just recently and one who refused to be examined got six months. The other one got six months but because

---

6   Two shillings and sevenpence would be worth around £8 in 2018. Accepting this as pay would have represented agreement with his conscription, though the next day Frank accepted it in lieu of his rations.

7   Hancox was Frank's manager for the insurance collections.

he had been reasonable and allowed himself to be examined, his sentence was commuted to 4 months. I have thought it over and I think I shall take his advice as I shall then know as to what sort of condition I am in but I'm sure whatever the decision I shall not serve.

I had a bit of fun with some of the chaps who were served out with their clothes. The puttees[8] seemed to give them a lot of trouble so I helped them put them on and great fun we made of it. By the way Hancox is coming over to Hitchin on Tuesday and he and Lindsay will go round with you on the debit and he will relieve you of all that but if you do the Letchworth bit that would keep the agency open, but I leave it entirely to you. He will also bring my big coat back if I can see him tomorrow Monday.

So much about myself. I do trust you are keeping all right and please do not worry about me. Things have changed in the army for the CO. They do not want us chaps to go into the training depots and so the business is done from here which saves a lot of time for everybody.

Kiss all the youngsters and tell them their Daddie is not a soldier and will soon be home again. There many kind friends around and lots of goodness in the world even yet.

    Lots of love, darling to you all. Write to me soon.

Address FT Sunderland Bedford Barracks

Kempton Barracks, Bedford
Sunday afternoon [November 5th 1916]

Dear Wifey

I trust you are better than when I left home. I am pleased to say that I

---

8 Part of the private soldier's uniform were these strips of khaki flannel wound around the legs below the knee, partly for insulation, partly for ease of movement.

am feeling better than I have done this last two days. I saw the Colonel on Sat morning and he has no orders about me and has now sent to the War Office to get instructions. He was quite nice to me and asked me how I got on in Wormwood Scrubs. I told him about my fit of madness[9] and he said he could quite understand it as he has had a lot to do with prisons himself and knows all about them. I tried to get home but could not get a pass so had to content myself in Barracks. Most of the Sergeants and some of the men recognised me and are sympathetic but of course they all advise me to join up. My fate is still in the balance. I wish the issue was a clear one, then it would be easy. However I know that you will stick to me even though I have to put on the khaki.

I heard from Brunt and Myles this morning and their letters cheered me up. It is nice to get an acknowledgement of duty done even though we cannot always live up to the highest one knows.

[...] I called to see Hancox on Friday night and gave him quite a shock but he survived. His wife got some fish and chips for my supper and he came to the barracks to see me safely landed for the night.

On Saturday night I went to the Picture Palace and passed the time away. The films were good and I enjoyed it but the weather is awful. Sat round the fire all this morning listening to yarns from the Front but had better not tell you anything in case the censor reads this.[10]

I together with two other chaps went for a walk this afternoon round the town, then to a PSA oh yes and into a Soldiers Home for tea which was cheap and nice. We three are now writing our respective dutiful letters to our respective homes. After which we shall wend our way

---

9   Nothing is known about this episode, which seems to refer to an earlier prison sentence, at Wormwood Scrubs.

10 John Hoare, another CO from this period, noted from his imprisonment that 'they sent back a number of others [...] on the grounds that in their private correspondence they were indulging in propaganda'. Richard Hoare ed., *John Hoare. A Pacifist's Progress. Papers from the First World War* (York: Sessions Book Trust, 1998), 16.

to a <u>free</u> concert for <u>soldiers</u> [...] I got my prison discharge papers but am afraid it will not help me in any way. My only hope lies in the War Office Offer.[11]

[...] I hope you will not be stranded for money but if you do not get any we must use what we have in the bank. I am not drawing any pay of course so I shall <u>husband</u> my slender resources as much as possible. I hope Mrs Webster[12] has received some cash by now and that you are all still happy together. I'm right glad of the soap and towel also the knife and fork. The Guard room has three COs in and one was court-martialled on Saturday.

Don't forget to send my letter to Mother will you. I'll finish now dear and let you know as soon as anything develops.

  Oceans of love and kisses to you all, not forgetting the baby.

          Frank

               Bedford Barracks, Bedford
                    Nov 7 1916

Dear Wifie

I am at last in the guard room and my <u>crime</u> is refusing to don the Kings Uniform I shall be court martialed as soon as they can arrange it. I am not alone as there is a chap here who is also in for the same thing. He is the chap who I met in the Skittles one night.[13] Everybody

---

11 The War Office, the Home Office and the Admiralty could make offers of alternatives to prison or military service to COs, for example clerical or agricultural work. Frank was uninterested in anything except absolute exemption.

12 Mrs Webster was Lucy's lodger, soon to have a baby.

13 Skittles was the Letchworth inn, serving only non-alcoholic drinks, and was the centre for Letchworth's flourishing society, club and committee life. The Letchworth Adult School held its lectures there.

here is very nice to me and I've nothing to complain of although the accommodation is a relic of barbarous ages. I consented to go before the Dr and have passed for C3 the lowest scale of all so I must be an old crock. The Colonel offered me a job at the barracks here as a clerk and it was a great temptation to me to take it and save all the trouble but I couldn't do it and so here I am. Another chap went to Wormwood Scrubs yesterday for refusing to serve. I can have anything sent to me while here and I shall be here for quite a week yet. I saw Hancox yesterday and he knows my decision and I expect has told you by this time.

Just please yourself what you do regarding the work and do write to me as often as you can. Could you send for the collars as I would like to keep respectable as long as poss.[14] I think the worst is over now and it is just a question of endurance. Send me a writing pad so that I can scribe to you and to others. I have written to mother but not told her the whole truth about myself. We had fun in the guard room last night so loneliness won't come just yet.

I am always thinking of you Darling and I trust you will keep your courage up for I feel you have got to bear the brunt.

Lots of Love and Kisses to You and the Children

Frank

91 Shrubland Avenue
Berkhampstead
Nov 7th

Dear Frank,

In reply to yours of today I was pleased to hear you are in good health, but more than sorry to hear you have been arrested, you do not say

---

14   Men at this period wore detachable collars with their shirts, often changing collars twice a day depending on their activity. A clean collar could give an impression of clean clothing overall.

what for or anything about it but I suppose it is for being an absentee. The last time we heard you had to go to the County Tribunal: have you been and how did you get on?

We shall be waiting to hear how you get on and what it will mean as I suppose you are kicking against being a soldier but suppose you will go to work if sent the same as some of your men are doing?

You do not say anything about how Lucy and the children are going to live and keep going while you are away, if you can you might let us know as soon possible. We were glad to hear the nippers and Lucy are keeping well, during the rotten weather.

Now best love from Mother and wishes for your good health and release soon in which Mother and Lil join me

your affect bro.

Alf

PS I enclose you a couple of stamps

may be useful

---

32 North Avenue, Letchworth
Nov 8th 1916

My dear Frank

So glad to have your letter, just a few lines now more later, want to catch this post 9.30.

Got on all right with work Lloyds and everyone. Made out sheet and sent to Hancox. Shall quite cut you out yet.

Am sending stamps for you to write as many letters as you like.

Will write again presently

Lots of love from us all

Lucy

1. FROM LETCHWORTH TO WANDSWORTH PRISON

Guardroom, Bedford Barracks, Bedford
Nov 8 1916

Dear Wifie

Four letters to hand which I must say cheered me up very much and I felt the Hug from Chrissie. Perhaps Dora could practice writing by sending me a line. Kiss them all round and accept some yourself. I had Hancox call on me this morning and he brought me the things I asked him to get. Soap, towel, pen and ink, etc. He thinks I am wrong in my attitude but I am convinced it is right and could not accept the Colonel's offer as it was too easy a way out. However the die is cast now. Yesterday morning I was ordered to don the uniform and refused to do so. Am now in the guardroom waiting my court-martial which will be a matter of a few days.

They are feeding us alright but we get no exercise. [...] I wrote to Mother and told her something but not all so you will have to tell her if she wants to know. Did you fix up with Mr Lloyd alright and get the money? How did you manage about the bank? I'll write to Noel [Palmer] and Osborn but my supply of stamps is going to be taxed heavily.

[...] As to coming to see me I can see anybody if they say I sent for them and I've asked Mr Cubbon to call.[15] Do you think you can stand it seeing me here? I feel very weak on that point myself being as you know so emotional and I feel your influence here all the time. However I leave it with you. I can arrange to see you before going to Prison and will let the Friends know when the court martial is to be so that they can be there.[16]

If I am here another week I shall want some clean things for the place is filthy but will let you know. Mrs Bedford called to see me and sent me in some books and a loaf of homemade bread and butter to eat with it so I am still finding fresh friends. Got rather a stiff neck through too suddenly leaving the amenities of civilization but that will pass away.

---

15   Cubbon was a local Quaker and councillor.

16   The local Quakers made a point of attending courts martial to encourage the COs and support them in their pacifist testimony.

THE CONSCIENTIOUS OBJECTOR'S WIFE

I don't expect your letters to be very full but write as long as you can. I'll write every day and keep you posted with the <u>news</u>. This morning a draft[17] went away with the band playing 'Pack up your troubles in your old kit bag and smile boys smile'. I pitied the poor beggars many of whom did <u>not</u> want to come in to the <u>army</u>. My Pal and I are the only <u>free</u> men in the barracks.

By the way the Captain who is to give evidence against me is Capt. St Quintin from Clifton, strange, eh. He did not know me of course. [...] I wonder what your mother will say now, eh, that is if she gets to know. Have you heard from them lately?

Now I think I have written you a budget so will wind up by telling you that the guardroom now possesses a shove ha'penny board and I am getting an expert.[18]

Lots of love Darling and I'll soon be back to you and the darlings. I hope the motor still continues to give satisfaction and that the hens are still laying well.[19] [...]

Frank

⁂

32 North Avenue, Letchworth
November 9th 1916

My dear Frank

I hope you are able to write all you want now you have got the [writing] pad. I hope you can have the few goodies I have sent. Try and take the eggs in milk or even in tea if such a thing is allowed. My morning

---

17   A draft of newly enlisted soldiers.

18   Traditional board game played by sliding pennies (or half-pennies, which were much larger) across a marked grid.

19   Frank had made Morris a toy car, as seen on the front cover.

10

tea nearly chokes me because you are not sharing it (tho' sometimes you have refused it). I hope you will write to me every day as long as you can. I feel your spirit always with me. It helps me throughout the loneliness of the night. I haven't time to feel lonely during the day. [...]

I made up the Britannia sheet all right I hope, but forgot to enclose to Hancox the 18/7 and 14/1. I remembered it after and hurriedly sent him a £ note, how he will swear at not getting the right amount. Of course I have got it all right, couldn't think how I was so well off but I could not remember at all how you made the little slips out and I felt bad while doing it, the memory of you doing it every Wed, for so long was too much for me, then I had several callers. Miss Jeffries had been 5 times to see me and Miss Reynolds 3. I shall do better next week, tell Hancox if he grumbles about me. Am glad you can see him, but I wish he could see our point of view. Our people are all very glad you are holding to your principles, but it must be very hard. I cannot find Johnson's book, don't really know what to look for, do you?

Yes I got Lloyds' 15/- also 2/- from Veloce.[20] Most people pay up all right and when you come home I shall be quite an expert at the game. We shall be quite alright so don't <u>worry</u> about us. Look after your health as much as you can. You are no old crock, the Dr would pass you for what he liked. [...] I had a letter from your mother this morning, written by Alf of course, wants to know what you have <u>done</u> and how we are provided for. I have not answered, she need not worry, we shall not want. I am well and doing your work and you were quite determined not to serve, right must be right. Of course they won't see it so. I suppose my mother will get to hear soon, not from me though. They have not answered my last letter yet.

I think with you we could not bear to meet again to part once more, we must keep up and be brave, no weakness must enter into this. We have tried to face it in imagination but it is cruel when we are so much to each other and have been for so many years. If we might only continue to write even, it would be bearable, but as I have said before,

---

20   Johnson, Lloyd and Veloce were insurance clients.

our spirits are together till we meet in the flesh or in death, till then we go on with our work as it comes to us; yours for humanity, I for <u>our</u> children teaching them the gospel of love, freedom and liberty, hoping they may grow up to realize the happiness [...] that we are dreaming of and striving for.

Goodnight my husband and sweetheart.

My best and only love to you for ever.

Lucy

32 North Avenue Letchworth
November 9th 1916

Dear Daddy

We miss you very much and hope you will soon come back.

Mother has been out all the week but we managed all right we went to play on Saturday at Mrs Palmer with Nancy and Esther and we went to tea at Mrs Palmer as well and on Tuesday we went to dinner and we went to Mrs Lack to tea till Mother came home from Baldock on Monday we are going to Miss Benaleo tomorrow for tea.

With love from Dora Sunderland

Guardroom, Bedford Barracks, Bedford
Nov 10 1916

Darling Wifie

Of course you want a letter so will do my best to <u>spare time</u> to write one. We are very busy here you know. Had a shave this morning at the country's expense and feel quite clean. Our [Court Martial] has not come off today so perhaps it will do so tomorrow. Hope so at any rate. Our room is rather cold so we pace up and down like caged lions to get warm. We get plenty of air and precious little else.

I'm no longer a vegetarian as our diet is decided for us, and they gave us salmon for breakfast yesterday and batter pudding and mutton for dinner today; for tea we had bread and cheese and jam; a good mixture, eh, but there is not enough of it. Half a loaf between 4 men and one slice for breakfast this morning no butter but some bacon which I did not touch. I made up with jam from the day before. [...] I'm feeling well and the confinement will not tell on me much as our house is so airy.

Heard from the boys of the barn[21] this morning and also got your letter with the stamp in it. I have not yet heard from Osborn but have written to him. I'm looking forward to getting a really newsy letter from you so send it along. [...]

We have a very interesting man in with us (arrested on suspicion and been here since Monday) who is one of those who get the Wander Lust and has been all over England. He will be 60 before we have done with him I expect. Our Soldier chum was taken from us this morning and sent to Swanage. He did not want to go but they have a way in the army. Today they forgot us and we got no dinner until two o'clock and had breakfast at 7.30. [...]

Glad that Lloyd's [paid] up all right and thus you are doing my work so well. This is my last sheet of paper so will now finish. Lots of love and Kisses to you all

Frank

---

21   This is probably their private name for a particular group of friends.

THE CONSCIENTIOUS OBJECTOR'S WIFE

Guardroom, Bedford Barracks, Bedford
Sat Nov 11.16

Dear Wifie

Our parcel to hand as witness the paper which I have used. I'm so glad that you are settling down to the enforced separation but it won't be for long. I shall be home for Easter and every day brings it nearer. I have formally received the charge and expect to see the Dr. He has to report as to how much punishment and which sort we can stand. I hope he thinks I am only fit to <u>come home</u>. You might let me have the interpretation of Morris's letter as I can't make head nor tail out of it. I'll send back the cheque signed and you can then use it if you want to. Thanks for the money, it will come in useful and the apples have already gladdened the three of us here. Our fare is not of the greatest variety and next time you send eggs please boil them as we don't like asking too much from our <u>host</u>.

I had a letter from Mrs Harding this morning and she sent me a pamphlet to read. Rather good it was too. I'll describe the quarters in which I am living when I get back as then perhaps it will be more effective. Did I tell you that there is another C O here, also a man arrested on suspicion? He has been in here since Monday and nothing has been done for him yet. Poor beggar, he is feeling very sick about it and swears he won't soldier. He says he is over military age.

Thanks for shirts: my others are getting black, I can tell you, as army blankets never get <u>washed</u> and thousands of men must have slept in them on the ground, both outside and in.

Tell Dora she must work hard at her music because when Daddy comes home we shall have a big party and she must play to us all. Chrissie is to learn to cook and send Daddy some cakes and Morris must master the Motor to bring me from the station whilst mother must <u>keep smiling</u>.

The dominoes are jolly useful as we can see to use them when the day wears away and we cannot see to read or write. I think I shall have to employ an amanuensis if I am here much longer as there seem so many people to write to. Glad you have sent for the collars. I had a letter from Cuppuck and signed by all the boys and the solitary Lady of the barn. Liple tells me his brother in law has started boot-mending and is sorry I am not in the firm but there is plenty of time.

Has anyone unravelled the mystery why I am here and none of the other chaps, as I should like to know? I saw my case in the *North Herts Mail* and Mrs Harding is sending the 3 *Citizens Write* again tomorrow.

Lots of love all round and a special kiss for Mother. The cup of tea you may drink knowing that I am having breakfast about that time,

Ta Ta

Frank

✒

Guardroom, Bedford Barracks, Bedford
Nov 12.16 Sunday

Dear Wifie

This is Sunday morning and the sunlight is streaming through the long slip of window at the end of our room and making it look more cheerful than usual. I have been here a week and all the time has gone rapidly yet it seems an age. You want to know how we live: well yesterday we had mutton potatoes and carrots for dinner and then after waiting quite a long while, because the orderlies forgot us, we had tea. One slice of bread, margarine and a piece of cheese. That had to suffice until 8 o'clock this morning, when again the orderlies forgot us, and after a <u>little</u> delay they brought us a plate full of mutton and bacon and fried onions together with a piece of bread and a mug of tea. Not so bad that, eh, but please remember that I am not used to having to chew such hard stuff and my teeth gib at it a bit. By the time I get home again I shall have forgotten all about vegetarianism and become quite a carnivorous creature again, so that you see how illogical the position of the absolutist is.

I heard again from Alf this morning and he writes just as I expected he would. I enclose the letter for you to read. By the way his letter was the only one I had this morning. We have made ourselves a peg board out of a cardboard box lid so are now set up for <u>games:</u> not very intellectual and I'm afraid would not suit some of our comrades but I believe in making the best of things and our dwelling is not conducive of much mental strain. We had a long chat last night on religion and other things in which I of course had a prominent part. Re Johnson's book. It is an insurance book belonging to the <u>state</u> and is either on my table amongst the other stuff of that kind or else in the drawer, so now you know what to look for.

I have written to N Palmer but did not mention money matters.[22] You had better let him have that cheque, also Osborn's when you get it, and will settle when I come home, unless some good friend sends me a ten pound note while I am here; if they don't I save my <u>army pay</u>.

[...] I quite appreciate the piece of flannel you had put on my shirt but I miss my pyjamas at night. No you need not send them. I am looking forward to hearing Casey at Wormwood Scrubs. When I get there I shall be a real neighbour of Cissie and she won't know. Alf is very concerned about Jan and the Freddies so you had better write and tell him to do the bit of business which he has been so low about. Jan won't be able to complain about the length of the letters I am writing you although I expect you will say there is no news in them.

My neck is quite alright again now [...] As I want to write some more letters I will now close with fondest love and wishes to you all, kiss all the children and accept some for yourself

Your loving Hubby

Frank

---

22   Noel Palmer was the tenant of the bungalow that the Sunderlands sublet from him, thus they paid rent to him, and he paid it to Mr Marshall, their landlord.

1. FROM LETCHWORTH TO WANDSWORTH PRISON

32 North Avenue Letchworth Herts
Sunday eve. [12 Nov 1916]

My dear Frank

I have just come home from the Skittles where I went to hear Sylvia Pankhurst[23] but really to get reports from your visitors. Wasn't you surprised to see them? I hear you will have 2 more tomorrow, Clapham Lander and Kemp Brown, for the C.M.

I suppose by the time you get this you will know your fate for the next few weeks or months. I am not by any means settling down to this enforced separation, and never shall. If you died and was taken from us it would be the will of God, but this isn't. There, that's all I'll say but I feel very strong.

I had a strong argument with Mrs Bradley yesterday about your position. She is glad <u>her</u> husband will not come home with the stain of a convict prison and reap all the benefits that another man has fought for. Of course I had <u>plenty</u> to say about all that. Anyway the daughter thinks you are no coward, so I gained something.

Everyone has been glad to have letters from you and I daresay you have been glad to get them. People are very kind to me and the children. We went to tea with Miss Walkden yesterday and Mrs Tickle this afternoon, after Mrs Palmer and Mrs Wiltshire had been here to see me. We went to Miss Reynolds for tea on Friday so the children are getting quite used to visiting. If I am not back from Baldock[24] before dark tomorrow they are going to the Barn. I had all the boys escort me home tonight, quite a bodyguard. The children did not want me to go out, but I left them quite good and I could not wait for news of you.

It already seems an age since you went away and I long to have you

---

23   During the war Sylvia Pankhurst was no longer active in the women's suffrage campaign, which had been suspended for the duration of the hostilities, but was a political lobbyist for the international women's peace movement.

24   Baldock was on Lucy's collection round.

home again. I shall keep very busy and try to go on just in the same way and 'keep smiling' if possible. I really feel quite at peace because I am sure we are taking the right stand. If our thought is too advanced for the present state of civilization we cannot help that, but must be true to ourselves, even as Christ was too soon, but all new teaching must have pioneers and its martyrs although we little dreamt in talking about our future that you would be one.

Sylvia Pankhurst was good tonight and her closing remarks fine. No one can be an internationalist without being a socialist. You will be surprised to hear that Burgess has come back to Mrs Dent's after 5 years.[25] If he goes to the ILP he will probably hear of your present abode, then he might mention it to Katie. It would be rather strange if they had the news that way.

She also told us that Bruce Beveridge had died of consumption and Dick Hunter of wounds, she adds 'another sacrifice'. Also Maud Raven will be married this month, so she is the last of all our old friends left single. I am meeting Hancox again on Tuesday, hope it will be better weather than last week. Eastman has not been over yet.[26] I had a card from his wife saying he was away from home.

Have plenty of offers of work so need not be idle, but I shall be looked after. I feel quite well, am glad you are well in health and spirits, please keep so. Let me know if I shall come over, or if you would rather not.

> All my love for you from your true and loving wife Lucy

---

25 Presumably as a lodger.

26 Eastman was also connected with the insurance business, running a neighbouring agency so that Lucy worked for both him and Hancox, after she took over Frank's round.

1. FROM LETCHWORTH TO WANDSWORTH PRISON

Bedford Barracks, Bedford
Nov 13.16

Wifie Darling

I suppose if my daily epistle does not arrive you will discharge the postman so here goes. Yesterday was at home day at the guardroom and I entertained Friend Palmer, Symonds and last but not least Mr D D Brunt. They brought no end of good things with them and our larder is thereby replenished. They stayed quite an hour and saw our dinner and the manner in which it is served, but I would not prevail upon them to partake thereof, thus another example of generosity on their host.

The shirts came in just right as I wanted a change, so that I could feel fresh for the [Court Martial] which by the way came off this morning. We have spent quite a busy morning. Up getting, washing, shaving, medical examinations and then the grand finale. Friends K Brown, Clapham Lander and Mr and Mrs Mathews were present. It was very formal and humdrum, no <u>fireworks</u> but I raised a smile even in such an atmosphere by something I had written in my <u>defence</u>. We do not know what the sentence is to be and shall hear later on. Only one more ordeal that is the sentence is read out to us on the barrack square before all the soldiers present. Being used to face <u>vast</u> audiences and also being <u>married</u> I think I can face that alright.

By the way your daily letter is three days overdue; I trust you are not overworking. Wrote an apology to Miss Lawes and received her reply this morning. Also a letter from Osborn together with a socialist songbook so look out when I come home. I shall be singing all the red rag stuff.

Well, I could go on babbling all day like this but space and light forbids. Hancox called this morning but I did not see him. He left a book or two, all of which are acceptable. Lots of love and kisses, you can get the latter by proxy if someone is willing to take on the job

From your own loving & lazy Husband

Frank

[27] I plead guilty to the crime [...] of refusing to do as requested by the Sergeant. I am a conscientious objector to all forms of military service, and can therefore take no part therein. An act of parliament <u>deeming</u> me to be a soldier does not make me one, any more than an act of parliament deeming all citizens, from a certain date, to be left handed would make all citizens left handed: unless there is willingness to serve there can be no service. I made my claim to exemption before the Tribunals set up by parliament for that purpose, but with the usual stupidity of such bodies they refused my application, thus throwing this inconvenience upon the Military Authorities and compelling me to take the action which has led to this [Court Martial] to prove that my conscientious objection is a genuine one. I am sorry to be the unwilling instrument of such a lot of trouble but no other course was open to me I must therefore bear the punishment which it is your duty to inflict, with the same fortitude which upholds all those who feel it their duty to refuse to allow conscience to be subordinated to expediency.

Guardroom, Bedford Barracks, Bedford
November 13th 1916

Dear Dora

As I am away from home for a while I want you to be a good girl and learn your lessons. Practice hard at your music and do all that Mamma tells you. Help Chrissie and Morris to be happy. I am coming back soon. You may write me another letter I was pleased with your last one.

Lots of love from Daddy

---

27   This is Frank's statement to the court martial, which he sent to Lucy with his letter of 13 November.

1. FROM LETCHWORTH TO WANDSWORTH PRISON

Guardroom, Bedford Barracks, Bedford
November 13th 1916

Dear Chrissie

I cannot see you just yet but I hear all about you. I want you to be a good girl until I get home again. Take care of Mamma and learn to do the cooking and all the work. Try hard at school to do all your lessons and then I shall be pleased. I got your letter all right and expect you will send me another.

Lots of love from Daddy

⁓

Guardroom, Bedford Barracks, Bedford
November 13th 1916

Dear Morris

I read a piece of poetry which was written by a great man of your name.[28] He said we must try hard to do the right and then all will be well. I am trying to do that and I want you to do the same.

I received your letter but cannot tell what it means so please send me one and tell me all about it.

Try and be a good boy and don't go under the table.

Lots of love from Daddy

⁓

---

28 Probably Frank meant William Morris, the nineteenth-century designer and visionary.

THE CONSCIENTIOUS OBJECTOR'S WIFE

32 North Avenue
Nov 13 1916

My dear Frank

I received your 2 letters this morning. I could not enjoy them as much as I wanted, because I was having a rush to catch the 12.19. I felt very disappointed at not getting a letter at all yesterday, but I forgive you as you wrote it and I got both together. I shall go through them again tonight for my supper.

[…] We have got the collection done and done the dreaded sheet. I shall find it easy soon. I have signed the paper for the agency, now I am a qualified Insurance agent, paying 3d per week state insurance too.

People are rather concerned about me working so hard, but it will be an outing for me each week and does me and you good to go among people. I shall not earn a great deal but shall get plenty of needlework and Miss Pass wants me to go to the shop for the Christmas trade, don't know yet, we'll see.

Perhaps you will be home soon. I hope so, <u>the sooner</u> the better. […]

❦

Bedford Barracks, Bedford
Nov 14.16

Dearest

If I fail to fulfil my compact to write every day I suppose some awful punishment will descend upon me and as I am in for punishment enough I had better write, so here goes. In the first place I received your Sunday evening letter this morning […] We pass the time reading writing and arithmetic. The latter is necessary in dominoes, shove ha'penny and our latest is a Bagatelle Table installed by Dawson and Co. It is a great addition I can tell you. The letters I have written to the youngsters I thought perhaps you might keep for the years to come. So you are going with Hancox again, are you? It's a good job I know you, but I didn't think you were going to turn the tables on me like this.

1. FROM LETCHWORTH TO WANDSWORTH PRISON

[…] So you have heard from Katie. I'm surprised to hear about Burgess. I should like to know what his views are concerning the war. If I was sure he is one of us I would write to him; as it is one has to be cautious. Perhaps they, Katie and he I mean, may become friends: that would be funny, wouldn't it?

[…] We had an interesting talk on Printing last night, my fellow CO being a printer. He explained the workings of the large machines that print newspapers etc also the working of lino type and monotype machines. So my time is not quite wasted.

I picture you at home every night when I go to bed about 8 o'clock so please put on your thoughtwave process at full speed between 8 and 9 o'clock and I'm sure it will be good for both of us. I did not quite know how I was going to fill in three pages for you but it is now an accomplished fact. Kisses all round for our darlings and lots of love to the sweetest little wife man ever had.

Yours even in the next incarnation Frank

Guardroom, Bedford Barracks, Bedford
November 15th 1916

Dear Wife,

I got your long looked letter this morning and was pleased to hear that you and the children are well. I think we shall all enjoy good health to enable us to endure this ordeal.

I am expecting to go upon the Square to hear my sentence this morning and then we shall be shifted so this may be the last long letter you will get for a month. At present I am determined not to accept the Home Office offer but we cannot say what one will do.

So you are a bona fide Agent now. Well it will be a bit of <u>Pin</u> money for you but don't overwork yourself. Rowntree Gillett is the chaplain for Wormwood Scrubs so I shall see a friend when I get there.

THE CONSCIENTIOUS OBJECTOR'S WIFE

The sun is shining beautifully through the window as I write and the band is playing as a draft is going away. We have been to face the music in two senses and received our sentences. Six months each remitted to 4 months and we go today so this will be the last letter for a while. I shall not get your goodies but Mrs Taylor sent me some chocolate this morning which was very acceptable. Kiss all the children for me and tell them Daddy is always thinking of them. I'll leave all my stuff at the barracks for Warren to fetch away.

I can't write any more now dear but we will meet in spirit as you say. Think hard of me about 7 to 9 in the morning and I'll try and visit you then. For remember the old Scotch minister who stayed with us, well we try to be like him. He succeeded and so can you [...]

Once again farewell. Lots and lots of love my own sweet little Wife. We have had many stormy times together and we always stick together. These things only make us love each other more. Remember me to all enquiring friends and say I went smiling.

Bye bye. Yours ever, Frank

In Train going to London
Nov 15.16

Well Dearie

At last I am off, but cheer up, I have just heard that two men sent to W.S (Wormwood Scrubs) a few weeks ago are now at liberty, but whether they have accepted the W.O. scheme or not I can't say.[29] We had a good dinner of beef and batter pudding, potatoes and turnips, after which we had bread (Irish butter) and your dates so we shan't hurt for an hour or so, shall we.

---

29   Instead of a War Office Scheme Frank may have meant the Home Office Scheme which arranged for COs to be given work of 'national importance' to relieve space in the prison system.

1. FROM LETCHWORTH TO WANDSWORTH PRISON

The chap we left in the guardroom was very cut up at our leaving. We have an escort of Sergeant and two men, one of whom came to Bedford with me, and I took him to Hancox on the Saturday night. Strange, eh. I'll get him to post this if I can't manage to do so myself. We marched out of barracks with a squad of men who are off to Clacton for training. They wonder what strange fellows we are and where we are off to. I left a parcel for Hancox to fetch away and have written him a card. I left a pencil in the guardroom which I expect will be there when I come back.

I'm glad it is such a glorious day as it will be something to look back on. I am not nervous about the coming ordeal as the Warders are not bullies and the system is quite different to the army. We are on a non-stop to St Pancras and then on to Shepherds' Bush by tube so I shall see a little of London. If I gain <u>all</u> my good conduct marks I shall be home by the end of <u>Feb</u>. I am quite content so don't worry about me. Kiss the bairns and accept some yourself

Lots and lots of love
Yours ever
Frank

❧

32 North Avenue Letchworth
January 17th 1917

My dear Frank

Once more I write to you. I was very glad to have your letter. Please write every day. I feel rather worried about you. I suppose it is the suspense and the bad cold I can't seem to shake off. I had a letter from Alf yesterday so have written sending your letter and photos. Everyone is constantly enquiring for news of you and I have plenty of sympathy [...]

I don't feel like writing a long letter this time. I feel very much off; hope I shall soon feel well again. The children are all well and send lots of love and hope to see you soon. XXX

THE CONSCIENTIOUS OBJECTOR'S WIFE

Goodnight best love from your own

Lucy

❧

Kempston Barracks, Bedford
Thursday morning, Jan 18 1917

Dearest Wifey

I expect you are all on thorns about me so I must let you know all the news. By the way, there isn't any. Am still a prisoner in the Barracks waiting to hear from the War Office. Nothing to do all day but sit around the fire and listen to the yarns which are told by the old soldiers from the front. It is cold here but I am quite all right and I trust you and the youngsters are also. I am not writing any letters to any one until I know what I am going to do. A C.O. was given six months today and I expect goes off to [Wormwood Scrubs] tomorrow. He'll be glad to get away from the cold guardroom, I guess. The barracks is full up with men coming up to join, none of whom seem very happy.

❧

Bedford Barracks, Bedford
Jan 24 17

Dear Lucy

I have at last got some real news for you. I had an interview with the Captain this morning and he tells me that I have been posted to No 1 Coy Bedfords[30] as a clerk and am to don my uniform this afternoon. I told him I shall again refuse so I <u>expect</u> to go into the guardroom this afternoon. I am in good spirits and feeling quite well so don't worry, but send me something nice if you can spare it as I shall not then feel it necessary to share in with the rest. I am writing this in haste so it will be a short one.

30   'Coy' is the military abbreviation for 'Company'.

Lots of love from your Own Hubby

Frank

32 North Avenue Letchworth
January 24th 1917

My dear Frank

Your letter received yesterday afternoon. Am sorry I haven't been able to write before. I expect you are looking for one. I had an awful day out on Monday, had to walk so slowly and even then had one tumble. The streets and roads were like glass all day. I went to Baldock in the afternoon so got all done. A good job I did as Hancox came yesterday so [he] took acc. back with him. Now I have got the Planet to do today. Am going to see Mrs Gregory this afternoon.

Your visit home[31] did me a lot of good but my head is dreadful, I can hardly hold it up nor my eyes open, and still I have to continue work. Am sorry to say all the children are queer, bad colds I think, but Chrissie is a dreadful colour, pinky red, I hope she is not in for Chicken Pox or anything else. They are all in bed, of course. It is Morris's cough that is bad and Dora's too, but Chrissie has got pains in her legs. You don't mind me telling you, do you? Don't worry, they will be all right again soon.

I have had a letter from Mother and one from Katie. If you don't come home soon I'll send them to you to read.

---

31   This probably refers to a visit home by Frank that took place when an opportunity unexpectedly arose, so that there was no opportunity to refer to it in letters. He does this later on, when he was mistaken for another inmate who had a pass to leave the barracks.

I went to school yesterday[32] and Miss Jefferies asked me to give you a message and I told her to write to you herself. Mrs Palmer says she is delighted with you and your attitude. I hope your letters to the 'Lords' will have some effect.

Now this must do for today.

Lots of love from us all

Lucy

Guardroom, Bedford
January 25th 1917

Dear Wifey

Your letter to hand this morning. I was glad to get it as I am feeling a bit down. It is cold and dark in here. I can neither keep warm, nor see to read. I am in for another Court Martial but am quite satisfied it is the right course to adopt. They did not expect me to do anything else here so we must keep the flag flying.

I am glad the youngsters are better and trust Morris's cough will soon be well again. I'm sorry you had to turn out on such a day as Monday – hope you have not bruised yourself much. As to the building the futFure we must wait and see, so we are not out of this yet. […]

There is another C.O. in here with me, quite a young chap and he is making a good stand. He will be all right. Has had his C.M. and is now waiting to go to Wormwood Scrubs. I am pleased to say that I have got the biscuits and pillows this time, so shall not have the books until I get to Prison again. I have not yet heard from the HQ or the War Office but perhaps something will turn up. It will give me hope all the time, at any rate. Had I joined up my troubles would have increased as all men have to be vaccinated and inoculated etc which would have meant more trouble.

32   Adult School, evening lectures for adults on a variety of subjects. Lucy would be running the School in the following year.

Reg Gardener has left his mark in the guardroom in the shape of a […] motto which is quite artistic and the walls are covered with texts, poetry etc written by […] chaps so it gives a homely feeling on looking around. Mr Webster's piece of poetry is still here too but I am afraid they will be whitewashed over when this job is over.

Darling: your parcel has just arrived: for which many thanks. Also a new arrival. A man from Watford who has refused to don khaki. The other chap has just got the sentence–112 days– as I expect he will be going off to [Wormwood Scrubs] today.

We have sampled the apples and they are good. Kiss all the kiddies and accept more for yourself.

Lots of love from your loving Hubby

---

32 North Avenue Letchworth
Wed morning January 25th 1917

My dear Frank

Just received your brief note. Glad to know you are over the waiting period. I am going down town this morning so will send you a parcel this afternoon, so you can look for a nice feed tomorrow: don't forget to write every day and let me know if you want anything, and you shall have it at once. I shall call in to Mrs Palmer's on my way, to let her know what you are doing […]

Dora has gone to school this morning and the other 2 are no worse. They are in bed still. Am going to get some 'Liquefruits' for their cough. Will write again in the parcel.

Love from all and thoughts and wishes from everyone.

Lucy

32 North Avenue Letchworth
January 25th 1917

Dear Frank

I hope you will enjoy this box of good things. If anything further is required let me know at once. I'll send your clean shirts, pants and new vest washed, tomorrow or Sat afternoon, then I will put a few scones and anything else I think of. Mrs Palmer is very pleased and sent you the candles, biscuits and almonds. She said Mrs Brunt was quite excited about you taking this stand. I hope you will keep well and fit. I am afraid I cannot come to see you before next Wednesday.

The children are recovering I'm glad to say. I bought Dora's boots this morning – 8/11 – real nice soft brown ones, broad and flat. She is quite pleased with them and has gone to school in them. I have settled my accounts and have got 5/- left to keep us till Sat. Still owe Co-op a bit and Palmer's. We shall have honey soon and I will pay him a bit each week for that. You won't need to worry about the funds this time [...]

Mrs Webster has been to the Dr this morning and he sees a great improvement in her. She has an idea of later on going to live with her sister in Liverpool. She is expecting her first baby in the summer and her husband is standing out as a CO. Don't forget to write to Mr Thomas (when you have time) and Rowntree Gillett if you feel like it.

I think I must stop now.

Goodbye lots of love from us all

Lucy

Please return Mr Palmer's book. I thought you might like to read it. Should you like a tin of ideal milk cream?

1. FROM LETCHWORTH TO WANDSWORTH PRISON

Ingle Cottage, 29 Norton Way North, Letchworth
26 Jan 1917

Dear Comrade

We are very sorry to hear that affairs have taken an unfortunate turn, but we trust that it is only temporary and that your representations to the Home and War Departments will set the machinery in motion which will procure your release for which you are entitled. Meanwhile it is splendid to hear that you have again risen to the occasion and vindicated yourself and the cause. Once more we congratulate you. I sincerely trust that this time it will not be necessary to go through the whole hateful business to the bitter end. You must persist, and of course I know that you will – that you are not a soldier: your legal status now is quite different from the previous time: you are subject to Home Office conditions which you have not broken and the action of the War Office is therefore quite *ultra vires*. Ascertain if possible and press your question, why you are recalled. If it is because of your petition made under duress in Wormwood Scrubs, stick to it that you were not in a responsible condition when you made it and that you now entirely disavow it. You cannot serve two Departments at once. Until you have definitely rejected or infringed the Home Office conditions you are their man, and the military are retaining you illegally. Do not let the Home Office drop you even if they want to: hold them to the conditions as you have held to them so far as you were able. If you do not get a reply to the letters you sent in on Monday, write again, both to the Home Office and the War Office they are bound to give you satisfaction if you keep on at them. Send the replies of each to the other if you find you can do so to advantage, not forgetting your own comments on both.

We are very glad you feel bucked up again and able to hold fast. I reported at the Branch Meeting this evening and Myles did so too. They were all very glad and applauded your attitude. I hear that Wiltshire has been transferred to Wandsworth. Mr and Mrs Bowry have been to see their son there and Mrs Clark and Mrs Williams have received letters from their husbands. White has accepted the Home Office Scheme.

Mrs Sunderland came in to see my wife yesterday: she is very pleased at the line you are taking as you doubtless know.

Well, I hope we shall soon see you here again and that your troubles will be finally settled. Yours has been a muddled case all through: the only consistent feature of it has been your own good faith which has been unmistakeable and would have convinced anyone but the set of blundering tyrants who seem to have got us in their grip at present.

Good luck and kindest regards from us both. We shall constantly keep you in mind and so will the other comrades.

Yours fraternally

Sydney W Palmer[33]

---

32 North Avenue Letchworth

January 27th 1917

My dear Frank

Why don't I have a letter? not a line since Thursday morning and that was Wed news, now this is Sat. Have you got the parcel I sent? I sent it by train for cheapness.

We are all much better, I'm glad to say. I haven't any news for you. Am sending off your clean vest, towel etc. I thought you might not get it till Mon so writing letter by itself. Do please write at once. I shall come on Wednesday DVWP[34] hope it will be in time to see you. Let me know all the news and I will write often. I do want to see you and long for your presence constantly, but we shall be together again one day. Morris's birthday tomorrow. Now goodbye I've got tons of work to do today. Wish you had.

---

33 Sydney Palmer was a friend of the Sunderlands, and would remain an important figure in their lives, supporting Lucy and the family, and giving advice and practical help when needed.

34 Deo volente (God willing), weather permitting.

1. FROM LETCHWORTH TO WANDSWORTH PRISON

Love from us all

Yours ever Lucy

✢

32 North Avenue, Letchworth
Sunday afternoon, January 28th 1917

My dear Frank

I found your letter waiting for me when I got back from rounds yesterday. Glad I was to get it too. It makes me feel very bad to know what you are going through. Am glad you feel it is the right thing to do. I have decided to come on Tuesday, and have written to tell Hancox, perhaps he will come with me. I shall get all the collecting done on Monday so I can bring all with me. If you want me to bring anything write at <u>once</u> and mark it <u>Urgent</u> or I shall not get it. Am sorry I forgot to put shirt in parcel, but I posted it after so I expect you have got it or will soon [...]

I believe White has accepted 'Alternative Service' and Wiltshire has gone or is going with 50 others to Wandsworth Prison, I wonder why. Mrs W had a letter from him on Friday but have not seen her yet. Mrs Williams had one on Wednesday, 3 large sheets. She is very pleased; he is quite determined to stand firm if it is 2 years next time; he expects to be kept quite 6 months after the war is over.

Am going to the Skittles tonight DVWP. It is colder than ever today and it was awful yesterday, so cold. Goodalls came in to tea and brought Morris a pair of Goloshes for his birthday, and me some money last Thursday which was very welcome. I was nearly stoney broke. I bought Morris a Teddy Bear and a knife, fork and spoon for him from you. He is ever so pleased, especially with your present, you will pay me some day.

Cheer up dear, we shall come through all right I have no doubt. We are all better again except my head which is very bad at times, like neuralgia behind the eyes. I can hardly bear it. I suppose it is the last of the cold: I hope so.

Hoping to see you soon, am very glad to think you have got a bed. Sorry you cannot keep warm. It is awful to think of you cold and I can't help you.

Good bye dear. Lots of love from us all.

Your ever loving Lucy

Guardroom, Bedford
Sunday morning, Jan 28 1917

Dearest Wifie

I got your nice long letter last night and it cheered me up wonderfully. I must admit I have been a bit down in the dumps all the week, but perhaps it is the cold weather and the rotten surroundings. I still adhere to my opinion that I am not cut out to be a martyr. I am writing this letter by the candle light and with a blanket round my legs. I had an egg and your delicious scones for breakfast and now feel much refreshed.

I think the men in the barracks are surprised at my second stand[35] but I could do no other. We are getting plenty of food now, really more than is good for me, perhaps, as I have had the wind so bad, but feel better now. I am glad the children are better and trust the weather will soon alter and the sun shine and then you will all be bright and merry. I had a nice long letter from Syd Palmer when I received yours and he gave me great encouragement. It is impossible to describe my feelings but the central fact remains always clear and that is I must stand fast all the time. The clouds will break and we shall be together again and many happy years will be ours.

---

35 This is perhaps a reference to Frank refusing to accept alternatives to military service, following his absolutist principles.

I have not forgotten Morris's birthday and will enclose a letter to him for himself to keep. Our biography will be worth writing won't it eh. I have been reading *The Valley of the Moon* and it has cheered me up. The adventures of that young couple were similar to ours and we have not yet found our valley but it will come along yet.[36]

Your parcel of good things is just a wonder as I keep finding great treasures in it, and the candles are worth their weight in gold to me.

My companions are Christians. One is a young chap of 19 who comes from Aston and is a member of the Open Brethren. He is quite happy and as long as he gets plenty to eat has nothing to worry about, thanks to being without responsibilities. The other chap is 25 and a married man with one child. He comes from Watford and has been a painter on the N W Railway but he became converted to the faith of the 7th Day Adventists and they keep their sabbath from sunset to sunset, Friday to Sat. He therefore had to leave that job and by doing so rendered himself liable to military service and was called up. He has refused to soldier on C.O. grounds. He is not a member of the NCF[37] and his wife is depending on what she can earn and what the Brethren will give her. Perhaps some of such people can get in touch with her, or Jack could write? His address is Mrs H Howard, 16 Nevil Grove, Watford. Those two are always reading their Bibles and discussing it between themselves. I think the single ideaed people are the most fortunate as they only see just a small portion of the fight and it is not so complicated to them.

By the way my [Court Martial] comes off on Tuesday at Northampton[38] but I have made enquiries and I find that I shall be brought back here again. As to the reason for this I cannot find out.

36   Jack London's *The Valley of the Moon* (1913) was a novel about the aspirations of a young couple to leave their squalid and immoral mid-West surroundings, exchanging the city for the countryside, to live in freedom rather than being in bondage to industrial systems and violence.

37   No Conscription Fellowship (see Introduction).

38   This brought about the first of two extensions of Frank's prison sentence, presumably because after several months of his first sentence he still refused to join the army, or do any kind of military service.

[...] Our prison walls are covered with the work of Letchworth COs and others who have tried their hands at sketching. Last night a corporal brought in the box of dominoes which Dora sent me last time I was here, so we have a little amusement if we care to play. Remember me to all enquiring friends but don't laud me to the skies as I'm a poor specimen after all. [...]

Love and lots of it from your own

Hubby

Guardroom, Kempton Barracks, Bedford
Monday Jan 29 17

Dear Lucy,

Your parcels and letter to hand safely. I can now have a change of clean linen and shall feel much sweeter. I am surprised to hear that you have altered your mind and intend to come on Tuesday as I am going to Northampton for my Court martial that day and so shall be away from here. I do hope you will know in time to prevent you coming on a pointless journey. The lad here is being sent to St Albans prison, not Wormwood Scrubs as we expected, so I suppose there is a new move on foot. You can content yourself at night as I sleep quite well and warm. We make the bed up for the three of us and thus have 12 blankets between us 4 on the bottom and 8 on top. How's that for warmth eh. I have not yet heard from the War or Home Office but something will turn up I expect. Kiss all the youngsters from Daddy and accept some for self Ad Lib

Lots of love from yours Ever

Frank

1. FROM LETCHWORTH TO WANDSWORTH PRISON

Guardroom, Kempton Barracks, Bedford
Jan 31 1917

Dear Wifie,

I'm settling down to write you a nice long newsy letter. Your visit cheered me up right well and I now feel quite prepared for the future.

[...] You remember the man that went in as we were talking together in the outer room? Well he was brought from Luton under escort and thought he was going to be a butcher in the ASC.[39] They passed him for general service and told him the ASC was full up and tried to bully him into accepting – ordered him to draw his kit and put on his uniform, and got his back up. He refused to do so and now has refused to soldier altogether. So the guardroom influence tells at times. He is now awaiting [a Court Martial] [...] He is a slaughterer and horse dealer, breeds pigs and keeps fowls etc. He got no time from the Tribunal and had to sell out after working up quite a good business. He comes from just beyond Luton, a place called Open Ridges and is the brother of Wright the baker in Letchworth: strange, isn't it, how we come across all these chaps. He is quite prepared to go to prison and does not mind a bit. If you see Wright you might tell him as he would be pleased to know.

[..] Your candles are much appreciated and make our dark hole of Calcutta look quite cheerful. Could you get a book or two for me as I have nothing to read. By the way, just you read *The Valley of the Moon* again, it will do you good, especially if you can imagine that you and I are Billy and Saxon and are looking for our Valley of the moon [...]

Let me have a nice long letter if you can spare time to write one. I'm writing to Dora so perhaps she will write in return.

Lots of Love Darlings and keep your Courage up.

Yours Ever

Frank

---

39   Army Service Corps, with responsibility for catering, supplies, communications, etc.

THE CONSCIENTIOUS OBJECTOR'S WIFE

Guardroom Kempton Barracks Bedford
Feb 1st 1917

Dear Wifie,

[...] We had quite a full house yesterday as another CO has been brought in and is now awaiting [a Court Martial]. His name is Gregory and he comes from Letchworth. He is a Christian and is (or was) only opposed to killing but has now come to see the thing in its entirety. Mr Wright is quite determined not to soldier and now awaits [a Court Martial], so this makes four of us. Gregory knew me by sight and knows Cubbon but is not a member of the NCF, so we are doing well here, aren't we? Another soldier came in for a while this afternoon, a poor devil who has been buffeted about; he's done 9 months imprisonment out of 12 service. How's that for the army?

[...] We pass the time away fairly well. This afternoon we have had a good discussion on Socialism etc, also the future, and the coming communities had a good place in our tale. The butcher calls the guardroom the house of knowledge and upon my word it really is true that one can learn everywhere; of course Howard is trying to convert me to his conversion by faith theory, and he and Gregory have been having Bible lessons together.

[...] Kiss all the Kiddies from Daddy and tell them to remember him in their prayers. Bye Bye Darling

Yours Ever

Frank

1. FROM LETCHWORTH TO WANDSWORTH PRISON

Guardroom, Bedford

Dear Lucy,

I am writing as per promise although I'm not getting your letters as regularly as I should have liked. I enjoyed your nice long letter and shall treasure it up in my memory whilst I am waiting for your nice long letter you will send me in two months' time [...]

I have just been read out and my sentence, now don't faint, is two years. Just what I expected, so I am not disappointed nor surprised. I am in excellent health and spirits and do not fear but am full of faith. The parade was a large one and I felt a wave of confidence come over me as I gazed at the body of men in front of me. We are right and have got the divine laws on our side. In such crises we are given a glimpse of these things and they carry us through. I'm afraid I can't write a long letter but I assure you of my true Love to you and I feel that though we are parted in the flesh, Love leaps all boundaries of flesh and we are still together. Be brave little woman and I'll try also, and together we shall gather strength to walk through the maze of sorrow and tribulation. I have written just as I feel knowing that you will be able to read my heart.

Tell the children that Daddy loves them dearly and though absent has them in his thoughts. It will be a good example of the Father's love and perhaps help to get them to understand fundamental truths. I am glad we have not had a parting meeting and I can always see your cheerful smile as the train wafted out of the station. I am sure we shall meet again right soon so once more *au revoir*. I send you all the love I am capable of sending and I think it is the greater part of me as you know. I shall be happy all the time. My only anxiety is your dear self, having to work so hard but be sure and let me know if any time the strain is too great to bear.

Best wishes to all friends, and kisses, affection, and Love in all its forms for your Dear Self and our dear children.

Yours Ever Lovingly

Hubby Comrade and Lover

THE CONSCIENTIOUS OBJECTOR'S WIFE

Guardroom, Kempton Barracks, Bedford
February 3rd 1917

Dear Lucy Love

I have just received your parcel of good things and the candles were just in time for us and the books are just the thing [...]

I have not heard yet whether I am to go away today or not. We had a good breakfast of bread and sausages and feel quite fit for anything [...]

I'm glad you were able to make Tickle[40] understand how impossible it was for me to join up. He sent me a letter in which he explained how much I should get as a farm labourer under the War Office, but he does not seem to know that I should have to pay all the expenses incurred by the [Military Authorities] through me, which by now amounts to a tidy bit I expect [...]

I had to go out into the arch to hear my sentence read out. Just a dozen soldiers stood up opposite me and they were all shivering with cold. A little girl stood at the gate with wonder in her eyes, and an old ginger tom cat was playing round my feet and helped to relieve the monotony of the scene. I was not surprised at the sentence but of course I was a bit upset. I do not feel it now as I know <u>what</u> I have to meet and my <u>Faith</u> is firmer. We had quite a Bible class last night in here; as you know, my Adventist friend keeps his Sunday from Friday night until Sat and he started to read his Bible, so of course we all chimed in and our discussion ranged over the whole gamut of religious controversy. The butcher also had his little say and added the usual valuable contributions of a man who sees things from the outside.

I am so sorry Mrs Webster's baby still is bad. I should be pleased to know she had left you and that you had got somebody really nice to stay with you, but <u>nice people</u> are so rare. That's why you are such a treasure to me. Dearie, I love you more than ever and that is saying

---

40   One of the Letchworth provisions merchants with whom Lucy dealt several times weekly.

something. The old book is right when it says a good woman is worth more than precious stones and her measure cannot be taken in Rubies. If this quotation is incorrect you may look it up and correct me [...]

Kiss all the youngsters from Daddy and tell Dora I got her letter and liked it very much.

Lots of love and kisses

Yours <u>for Ever</u>

FTS

Pardon the FTS it slipped from my pencil and should have written

Frank

HM Wandsworth
5-2-17

Dear Wife,

I am now in this prison and I am in good health If I behave well. I shall be allowed to write another letter about 2 months' time and to receive a reply, but no reply is allowed to this.

I have 12 months

Signature F T Sunderland

Register number 2272

2. In Wandsworth Prison and Bedford Prison, April to August 1917

April 2nd 1917

Dearest Wifie,

[...] I may say that I am in excellent health and that my nerves are much better. I am as happy as one can wish under such circumstances. On arrival here I petitioned at once for the old conditions but they have not been granted, and as I cannot take the alternative I shall do my sentence.[41] I have little to say about myself, although I know you are very anxious to know how I am getting along. My indigestion is much better although it was rather bad when I first came in. My appetite is still good. I am cheerful and do not get despondent. I am very pleased to have received the children's photo. It gives me much pleasure to see their faces looking down at me from the shelf as I take a tramp (in inspiration) across the Heath, or down Wilbury Road. I really must have your photo to go with them. Although you are enthroned in my heart, and the memories of the pleasant times we have spent together, are the most happy comparisons I have here, I should like your face always before me, so send it along as quickly as you can please.

I hear that potatoes are very scarce and am glad to know that you are well off in that way. Tell me all the news when you write but read the regulation on the front of [the] letter and don't trouble about sending anything of public interest. I'm glad that Goodalls are with you as he will be a help in the garden.[42] Tell him I appoint him head gardener, under you of course, at a salary to be determined at a later date. [...] Remember me to the Adult School and tell them they are often in my thoughts and I look forward to the time when once more I shall take my share in the work of the school.

---

41   The alternative would have been the Home Office Scheme to transfer sentenced COs to land work or clerical work, among other options.

42   The Goodalls, a Christian couple, were Lucy's new lodgers.

h v c   due monday   for S W

In replying to this letter, please write on the envelope :—

NUMBER 2242   NAME 4 Sunderland
                       WANDSWORTH   PRISON.

The following regulations as to communications, by Visit or Letter, between prisoners and their friends are notified for information of their correspondents.

The permission to write and receive Letters, is given to prisoners for the purpose of enabling them to keep up a connection with their respectable friends and not that they may be kept informed of public events.

All Letters are read by the Prison Authorities. They must be legibly written and not crossed. Any which are of an objectionable tendency, either to or from prisoners, or containing slang, or improper expressions, will be suppressed.

Prisoners are permitted to receive and to write a letter at intervals, which depend on the rules of the stage they attain by industry and good conduct; but matters of special importance to a prisoner may be communicated at any time by Letter (prepaid) to the Governor who will inform the prisoner thereof, if expedient.

In case of misconduct, the privilege of receiving and writing a Letter may be forfeited for a time.

Money, Books, Postage Stamps, Food, Tobacco, Clothes, &c., should not be sent to Prisoners, for their use in prison, as nothing is allowed to be received at the Prison for that purpose.

Persons attempting to clandestinely communicate with, or to introduce any article to or for prisoners, are liable to fine and imprisonment, and any prisoner concerned in such practices is liable to be severely punished.

Prisoners' friends are sometimes applied to by unauthorised persons, to send Money, &c., to them privately, under pretence that they can apply it for the benefit of the prisoners, and under such fraudulent pretence, such persons endeavour to obtain money for themselves. Any Letter containing such application, received by the friends of a prisoner should be, at once, forwarded by them to the Governor.

Prisoners are allowed to receive Visits from their friends, according to rules, at intervals which depend on their stage.

When Visits are due to prisoners notification will be sent to the friends whom they desire to visit them.

No. 243   (8254—20-4-00)

5. Letter-writing instructions, Wandsworth Prison.

All the Letchworth men, but one, have left here and I expect they are now at Bedford where I hope they will have a good time. The Quaker Chaplain is the same one that visited Arthur Francis in Lewes. He cheers one muchly.

[...] I am entitled to a 20 minute visit and I should like to see you if you can manage it. Now I shall be able to write every month, that is if I behave myself, and you will too, so the time won't seem so long. I hope the war will soon cease [...]

Kiss all the youngsters from Daddy with his best Love, and accept some for your dear self from him who loves you dearly

Frank

39 Maitland Park Road
22/4/17

Dear Lucy

I am glad to know you are all well and going on all right. I think you are very plucky to carry on as you have done all this time; at the same time I think that the men of the CO class have no thought of wives and families, to leave them to the mercy of other people. I do not know where we should be if all our men was of the same opinion.

I am <u>proud</u> of the men who are fighting for the safety of our country and people. If we were to allow the Germans to come here we should have had to go through the same torture as Belgium and France has had to experience. I consider that the COs who have deserted their homes and families for the sake of pride, of the so called Brotherhood, then I do not see where the manhood comes in: we know war is a terrible thing, especially the frightfulness of the Hun's methods, Zepps and submarines bombarding of the coast of no military importance, which is not warfare at all, but let us hope that it will soon end and bring us back to normal conditions again. I hope you will keep well now the fine weather is coming; after the long and trying events we have had it will be a pleasant change. You might let me know how you are getting on now and again. Mother was very poorly last week. Katie came and stopped here several nights, but she is better now but not quite right. You must not mind me being outspoken as I say what I think.

Love to all

Your affectionate father

E J Clifton

North Avenue Letchworth

May 4th 1917

My dear Frank

I was very glad to get your letter this morning. Also glad to know you were alright so far. I hope you don't expect a long letter this time, I am just going on the round as usual but thought I had better write you a note so you get it in the morning [...]

I will write again tomorrow. Excuse scribble and haste. I had toothache very bad in the night, also headache, nerves I suppose. I shall be alright in a day or two; the children worried a bit yesterday and I was wanting a quiet think all about you. Perhaps it is selfish to love you so much but some day we shall have our own happiness all the time when we are reunited after the war [...]

Lots of love from us all

Lucy

THE CONSCIENTIOUS OBJECTOR'S WIFE

32 North Avenue Letchworth, Herts
Tuesday May 8 1917

My dear Frank,

How we long for this opportunity of writing to each other. The longing to speak to you and look at you sometimes is almost unbearable. I expect you feel the same. You are <u>never</u> out of my thoughts. I hope you don't mind for me to write this, but I must express this feeling to you, to all the world I hide it. Our love is no less for this separation. I know now how much you are to me, my every being is bound up in you. Perhaps I have relied too much on you, and your judgement on all matters. Now I find I have to talk to people instead of you. I manage very well but you know I am not a talker and I often wonder how I <u>do</u> manage to say what I mean and think. It is like the 'mantle of Elijah' fallen on me, or perhaps you are with me in spirit as I go my rounds and so help me.

People are all very nice to me and I like to keep the work on, but sometimes I am fed up. I shall be glad when the war is over and you are back to work for us all. I cannot see how women are continually going to take the place of men, especially when they have the care of children.

[...] I am just off to Adult School, it is held on Tues. eve now, so it suits me much better.

Thursday

I enjoyed school very much. Mrs Myles gave us a talk on beans and peas and how to dry them for winter use, so now we know we shall be able to do it, provided we can grow them. Dr Crowley has sent me an outline of the 'Proposal for the establishment of an agricultural and Industrial Cooperative Town'.[43] There are six pages of closely typed words, so I cannot give it to you unless you wish to know or dwell on any particular idea of it. Mrs Matthews tells me that Mr M is on the committee for the commencement of it, they are already looking for a site and hope to commence operation in about a year, so things are

---

43   This would eventually be built as Welwyn Garden City.

moving on. Of course there are numbers of people here interested and I believe eager to start.

Mrs Matthews came and told me this on Sat. I have seen very little of her, but I must tell you of her kindness to me and you must never say a word about her again. I was feeling a little depressed about you, (I feel it more the better weather coming) she saw I was nearly done up but said nothing, only asked me to take the children round in the evening.

I went and to my astonishment [she] asked me to stay the night and spend Sunday, of course, I refused, how could I leave the children, however she had seen Mrs Goodall and got her to promise to get dinner and tea and see to the kiddies on Sunday, so in the end I went after breakfast about ten and she put me to bed on the veranda with a hot bottle and left me to myself rest and quiet bringing my dinner to me. You don't know how much good that did me and how much I appreciate her thought. I did not want to be talked to. I feel much better now.

It is very wonderful how all ways seem to be made smooth for me. I knew the one thing I was wanting was rest and quiet, even according to Christian Science, but did not see how to get it, and there it was.

Then Dora's boots have given out, and there came two pairs of shoes from Miss Poynting or rather Mrs Jacques, I never dreamt of her sending me anything and they just fit. As Dora said, if we do as we feel right no harm can come to us and we shall not want for anything. Altogether we are happy and contented that things are as they are, if only the dreadful slaughter would cease [...]

Wandsworth Prison
May 14 1917

Dearest Lucy

I again am privileged to write to you. I am sure you would have me state as to how I am [...]. As to health I am well and the indigestion has left me entirely, so I suppose that a restricted diet is a blessing in disguise. As I write the sun is streaming in at my window and making even my abode look cheerful. [...]

The weather has been so glorious lately that it puts new heart into us and we can go on strong in the strength the Master sends us. We have had good times here at the Quaker meeting. I was with you in spirit last Sunday afternoon and pictured the scene to myself. I hope the children had a good time during this holiday. Tell Morris that he must be careful not to run over anyone with his motor and perhaps Mr Goodall can put a bell on it for him.

I suppose that the Maypole dancing is to be carried out as usual and I hope the youngsters will be in it. I remember last year; what a good time we all had. I actually danced with Katie, do you remember. I guess it will be a little time before we all meet there again. I miss the Letchworth chaps from here but if my sentence is commuted I shall soon see them again. Write and tell mother I am well and as happy as can be under the circumstances. [...]

I hope your mother and Dad keep well remember me to them when you write. It must be an awful blow to their ideas of respectability to have a Son in Law in Gaol. [...]

The library here is a good one and I get some good books. I have been reading Longfellow again and it is sweet to read of love and God's works. I have also got the Inner Life by Rufus Jones and advise you to borrow it from Miss Jefferies if you can as it is good [...] [44]

I hope you have got good neighbours. I am glad the chicks have done so well, you must try and get some young ones to maintain your stock. [...]

I send all my Love to you and a Father's Love to the children. Kiss them all from me and accept some for yourself.

---

44   Rufus Jones was an American Quaker and theologian, prominent in writing and publishing Quaker thinking. *The Inner Life* (1916) was one of his many works on spiritual thinking and living.

Yours as Ever

Frank

̴

June 8.17

My dear Frank

I am writing this letter now hoping you will be allowed to receive it before you write yours to me. First I must say that this month has passed much quicker than the others have gone. I have been very busy, all sorts of jobs as usual: collecting first, of course, sewing in abundance, also gardening, cleaning (some), washing also, some and mothering. I really think that should come first don't you, because I'm that all the time. I go out a lot too in the evenings to meetings.

I have enjoyed those Wednesday evening meetings very much and am learning such a lot. I feel to be just finding myself and putting my thoughts and opinions in order as it were. [...] I believe that having the experience we had then really led us to the wider love of the brotherhood of the world, and makes one want to be helping humanity all one can. The words 'Faith without works is nothing' have been in my mind all the week, you will see why in a few moments.

I am rather disappointed in Goodalls. They are too full up with Mission[45] and so on to spare time or thought for the nation or the public good. I gave him a regular 'Frankonian' dressing-down today at dinner because he never goes to any meetings, and one day, talking about the women question, she said she knew nothing whatever about those things and didn't want to. However they are young yet and have a lot to learn before they catch up to us, haven't they? We have been through more than some people's lifetime experiences in the last 12 years [...]

Last Sunday was Sunday School anniversary at the Mission; the girls went in the morning and wanted to go again in the evening. Morris

---

45   Mission Hall, a nonconformist and evangelical church in Letchworth.

wanted to go too if he could have a hymnbook and sing, he said. We went again on Monday evening for prize distribution. It was really more than I could swallow, I felt I had gone back years and years and I nearly shouted out, more than once: it would no doubt have created a sensation. I know I shall break out one of these times. I told Goodall if those people had lived up to their Christianity we should never have had war, even now they might write with those who are trying to get peace, but they won't [...] We had a nice meeting at the Adult School on Sunday afternoon altho' very few there; not one of the Barn men and not Goodall, of course. Did you know he was Sec. during the absence of Wiltshire? The Howard Hall [adult] school had been invited but only about 6 turned up. Peter Myles spoke, and among other things said thoughts were of great importance in life and had great influence. He was very interested when I quoted to him that part of your letter referring to thoughts. I do really feel you with me so often, I know you are thinking of us almost constantly.

On Wednesday eve. the ILP had a garden party at Mrs Harding's. She sends greetings to you. We had a nice time: I took Dora and put the other two to bed, we had from 6.30 to 10.30 and I danced two or three times once with Mr Ray [...] I heard then that Mr Osborn has got until Aug 2 now [...] (Mr [Noel] Palmer's appeal comes off on the 15th.) Mr Brunt sends greetings and particularly wants to know if you are working in your cell or in company of others.

Mrs Noel Palmer has a daughter, last Monday, she was very ill and is still. I took the children up to see the baby this afternoon, 5.30 bus and I was allowed a few minutes with her though visitors are not allowed yet. I suppose I am one of the family. The baby is Katherine Isobel [...] There was a splendid meeting at the Skittles last night to hear reports from delegates to the Leeds conference. Eben Howard,[46] Simmonds and Miss Lawes, they were very encouraging and makes one feel hopeful that something *must* soon be done to stop this world madness. When you hear reports from those actually there, it seems very different from what one reads in the paper [...]

---

46   Founder of the Garden City movement.

The chickens still keep on laying; One seemed to be gone broody so I got 6 eggs to sit her on just for the children, however moving her from her corner where she has sat all the week upset her, so she ate one of the eggs and went back to her corner. I had boarded up the side of the small house, but she pulled it all down: so much for my first attempt at sitting a hen, however I shall try again. I don't like to be beaten.

[...] Morris is as brown as a berry, no shoes and stockings as usual most times. Chrissie feels the heat rather and is a bit off her feed, but an egg or two puts her right. On our way back from Redcroft we called at Miss Gregory's, they were in the garden: she gave me a lovely bunch of syringa, we must have a tree of that in *our* garden some day![47] She wished to be remembered to you. I think she gets a bit lonely sometimes. Mr G only gets home for weekends now, the increased fares make it expensive for people to get about.

We are having a meeting next Wed. Skittles, speaker E D Morel;[48] of course I shall be there. Morris particularly wants me to tell you he has got 3 silkworms and he will look after them alright this year [...]

I was so glad to have Mr Palmer's report of his visit. I suppose you would like me to come and see you? I expect it to be the Wed. or Thurs of the week after next. I shall have to see when suits Dr Crowley: I believe, now I think of it, he said he was only in London Fri and Sat, so we must just come when we can. I only wish it were possible to meet you in the open. The men at Bedford are being visited next week, they are all well [...] Clifford Allen has got 2 years.[49] Mrs [Brockway] has been with the 2 children to see her husband [...]

I have not heard from your mother since I wrote after receiving your

---

47 They did. Dora had some in her wedding bouquet, and the tree lived long enough to supply cuttings to Dora's daughter Elizabeth.

48 Morel was a prominent pacifist, best-known now for his work with Roger Casement campaigning against slavery in the Congo Free State.

49 Clifford Allen was the chairman of the No Conscription Fellowship and a leading Independent Labour Party politician. He was imprisoned as a CO three times.

last letter. My mother told me that Carrie would like to come and see you: shall I ask Alf and her to come?[50] Think it over and let me know when I see you [...]

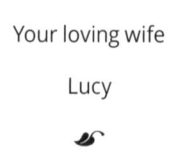

Your loving wife

Lucy

June 11 1917 Wandsworth Prison

Dearest Lucy

Your letter, as they always do cheered me muchly and has been a bright star in the clouded sky of confinement [...]

I am keeping well but find the hot weather more trying than the winter was and that was bad enough. I have caught the children's complaint and cannot sleep until it gets dark and I always wake at daybreak and lie listening to the birds singing their morning song and thinking of home. There are quite a number of birds around here as we are so near a big common. We are having a spell of lovely weather and have had no frost so I should think the potato crop will be a good one. Sorry to hear you will have fewer apples this year; did you get the trees pruned? Glad the chickens have been so dutiful to you.

When we get started again perhaps we shall be able to launch out on a bigger scale. These last few years have been full of experience to us and it will all come in useful in the future. I often think of the future but it is very dark. I am not a Prophet but I feel sure England is to see even darker days than she is experiencing now and trouble bigger than the war is looming ahead. God grant we shall see intelligent men and women arrive to grapple with the problems that are slowly forcing

---

50   Frank's brother and sister.

Opposite page:
6. Lucy's message on the 1917 family photo to Frank.
7. Chrissie, Dora, Morris and Lucy, June 1917.

2. IN WANDSWORTH PRISON AND BEDFORD PRISON

*To My dear Husband
With love and birthday Greetings
from. Lucy. May 10. 1917*

*Kind thoughts from all.
and loving wishes for the future
from Dora Chrissie and Morris
to Daddy
I am not so worried as I look   all well*

their way to the front. But enough.

Tell Dora that Daddy is now living on the dead body of the young man that Hiawatha wrestled with and buried in the earth and then watched the place for a long time. This will give her something to think of, and fix her memory perhaps. I am glad to hear of the good account you give Morris. He is a bonny laddie and our two girls are bonny lassies but the bonniest of all is their Mother. Your photo [see Figures 7 and 8] occupies a place of prominence in my abode and smiles down upon me as I lie awake at night [...]

Sidney Palmer's visit cheered me, as seeing his kind face was like feeling home again. He read your letter to me and I was glad to hear you are going out with the youngsters as we used to do. I hope you had a good time at the ILP Social [...]

I am glad to hear that Katie is still trying to be brave. She won't be happy until she has broken with convention. I suppose she is referring to us as those who do not trouble about what other people say. Well if we had done so I'm afraid our lives would not have been quite so happy and certainly not so full of adventure and experience. You will never convert your people so don't try, it is sheer waste of energy at their time of life. I thought somehow the war could not be carried on without Harry's assistance but everything will be all right now [...]

Kind Remembrances to all and lots of love and kisses to yourself and youngsters.

Your loving Husband,

Frank

Wandsworth Prison
July 10th 1917

Dearest Wife

Your letters are always a delight to me. You have such a concise way of saying just what is wanted. To put your mind at rest, I am in excellent health and received your letter yesterday. It was a welcome addition to my tea table. My Spirit is calm and my mind is quite easy. I sometimes wonder where all my troubles and anxieties have disappeared to. In the early days I tried to carry them alone but I found I could not bear them so I have just handed them on to Him who holds us in the hollow of his hand and such a peace possesses me now that it is impossible to describe. You I know do the same but living in the World as you do perhaps the reality is not so present with you when you are busy with all the duties to which you are called.

I received the photos and I […] think they are champion and Chrissie's face is worthy of a place in the National Portrait Gallery alongside the Laughing Cavalier.[51] It is such an exact picture of home as I see it when I am thinking of you all and drawing imaginary scenes of your life to satisfy my longing. Your visit cheered me immensely and I think you look as young as you did when we married. You must thrive on troubles as some children seem to thrive in dirt. Peter Myles too went straight to my heart. He is such a lovable chap and we understand each other so well. Better than anyone else in Letchworth I think. I hope when we migrate to the new colony he and his wife will go too.

As to making plans for the future, dear, and leaving the Bungalow[52] I say do nothing as all is so dark and uncertain that we can only wait with patience. A way will be made for us. Fancy me talking like this eh but prison has done me good. The being thrust aside and compelled to be idle has helped me recover my spiritual balance as it were. A naturally busy and energetic soul like me often wants to do his own will, not recognising the overruling power […]

I am glad you had the rain you needed so badly but I see you are like all the country folk, there has to be a fly in the ointment. Before I forget, my exchequer is nearly empty. I possess but one copper coin of the realm […] so if in your mercy you will send me 5/- I shall not be quite a beggar no matter how I look. […] The church service is bright and the Chaplain tries to bring a cheerful note into our lives. He preached on

---

51   See Figures 1 and 2.

52   Their rented home in Letchworth.

the Virgin Mary's Song of Joy in Luke, but I can't help feeling sceptical as to whether it is her work even though it is in the Bible. It is such a fine piece of poetry. There is a bone for you to pick.

You mention that you have been making jam. What is it? Something to eat? I have a dim recollection that it is […]

Lots of love my darling from your own loving and happy Husband. Happy in being so rich in love and loved ones. x

32 North Avenue Letchworth
July 25.1917

My dear Frank

I am sending 10/- for you. I should not like you to be without money. I hope you enjoyed Osborn's visit, I have heard from him since. I am looking forward so much to seeing you once more. Although I try to prepare myself for another separation Our life is made up of joy and sorrow and partings.

Some day we shall meet and part no more.

I hoped to write a nice letter for you to have […] but the words won't come readily, for one thing; this is Wednesday and I am doing accounts, and it is so hot.

Mrs Thomas's sister went home on Sunday so now we are 8 – plenty of us – Mother is going on Sat afternoon: she badly wants to stay on, can't see why not, but I have been very firm and she has just written to Dad and Katie to meet her, so that is settled and I am very glad.

Now I can't write any more; hoping with all my heart and soul soon to meet you in the flesh, you are always with me in spirit adieu, lots of love from us all

Your ever loving wife

Lucy

2. IN WANDSWORTH PRISON AND BEDFORD PRISON

Bedford Barracks, Bedford
August 3rd 1917

My Dearest Wife

I am sure you are looking forward to some news of my doings here. As you know I caught the train all right and sat by Donald Brunt and Jonny Hunter.[53] We had a pleasant talk about things in general. After getting to Hitchin I found I had fifty minutes to wait so I walked down to the centre of the town with Donald. I bought some stamps and then got back to the station. With still some time to spare I got into conversation with two men (workers) and then passed another twenty minutes.

I arrived at the barracks at about 11.30 and went to the Orderly room. The Sergeant greeted me with a smile and said 'Well you have come back again'. I thought I was for the Guardroom but the Corporal of the G Room took me to the [Company Sergeant] major and he put me on my honour not to run away again. I told him I was satisfied having had a holiday and would not give any more trouble. He then told me I would go the Barrack Room and consider myself a prisoner at large. I shall have to go before the Captain tomorrow morning. The Sergeant was very cross but he didn't disturb me much.

I went to the room, and some of the men who were there on my last visit came up and shook hands. I have had several conversations with men here and find most of them dissatisfied. While sitting there a soldier came up and cordially greeted me. He turned out to be Webster. He seems well but says he still feels very unfit [...]

I have been given to understand that my long stay was allowed because someone thought I was on Pass. It seems that Webster has a sleeping-out pass and that the Sergeant has been reporting me present by confusing Webster with myself. As they all call him the CO I have by that means profited by him being here but I am afraid no other CO will get the same benefit. What do you think?

---

53 Frank took an unexpected opportunity to come home to Letchworth for an unauthorised visit at the end of July 1917.

I shall be sleeping in the Barrack Room tonight but I guess it will be Guardroom tomorrow. I do not mind, however, as I got my holiday didn't I? I shall get as much fresh air as I can whilst here and dwell on my few days at home for many days to come [...]

Don't fret about me, as I am quite content and even happy, far happier than many men in these barracks: even if they do <u>think</u> they are free, I <u>know</u> I am free, and that makes all the difference [...]

As I write two squads of men are drilling in the square and the raucous voices of the Sergeants remind me of Wandsworth, but I do not think they bully so much and are not swearing so I suppose this a quite respectable barracks. The squads are recruits so perhaps that makes a difference [...]

Webster seems to be happy here. He says has not been posted to anything and gets no military commands but just has to help in the dining room with the meals. He undoubtedly can do good propaganda work here among the men he meets and I think he takes these opportunities.

Get to as many of the Summer School events as you can and write me <u>full</u> accounts of some, and if I can I will endeavour to give my point of view upon some of the subjects at any rate. I bought a pen and some ink this morning but shall not trouble to use it until I am <u>inside</u>.

Once more I send you loving greetings.

Yours not to be beaten or down-hearted

Frank

PS Shall we start a not down-hearted association of two? Please reply.

2. IN WANDSWORTH PRISON AND BEDFORD PRISON

> Guardroom, Bedford Barracks
> August 4th 1917

Dearest Wifie

I will resume from where I left off yesterday [...]

I rose soon after reveille 5.30 and was called on parade together with several others. I went knowing it was just for fatigues and as it was raining the corporal sent us to the bath house to clean the taps. There were seven of us men and six taps so I suggested they each cleaned a tap and I would watch them as my share being the organiser of the distribution of labour scheme. Soon afterwards the bugle blew for breakfast so it was a welcome sound. Menu – Tea, Bread, Margarine and boiled bacon. There was a good supply and I ate fairly hearty but there seems to be no staying power in the food.

At nine o'clock I was taken to the stores and ordered to don the khaki but refused, so of course I am now inside, as they call it. I was taken in front of the [Commanding] Officer and charged with being absent without leave, also refusing to put on uniform, both of which charges I admitted. He asked me where had I been and I said 'Home'; also, was it for the same old reason that I had refused, and I said yes. I was then put in the guardroom after getting my things from the barracks room, where my new friends shook hands and wished me luck. About an hour afterwards I was taken before the Colonel and the same performance was repeated. The Colonel said that we chaps had nothing to complain of in the treatment we got at Bedford and I said I agreed but nothing we can do will satisfy the Authority which he represented. He ordered me to be stopped seven days' pay for my first offence and to await the Court martial for the second, so I am now back in the Guardroom.

I do not feel very happy as the day is so bad and the light anything but good. I have had my dinner beef and potatoes and bread but little satisfaction. Meat does not satisfy me now, somehow. I have two companions in distress, one of whom is a C2 man who has been working on a farm, and having finished work on that farm failed to report himself and took holiday without permission.[54] He is doing three weeks in the guardroom. He is a quiet inoffensive specimen of the <u>hard</u> working class. The other is a soldier who has been out to the front and wounded rather badly, and walks on a crutch and stick. His offence is being absent, also having a forged warrant for travelling and he is awaiting a [Court Martial]. He is bright and cheerful but very dogmatic and opposed to COs. I do not think he is opposed to me as I refuse to argue or defend my position. Fancy that a change is certainly coming over me, eh. [...]

I wish I was able to be at liberty to work for you and our children. I cannot say what an awful feeling this feeling of helplessness is. It is no consolation to tell we chaps that we are fighting for great principles when all we want to do is just work quietly for those we love, but there the poor beggars who are dragged into the army are wanting the same thing, aren't they? [...]

Lots of love.

Yours ever even though in durance <u>vile</u>

Frank

🙞

32 North Avenue, Letchworth
August 7th 1917

My dear Frank

I have just had dinner by myself, the children and Mrs T having gone with some food to the sand beyond the Station in Icknield Way. They will enjoy themselves. I am preparing a meal for their return and am

---

54   Category C2 was a fairly low measure of fitness given by military doctors when assessing recruits' and conscripts' ability to cope physically and mentally with military service. Frank had been classed as C3, which he said was the lowest grade of all (7 November 1916).

off again, Howgills,[55] then to Baldock [...] Mrs Palmer and I went to ILP at Skittles on Sun evening: Eb. Howard on Housing after the War.[56] His is a Co-operative scheme too and Mrs T was interested. Am sending you Dr Crowley's paper. Let me have it back before you go to [?] don't like it much.

We all miss you very much; it seems such a long time since you left on Friday. Dora will write to you, perhaps this evening. I was amused at you having seven days' pay stopped. When will you draw what is owing to you?

I still think of writing to Lord Robert Cecil.[57] I wish you would be let off at the Court Martial. I also wish you could have liberty to work for me and the children and give me liberty to work in the house, garden etc, but we rub along quite alright. I must not complain about doing our duty [...]

Now I must stop again, duty calls so pleasure must obey.

Goodbye dear. Love from us all,

Lucy

Guardroom Bedford Barracks
August 7th 1917

Dearest Wifie

I was glad to get your letter [...] I must tell you all about the food here of course. We had bread and Mar and tinned bloaters. Quite good they were and the tea is <u>excellent</u>. For dinner we had roast mutton, potatoes,

---

55   Howgills is the name of the Meeting House of the Letchworth Quakers.

56   Ebenezer Howard, urban planner and founder of the Garden City movement.

57   Prominent pacifist and Member of Parliament, at this time serving as Permanent Under-Secretary of State for Foreign Affairs.

cabbage and batter pudding so we are doing alright eh. The cabbage was good and it was the first I had eaten for quite a long time. What we will get for tea I cannot tell as there is always something different so the surprises and combinations are really wonderful.

As I write two of the soldiers of the soldiers are yarning and as I am sitting between them I am having difficulty to keep my thoughts collected, for if I was to put in any of the conversation I am sure you would be shocked for even advanced women like yourself could not stand the luridness of the language [...]

The Guardroom is much sweeter for its scrubbing and the sun manages to find its way in so it is not so dark and miserable as last time. My companions are a cheerful crowd but not quite the sort I should choose, were I given any option.

I have not written to [?] nor to anyone else but you since I have been here and I do not feel inclined to do so. I cannot explain this diffidence but perhaps you can understand. I feel absolutely cut off from the world to which I belong and dumped into a world to which I do not belong and don't fit in as it were. I can only try to accommodate myself in a sort of outsider fashion and wait for better things to come along. As to candles and matches I am pleased you mentioned them, but there is no need to send anything as I can get such things quite easily. I have but few wants as you know and since I have been in this business even they have got less.

I have written to you every day but as the letters may not have been posted in time to catch the post you probably have not received them quite so regularly as you would like them [...]

Have you heard from your Mother yet? I should like to know what she says when she knows I am for another dose of prison. I should think it would be as good as a bottle of wine to her and make her heart rejoice to know another coward has got his deserts. [...]

Yours lovingly Frank

2. IN WANDSWORTH PRISON AND BEDFORD PRISON

August 8th 1917

My dear Frank

I received 2 letters from you this morning. Of course I am very interested in your doings and your food, am glad you are feeding well, it will help you when you are put on rations at his Majesty's guest house.

I have survived the work of yesterday but was quite knocked last night. I went to Howgills just in time to help cut bread which I did well and others could not do at all, as it crumbled so. Mrs Myles had made it, but could not cut it in decent slices.

Arlesley [Adult] School and Baldock turned up and we numbered over 60. Mrs Jeffries was presented with a hand bag and we had a most enjoyable time in social intercourse. I shall certainly try to get to some of the lectures, there are more of the Summer School people we know […] I got home at 8.30 dead beat. The children had been having a lovely time and were still playing happily in the garden. I got them to bed as soon as I could and after a little rest and a cup of coffee went myself. Now I have a busy day with bookings up. O dear I feel a little tired of it, no peace.

Now I must stop again for this time. So goodbye lots of love from us all

yours ever Lucy

✌

Guardroom, Bedford Barracks
August 9th 1917

Dearest Wifie

I got your letter and circular this morning and was pleased at the cheerful tone of your letter. I know that cheerfulness is the greatest asset in getting through trouble of any sort and in our case we have the assurance of doing the right thing haven't we darling. Also we know that in any case I should not be allowed to remain at home with you and the children but should have to spend my days in this rotten barracks knowing all the time that I had sold myself to the enemy. As to finances I understand that I could get the separation allowance for you but I don't think it will come to that do you? [...]

It is a great effort to write letters here as there is always a [?] conversation going on, not very uplifting I'm afraid but I try to do my best to raise the level and get them to think of better things. It would be much easier if the old soldier was not amongst us but he is of a dominating character, and though I could undoubtedly beat him at that it would not do the pacifist cause much good. There is a chap here who is awaiting [a Court Martial] for being absent 2½ hours and he is making a stand against tyranny in the army. He wants to employ a solicitor as will you of Mrs Thomas. Look in the Labour Year Book in the bookshelves and find the address of the Secretary of the Bedford Trades and Labour council and send it on to me at once.

Things are moving for me. Yesterday evening I went before the Doctor and he examined me and said I have got Scabies because of the rash on my chest which happens to be rather bad just now. Due to the diet here I think. We had bacon for breakfast and curried mutton rice and carrots and potatoes for dinner. I eat well but the confinement in this place is not conducive of good health is it? We had some exercise last night but shall get none today as it is raining.

I was taken before the [Commanding Officer] today and the evidence against me was taken down so the ponderous machinery of real life is at work and I expect I shall get my [Court Martial] in a few days.

Do send me a few envelopes, as I am having to borrow now and that I do not like doing.

I am sleeping well and feeling alright so don't worry about me dear. We men are earning respect amongst the soldiers by our attitude by the stand we are taking and the word coward is not used now when they speak of the Absolutists [...]

Another man has come in today and he is a wounded man who has been classed C3 and then put upon light duty; after some little time he gets another medical exam and classes as B1. So much for the army methods, eh? The more one sees of this awful military machine the more one realises the necessity to fight it and to obtain our freedom, both for ourselves and for the lads who will follow us.

I have just received another letter from you and am glad you went to Howgills and had a good time, also to hear your visit to Mrs Tait was a useful one […] Thanks for envelopes. If you send one or two each time you write I guess I can manage […]

I'll close now. Lots of love and endearments to my own darling wife and bonny children.

Yours lovingly

Frank

Guardroom, Bedford barracks
August 9th 1917

Dear Wifie

I am sitting perched up […] Two of the other chaps are lying down trying to while away the time. We have all just had a good dinner of Roast Beef potatoes, bread and Duff, if you know what that is,[58] so we all feel in the Sunday afternoon mood, when the paper falls from one's hand and curtain pulls one's head and slumber falls upon the senses like dew upon the grass. I am taking advantage of the quietude to write my promised letter.

I brought Chesterton's *Essays on All Things* with me and it is proving quite a treasure, affording means of argument amongst us on many topics.

We had a lot of rain yesterday evening but today has been fine but little sun shining. I've been interrupted by a pillow fight which has just subsided. These things will happen even in the best regulated

---

58   Duff was probably 'plum duff', a steamed pudding with dried fruit in it: cheap and filling carbohydrate.

guardroom. I'm also half a further lesson in the driving of a motor car so my education is still going on what with one thing and another [...]

One of the chaps here has a brother who is a CO and he says that he has had many an argument at home, but he now sees that we are right and all of the men here are sure that will be no peace without negotiation. [...]

I cannot write a long letter today but will try to do better tomorrow. Give all the kiddies a kiss from Daddy and accept as many as you desire for your own dear Self.

Lots of Love

Yours ever

Frank

🌀

Guardroom, Bedford Barracks, Bedford
August 10th 1917

Dear Wife

Your two last letters received this morning. As to Chrissie I trust nothing serious is the matter and you will do rightly to have advice about her. Perhaps she has got overheated and caught a chill, that might cause it. However do not worry, as all must be well for us. We are not given more than we can stand. So you are going in for public speaking, eh? Qualifying for the caravan and meaning to go with me and be my partner in that as well as everything else I do.[59] Ah Darling, you are my true partner, the better half. I am sure I should never have been the man I am had I not had your loving influence to sustain me. I was glad to get the youngsters' letters and have replied to them all.

---

59 This may have been a private joke between Frank and Lucy about taking to the roads to proselytise from a caravan. They were not Quakers, who do not proselytise, but came from a nonconformist background, which does.

2. IN WANDSWORTH PRISON AND BEDFORD PRISON

Last evening four of us had an hour's walk in the barrack yard and found it most enjoyable. It had rained in the afternoon and the air was cool and fresh. It is so nice to see all the clouds floating by and hear the wind in the trees, which look so fresh and green and calm and stately. There is a fine row of elms to be seen as one walks up and down. We have Guard over us but he does not interfere in any way and talks to us in quite a friendly way. Different from the prison system of doing things ie to be in one's own clothes is a delight. One feels oneself as it were [...]

I do not feel inclined to so much writing to our relations, so that must stand over and we will reply when they write to us. Not very charitable, perhaps, but I plead guilty to not feeling very much inclined towards them. Perhaps if you were here to reason with me I should muster energy enough to accomplish the task. My fellow confined thanks you for the address. Last night we had a discussion about Women and some lurid things were said and many strange incidents told, but I succeeded in making it clear that the same moral standard for both parties to the marriage tie is the only fair and honest one and they ultimately agreed. The divorce laws came in for a deal of criticism. We then discussed child life and the relation of the State towards them. Opinion divided on this subject. This gives you an idea that our time is not altogether wasted [...]

I send you lots of love and today will try and find a different ending if you are tired of my usual one. With all my affections I greet you Darling Wife.

Yours true to the end

Frank

PS Thanks for the envelopes and stamps. I am running short of scribbling paper so perhaps you could put in a few sheets with my washing.

THE CONSCIENTIOUS OBJECTOR'S WIFE

August 13th

My dear Frank

I have just got the children to bed and want a quiet time after the day's work, so cannot do better than write to you. I couldn't talk to you if you were here as I have got a swollen face, an abscess I expect, so don't feel at all the thing. I think I must have caught cold during the wet weather. The rain seems to have done a lot of damage to the crops, they are all beaten down and what are standing are losing all the corn out of the ears or else growing, so we have not a good prospect of living on the English harvest. The potatoes are also likely to be diseased through so much wet. It seems like a judgment I believe, and shows we are in the wrong to go on with this war. Have you heard about the resignation of Henderson and the anger of Lloyd George?[60] I wonder what you think about it. The government have refused passports to Stockholm! so we shall continue to fight till we stop.

Mr Brunt told us at the NCF meeting last Friday about a new sugar system: each house is to receive a paper to be filled, stating names, ages, sex and occupation of every member of each household – Well! Mr Brunt considered it a sugar pill really, covering registration for continued conscription, and no registration is available of lads of 16 and under. This is Lord Rhonda's idea, of course, as food controller;[61] each district has a committee and on ours are Mr Brunt, Mr Furnster and Miss Bartholomew, of course with others. They have seen through the trick and are disgusted. They have written to Civil Liberty people and others, and Mr Brunt says he will have nothing to do with such a thing.

---

60 Henderson resigned from David Lloyd George's Cabinet after Lloyd George refused to allow Britain to participate in an international peace conference in Stockholm, and those wishing to attend it had their applications for passports refused.

61 D A Thomas, 1st Viscount Rhondda, was a Liberal politician who served as the Minister for Food Control in Lloyd George's government, and introduced rationing.

2. IN WANDSWORTH PRISON AND BEDFORD PRISON

They were very interested about you and Mr Myles told me he was afraid the others will not get the same chance, you have spoilt that.[62] They will be put on their honour at once. […]

Mrs Thomas has got a book out of the Alpha Union Library[63] about Woman's Position. She has not come on very far and cannot enter into the communal household scheme; she says she could, but could not trust others to do likewise. She thinks I would, but knows no other people like me […]

There has been a raid over Southend and Margate, 2 killed at Rochford. I have not heard from Katie. You know she is there or at Westcliffe with her Jack. I hope they are alright, it does seem dreadful doesn't it, places full of holiday makers too. I think they made for London though, 20 of them (aeroplanes) […]

I have sold your old bicycle for 5/-, so shall buy you some new socks, or perhaps a pair of cycling stockings. I shall see, you will want them and I would rather buy something for you and everything will get dearer soon. I have paid Perry what I owed him and ordered another ton of coal so we shan't be cold for a bit. I like my new griller. I can bake scones (did you know?) when I have time. Of course things will be a bit easier when we are alone again, I don't think I shall let again.

Dora is getting very useful, yesterday she made a lovely pudding like we had on Christmas day; she scraped the potatoes and made the Batter pudding and on Sat she made the Nut Roast. I don't think I have any more news. I must tell you once more how much I miss you and long for your return. I am not thinking of the caravan idea just yet as I do so want a quiet peaceful time with you and the children. I seem to be doing so much now, I long for a holiday, which of course is impossible and I don't expect it. I am so glad we have grown together and not apart and understand each other so well and love each other so much.

---

62 Frank's lucky opportunity for leave by the guard mistaking him for Mr Webster.

63 The Alpha Union was a non-denominational educational and Utopian society, based at Miss Lawrence's house in Letchworth, where the Library was located (Hughes 1909).

I love the children but never before you (as Mrs Thomas says she did with Dorothy, she could even learn to do without her husband. I told her life for me would not hardly be worth living and I thought you were the same).

Fancy writing love letters after 12 years of married life and 20 years of courting. I'm surprised at you.

Now goodbye my dear husband, keep well and strong and come back soon to work for us and love us

>   lots of love from us all
>
>   Your loving wife
>
>   Lucy Sunderland

>   Guardroom, Bedford Barracks, Bedford
>   August 13th, 1917

Dear Wife of my heart

I received *Labour Leader* this morning[64] and was pleased to read of the movement once more. It is nice to feel that even though shut off from the world as we are at least we are part of the 'Church Militant' but not military [...]

Now for the news. My [Court Martial] is over. It took place at Bedford Barracks this morning. I was examined by the Dr and declared fit to pass through the ordeal. I refused to admit the right and ability of the court to try me as no man can try another for his conscience but when asked if I had any complaints against any of the officers personally. I of course had to say [no], so the President said I should have to submit to the jurisdiction of the court. I pleaded not guilty to disobeying any

---

64   The *Labour Leader* was a weekly socialist newspaper, that had been strongly pacifist from the beginning of the war under Fenner Brockway's editorship. The socialist politician Katherine Glasier (née Conway) was the editor from 1916.

military order as I considered that I am a free man detained by force. Then to facilitate the work of the Court I pleaded guilty to refusing to don the uniform. That cut out the evidence of the Ser[geant] and Corp[oral] against me. I gave them a little homily on the evils of militarism and said that it failed to accomplish the supposed object and just augmented all the evils it sets out to destroy. They listened patiently but I doubt it made any impression on them.

The [Court Martial] took place in the billiard room, and the windows being open I had a good view of the trees and fields opposite the barracks and my thoughts wandered from the business in hand, and I thought of the bounteousness of nature with all her beauty and contrasted God's work with the wilful and wicked destruction of man. A team of mules went by and the sleek fat animals looked so fine with their harness glittering in the sun, that the horror of war again thrust itself before my view. When will men organise for the common well-being? I suppose that they will do so some day […]

I expect to get my sentence by Thursday and go away at the latest by Saturday. A Corporal told me that he was going to [Wormwood Scrubs] today to bring back four COs. I wonder who they are […] I look upon this stage here as a pleasant break in prison monotony and it certainly has done me good both physically and mentally but of course one cannot expect <u>much Spiritual</u> upliftment in such an environment.

Yours full of love for thee

Frank

Guardroom, Bedford
Aug 14.17

Dearest Lucy

Since I wrote the last letter things have been moving here. Our family has been augmented by four more COs. They are not a prepossessing lot, by any means. All of them had been arrested at their work and their clothes are of course not of the best. Wanting a shave also makes no improvement in their appearance. It makes one think of the rottenness of the system that does not give them a chance to keep himself decent. These men are all strangers to me and they are all just plain workmen, the stuff out of which the revolution must come and I am one of them but I'm afraid I'm a particular kind of chap [...] One is a socialist, but as to the others I have not yet analyzed them yet. I expect during the course of conversation their views will come out. Two of them come from [Lincolnshire] and speak awfully broad. They are all young men and look fairly well considering their confinement.

[...] Yours still in love and no illusion

Frank

New Guardroom, Kempton Barracks, Bedford
August 15th 1917

Darling Sweetheart

I received your nice long letter last evening and it was good to read. I felt as if I were with you and it brought on my news to you. I am now in a new guardroom. We COs have all been removed from the old <u>dungeon</u> and are now in a fine big hut which is perhaps fifty feet long by twenty feet wide. It has nine big windows in it and they are all open, also doors at each end and another in the middle of the side so it is well ventilated and not at all stuffy like the old place. We have a guard of six men and a corporal to [...] keep us from getting into mischief.

Friend Latman has finished with the ink so I'm taking advantage of it. All our fellows are younger men than myself and two of them do not fully understand the position but will undoubtedly learn a lot before they are finished. Latman intended to stick it and his spell in prison has not altered his determination. All the other chaps have come from [Wormwood Scrubs] and they have had a bad time. My stay in Wandsworth was a picnic to it but don't tell Mrs Thomas this [...] All the soldiers are interested and want to understand our views etc. I <u>preached</u> for nearly two hours last night and tried to explain in as simple a language as possible our ideas. The history of war, the effects of war, and the revolution which we want to follow. The effect is to be felt in the future – as all soldiers are young men they will not forget what I have said and it will come up in their minds when they get back in civil life [...]

I did not finish describing my new dwelling. From the windows we can see the sky and the stars twinkling down on us as we lay abed. We in daylight can see trees and houses and a good view of the surrounding countryside. All these things tend to make one forget he is a prisoner. We also go outside into the air to wash etc, which is much better than having a latrine under one's nose all the time. The soldiers in the old guard room were very sorry that I had to leave them. I shall refuse to believe anyone who says I am a fighting antagonist etc again, as I am really a very <u>mild</u> and quiet sort of chap [...] I do not fear my coming imprisonment and I want you to really feel that I am happy, filled with the joy of righteousness and that I shall be content if I know you are also contented [...]

Yours ever Frank

✢

32 North Avenue, Letchworth

My dear Frank

Your letter arrived this morning. Please write as often as you can while you have the chance. I try not to mind very much, but it seems so cruel to take a man away from his wife and children when they need him so much. Either to soldier and death, or to prison and the knowledge of right, both are bad for the wife, only the latter is going to leave the world a little better than we found it and so makes it worthwhile to stick to our Idealism.

Chrissie is not better I am sorry to say. She has 3 places on her forehead now; her hand and leg is better. I am bathing her with hot water and boracic powder, but I shall take her to the Doctor this evening or the morning. Morris has his cough again. I am sure now it is caused through the enlarged tonsils. I expect they will have to be done soon. I shall try and get my teeth seen to too.

⇜

Guardroom, Bedford Barracks
August 17th 1917

Dear Sweetheart

I am writing you another letter after my <u>last</u> as I have not yet been removed from here [...] I was reclining on some shed boards and had an audience of about a dozen and I was not preaching Socialism but was telling them *The Valley in the Moon* and other Jack London stories. The old bard who used to tramp the country and to stay at the castles he came to did not have a more attentive audience, and a mother telling stories to her children could not have a more insistent demand for more. Pleasant occupation for a man waiting to be sent to prison, eh. I had an economics class in the evening which lasted about three hours, and after it got dark about nine of us sat round the table and talked. We discussed nearly everything and I think some were impressed by the COs and finally retired to bed at 5.30 this morning. I think I have made the most of my last day, don't you?

Your letter just to hand: I am awfully glad to have got it as I should really have been disappointed and worried about you for I knew you were suffering. I am glad the abscess has broken and Chrissie is on the road to improvement. You will perhaps get your teeth done through the Panel. If so it will cost you either nothing or just a trifle [...]

I trust you will write on *business* to me as often as you can so that we can evade the regulations if possible and don't forget to send me a photograph at the end of the month [...]

Lots of love to you to sustain you and keep you for our love comes from the source of all love.

Lovingly,
Yours Ever
Frank

3. 'I never wanted your presence more than now', August 1917 to March 1918

August 31st 1917

Dear Mr Sunderland

You will be surprised at getting a letter from me but I am writing at your wife's request to let you know that 2 of the children are not well just now. They were very poorly the end of last week – Dora and Morris and on Monday Dora came out in a rash and the Dr said both she and Morris had scarlet fever and on Tuesday they were taken to the hospital. Your wife is also not very well as she has had a sore throat, which is often the case with those who nurse scarlet fever, but she has not got the fever and is already very much better, but she is staying in bed for a few days and getting a good rest which won't do her any harm. Her sister Katie has come to stay with her till she feels herself again. Chrissie is quite well.

As the house has not yet been disinfected it is thought best that your wife should not write herself. That is why I am writing, not because she can't.

Now don't worry the least bit about them, the children are going on quite well and we will take care of your wife. I go up to see her every day and she was sitting up in bed today and was quite jolly, and knitting […]

Yours very sincerely

K J Middleton

September 3rd 1917

Dearest Wife

I have just heard through Mrs Middleton of the illness of your dear self and our two children. I have been very anxious about you for the past three weeks, as I have felt that all was not well with you. I am relieved to hear that you are a bit better and on the road of progress. You must take a real rest now. It is a strange fact that the only real holiday or rest a working woman gets is when she is utterly laid prostrate [...] I am glad Katie is with you but it is rough for her to be at everybody's beck and call in their hour of need. She is indeed a ministering angel and deserves every happiness in exchange. So Chrissie has escaped therefore you have one little sunbeam still shining in the house to cheer you, and Katie. I am in excellent health and am now easier in my mind that I know the worst. Fear of trouble is always harder to bear than trouble itself. You must exercise your <u>Faith</u> and I'll do the same. Send your thought waves this way and I'll return them then we shall strengthen each other. Take great care of yourself Dearest as you know how precious you are to me.

I send you and the children all my love

Your loving husband

Frank

October 9th 1917 Bedford Prison

Dearest Wife

I am rejoiced to at last be able to write a long letter to you. I will say at once that I am in good health and as happy as one can be in such circumstances [...]

I received the photo and it now adorns my mansion and all four smiling faces look down upon me as I eat my meals in the quietude of bachelordom [...]

3. 'I NEVER WANTED YOUR PRESENCE MORE THAN NOW'

I have reread *Martin Chuzzlewit* and greatly enjoyed it. Dickens is always a delight to read but I am inclined to think he puts the paint too thick. For instance Pecksniff the humbug and Sairey Gamp are exaggerated and perhaps one loses sight of the beam in one's own eye by surveying Dickens' timber yard. I have also read Thackeray's *Vanity Fair* which as you know deals with 'High Life' and its follies […]

Thank Mrs M for her letters concerning your illness and the children. I cannot say how thankful I was because I knew something was wrong. The tone of your last letter to me at the barracks showed me you were suffering. I knew that your strength was being used up. However it is over now and I suppose you have got D and M home again. I hope you will all regain your strength. […] By the way I should like you to keep my bicycle in the house during the winter. I am not altogether wasting my time here as I am studying the construction of a motor etc. also going through a course of mathematics so tell Dora that Daddy expects her to master those tables so she can make good progress when she returns to school […]

Let me know about the progress of the [Cooperative] Town as my interest in it grows. I am convinced that it is the next step in the right direction. We have got to show the world that our ideals are practical and it is by trying to live up to them that we can do so. If we can show on a small scale that men and women can live together, work and own in common the means of wealth production and that harmoniously we shall indeed be a city set upon a hill. It is not enough to think on good things as the apostle Paul writes and the orthodox preacher is so fond of quoting, we must also practice them. Pardon my moralising but as these letters are my safety valve as it were I make no further excuse. My space is nearly gone.

If you are coming to see me please do <u>not</u> bring the children as I should not like them to get a wrong impression. If you do not come I can have a letter instead, but I leave it to you entirely […]

Darling wife I conclude my rambling letter by once more repeating that which I am sure you never tire of reading your Love sustains me and my Love I send you.

Ever your loving Husband

October 11th 1917
32 North Avenue, Letchworth

My dear Frank

I was so glad to have your letter this morning; you know how much I long for it, as you do mine. Dora and Morris are not home yet and Chrissie is still here. Dora will be disappointed, she is so wanting to get home. I suppose they are not quite ready yet. Morris has been rather bad, he will need a lot of care this winter and you know I shall give it to him. I hope to have his throat seen to as soon as possible, the matron says that keeps him back. I miss them so much; at first it seemed dreadful, the day they were taken away I felt robbed of my husband and children too, and felt so ill myself. They wanted to send me too and send Chrissie away, but I said NO.

It was so good of Katie to come straight away, by the next train after getting the letter, and Chrissie looked after me and herself, like a little woman, until she came. Mrs Middleton happened to look in just as the ambulance came so she wrote to mother and Katie, Mrs Thomas, Eastman and Kays for me. [...] Katie went home last Tuesday, she had been here 5 weeks, much improved in health and nerves. She had been spared some experiences and is glad of it. Mother came down the Tuesday before, she is still here and waiting to take Chrissie back, thinks it very unwise of me to send her, but I do not want her to get [scarlet fever] if I can help it. I know they are supposed to be clear of infection when they leave, but it has happened before and might again.

Mother just said give my love to Frank. We have many an argument. I am afraid I get very hot at times, but I can't help it. I am feeling about well now, have not had my teeth out yet. I shall pluck up courage one day, but I really have not felt strong enough. I don't think I was ever so long getting well as I have been this time.

I think I have done well by giving up the Britt[annia] in all ways, Eastman will now pay my State Insurance. Of course I drew the 7/6 weekly for a month [...]

[Katie] helped to get some of my potatoes up, enjoyed the novelty. George Stone has been today and finished them. I and he reckon they

3. 'I NEVER WANTED YOUR PRESENCE MORE THAN NOW'

have yielded 2 to 3 cwt: not bad eh?[65] They are a bit worm eaten and a little diseased, but everyone's are the same. I have ordered a cwt from Green for 6/-, so we shall do, and the waste will help to feed the chickens. I have still got 2 jars of pickled eggs and they have kept on laying. Dora and Morris have had over 40 and I have had them too, so they have been good,[...]

Your mother has been to London and stayed with Cissie and Carrie: she is back home, she went up to see Mother twice and seemed very well.

Thursday Aft

I have been up this morning to the Hospital to enquire how the children are, still going on alright. I took them some more eggs too. It is a long walk and I must be there before 10 o'clock. I met Mr Brunt, he sends greetings and told me to keep a good heart, I do try but sometimes find it very hard. [...] Stone has been in and planted 150 Spring Cabbages, so I am being looked after. Am getting some apples from Palmer.

Have brought your bicycle indoors.

Mrs Middleton has just been in, now I shall not catch the post with this, so you will have to wait a little longer. She has been very good when I was ill she came every day for nearly 3 weeks and did a lot of writing and shopping for a fortnight. It might have been worse. Mrs Middleton sends greetings and is glad to hear you are well and cheerful. She seemed to like Katie and invited her to tea with Chrissie and myself one day, of course we went. K. did not get much dissipation here, she found it dull, not even a book she could read and enjoy. She did read *No. 5 John St* and *The Last Days of Pompeii*.[66]

I am doing some needlework for Mrs Harding, that will be better than

---

65   2 cwt (hundredweight) is about 100kg.

66   Richard Whiteing's *No 5 John Street* (1899) was a very popular 'slum fiction' novel, describing heroic lives amid slum settings in London's East End. *The Last Days of Pompeii* (1834) was written by Edward Bulwer-Lytton, combining high melodrama and social commentary.

going out so much. I know I can get plenty to do, and I must not be lazy: you know I like to be independent as far as possible, if none of the others can't. It costs a lot to live just now and all food is scarce. Mr Pearce [at the] Co-op told me today there is a world shortage […]

I have no more news about Crowley's [new Garden City] scheme, but he is giving it at the men's [Adult] school next Sun, I hear, so it is still on the move. Miss Jefferies has gone to Golders Green and K. Brown has gone to America […]

I got all you sent by Mr Bowry and must admit was rather upset at the length of the [prison] sentence, but do not let my mind dwell on it, there is plenty to think about, so many problems one tries to study. I am on the joint committee of the Adult School. We are holding ours on Tuesday afternoons. Miss Reynolds is coming to give us one talk on citizenship, and I hope we shall have some good times […]

You will like to know that George Thomas is at Dartmoor. He refused the HO Scheme too,[67] he is quite well, but feels the separation from his wife and children very much. He has had a cheery hopeful letter from his brother Jack, and mentions you.

Mr Miles called this morning (Friday): Gardner has his discharge, and both Ogilvie boys have been arrested. Our various organisations are working hard for peace and have been very prominent in the press lately. I do not think this awful war can possibly last much longer. I was sent for this morning to fetch home Dora, she is pretty well, am sorry to say Morris is back in bed, a cold, the matron says. I was afraid he would miss Dora, but he has some nice little boys there who talk to him and I think he is well looked after, so don't worry about him.

Now I must stop, hope I have not written too much

    love and lots of it from Dora and Chrissie and your ever loving wife

                                  Lucy

---

67   Dartmoor was one of the two sites used in the Home Office Scheme, so Lucy may have been mistaken.

3. 'I NEVER WANTED YOUR PRESENCE MORE THAN NOW'

Mother has gone back home and I have not sent Chrissie

❦

October 24 1917 Bedford Prison

Dearest Lucy

It was with the greatest pleasure I received your letter [...] I am glad you are well again and that Dora is home once more. I can quite understand your loneliness. It is an awful feeling and quite takes the nerve out of one [...]

I should like you to send me a list of the subjects you are taking at [adult] school and perhaps I could help you a little in my letters. I am reading G[eorge] Borrow's *Life of the Gypsies* just now. It is interesting as they really are a strange and mysterious people. I have read *Pendennis* again too. Thackeray is always good, but out of date as far as his deductions go [...]

I trust you are all well and reunited, Morris home again and I look forward eagerly to your early reply. I shall be entitled to send my next letter on November 19th. I send you all my love and lots of kisses for the bairns and my only regret is that I cannot give them to you all in person.

Yours ever Frank

❦

32 North Avenue, Letchworth, Herts
October 26 1917

My dear Frank

I was greatly pleased and cheered at receiving your letter this morning. We have been much together in spirit this week, so I thought you were probably writing to me.

You will be glad to know that Morris is at home again, much better than

I had expected him to be, of course he is not just as well as I should like, and I had to keep him in bed all day yesterday, but he is better today and has been down the town with Dora and I this afternoon. We met Mrs Ironside and she says his throat can be cured without operation by a fruit diet. I don't quite see how it is to be managed with grapes 1/6 lb, oranges 4d each, dates 9d lb and so on, still, I am doing what I can for him and feel sure he will get well and strong in time. I think it is wonderful how well they both are considering their general weakness, he has grown, as has Dora. I had to fetch him last Saturday, Mrs Tickle lent me her push chair, but he walked most of the way, and was so glad to get home, and appreciated his nice meals.

As for our dinners which you ask for menus of, they are very simple: Sunday nut roll, brussels, potatoes, apples and custard. Monday cheese and tomatoes, bread and butter, dates apples and nuts. Tuesday veg soup, potatoes, marrow, suet pudding and treacle. Wed, lentil savoury, cabbage, potatoes, macaroni pudding, Thurs, Haricot stew, carrots, pots. and rice pudding Fri Soup and pots, boiled rice and apples. You see we get plenty of variety as usual, cheap and nourishing, of course not so much in quantity, but plenty enough. I get a [quart] of milk a day: the children need it, and I still have my ½ Irish butter, and everything else I need I have no trouble to get from the Co-op.

Mr Palmer is trying to get some oatmeal and 28 lb of rolled oats for me. Things are very scarce and dear, but one can live simply and do without what we can't get. Tickle agreed with me in talking one day and says they have no trouble. Bacon and meat and eggs (4¼) are a great item when people can't live without. I am sorry to say my carrots and onions did not come to much but I have some good Brussels and Cabbage coming on and parsnips are very fair; I expect some more onions from Clifton, have got a good few now.

[...] Mrs Thomas has had 2 cwt potatoes and bushel of apples from Green, so people are looking a little ahead you see. They all seem to think we shall be feeling the pinch of actual shortage after Christmas, but I am hoping the war will be over soon, sometimes I feel hopeful and sometimes depressed, and when I meet Mrs Williams, or Mrs Bowry etc, we cheer one another. I met Mrs Bowry this afternoon, she hopes to visit Bedford in a fortnight [...]

3. 'I NEVER WANTED YOUR PRESENCE MORE THAN NOW'

While we were sitting round the fire last evening I told the children, Daddy was thinking of us, we never forget you and after they have gone to bed I feel so lonely, now the nights are long and dark I don't get visitors. Sometimes I think I shall have to get a lodger for till the spring, I suppose when the time is up, there will be no choice […]

The ILP meetings seem to be attended very well. Moss is Sec. and treasurer is Mrs Moss: he likes to do all the work I think. Mrs Gregory has given up everything concerning it, not membership of course and Miss Lawes still does her bit, also Simmonds. I have the *Labour Leader* from Mrs Middleton now, when she has finished with it, also the *Herald*.[68] I know all about the meetings and what is talked about, but I could not leave the children to go, especially after the upset I had last week.

I was very much alarmed and not unduly seeing that three [bombs] were dropped at Walworth and so suddenly that the factories were still blazing away till after; they had no warning till the bangs came.[69] Mrs Tickle was here and I had just gone with her to the gate. Of course she came in again and waited a bit with me, then on her way home called for Bertha Wells to come in to me for a little while, I feel rather nervous every evening and go to bed about 9 and get to sleep pretty soon. Dora was awake and was very frightened the windows shook so. Chrissie slept through it. Of course I thought of Morris, but he slept though so near, then of you and the poor creatures in London. To think that such horrors can go on in these days of civilization and enlightenment it surely must stop soon. I am glad I did not let Chrissie go to London.

Katie is coming again soon. I wish she could stay: she is living with mother just now and I know is not happy, she won't be until she has her heart's desire. He is not a bit like what you would imagine she would like, but he seems very fond of her, in fact told me so, and will wait the

---

68 *The Daily Herald* was a Labour-supporting newspaper that was published weekly for the duration of the war. It would eventually become *The Sun*.

69 This may have been part of the 'Silent Raid' of 19 October, in which a single Zeppelin dropped bombs on London without detection. White 2014, 219.

5 years necessary for a legal marriage: it is now 2 but probably the law will be altered before then. I hope so, it might get weary work waiting, and he is older than her so neither of them are young. I expect he will come down again while Katie is here. I am glad you are interested in them.

Our [Adult] school does not seem to be quite satisfactory, somehow. I went last Tuesday and did not get the help and fellowship I was needing. Miss Crees took the Bible lesson; it was the temptation of Jesus, Luke 4 1-15. I liked what she said. Next week is the Friend of Sinners, Luke 7 31-50. I don't know what else we are to have, but it is likely Miss Jefferies will be here for a little, she has had some bad shocks from Air Raids and has not quite found herself among the new friends yet. I expect she will be surrounded but I must try and get a word with her […]

It will soon be a year since our parting. I feel to have lived years since then, one thing I believe I have grown, mentally I mean, I have just been reading the life of Mrs MacDonald: how splendid to have such an intellect and use it for so much good, but still I suppose I must not wrap up and put away my one or two talents, so now I have to keep them in use being on my own.[70]

I am so glad you have had some books you like. Dora is very interested in Gypsies and wants to know all about them so remember all you can for her. I think she will take to her music again presently. I have not started her to school yet, perhaps next week she will be quite well enough […]

The children all send love to dear daddie and I send you all my love to my dear husband Frank from Lucy

---

[70] *Margaret Ethel MacDonald* by Ramsay MacDonald (Hodder and Stoughton 1913). She was a feminist and social reformer, married the future Labour Prime Minister in 1896 and died in 1911.

3. 'I NEVER WANTED YOUR PRESENCE MORE THAN NOW'

32 North Avenue, Letchworth
December 12th 1917

My dear Frank

I was very much surprised as you expected I should be, and you can imagine how delighted to receive a letter from you this morning. I should have liked to answer it at once but duty called me out, collecting, and Adult School this afternoon. Now I have put Chrissie and Morris to bed early, it is now only quarter to seven and Dora is sitting reading so I can get a quiet time with you and I always do write as if I am talking to you. I hardly know where to begin. I think I must shock you first by telling I went (with Dora for company) to the ILP Social and dance last Thursday at Howard Hall. It was full and I enjoyed it very much. I had not thought of going but Mrs Harding sent me tickets. Mrs Tickle did not go; she said she was half inclined to, but hearing of the raid in London the night before unnerved her. I left Chrissie and Morris in bed and asked Mrs Stacey to go over if anything happened. I got home about 10 and found the house and contents as I left it.

The lecture on Sat was quite good. The Hall was more full if possible than before. Of course there was a great number of teachers and inspectors etc […] I felt in very respectable company. The subject was Nursery Schools, the speaker being Mrs Fisher, the wife of the man who is introducing the Education Bill.[71] She said she was more at home with Infant Welfare work and was evidently a worker among the poor. She considers these schools for children between the ages of 2 and 5 very necessary first from a medical point of view as the children can be watched and treated for the first sign of anything wrong with health; then from the mother's point of view. How could she look after the house and all the duties therein <u>and a husband to cook and wash and mend for</u> with 2 or 3 or more little ones round her (I thought of a part of

---

71 The economist and historian Lettice Fisher (née Ilbert), married to H A L Fisher, Liberal politician and President of the Board of Education during Lloyd's George's government. She would go on to found the National Council for the Unmarried Mother and her Child, now known as Gingerbread. His bill became the Education Act of 1918.

my history almost forgotten). Then the children themselves would be far happier and learn better habits than they would playing in a gutter or minded with 6 or more others by an old granny in a neighbour's back kitchen while the mothers went out to work.

This was really the summing up. You can pretty well tell what she said about each point. Of course I think the idea well enough, but we do not want mothers to <u>have</u> to go out to work. If they prefer it then have the schools for the babies. It was asked if it was to be compulsory and the answer was no (but I think it might become so). Then about the husband which I have underlined; it seemed he was causing so much work he had better be boarded out, I thought. Then it seems to me most women prefer to look after their own little ones and if houses were more convenient there would not be so much unnecessary work and husbands want teaching for boys to be useful and take a share of training the little ones. On thinking this over I still consider my old scheme of cooperative housekeeping the best; nursery school would be included. One hope in all this is that these babies who are trained from 2 years to good surroundings and care and amusement and fresh air and proper food will not put up with just anything and will want different arrangements for themselves and their own homes by the time they get married and have little ones [...]

I suppose you know we are living in the front room and have been since I was ill. I only light the kitchen fire about twice a week and occasional fires in the bedrooms. The girls have our room. I don't like it without you and the front is more cheerful in the morning when I wake up. I have decided not to have a lodger. We really need the room. The children are getting quite big now. We can't all crowd in together. I find I have more time for the house since I gave up the Brittannia and I could not have left Morris so much alone. Anyway I feel I do <u>quite</u> as much work as I am able. I don't want to wear myself out even if it is better than rusting out [...]

When I fetched [Morris] home on Sunday week afternoon I found he had got a very bad cold and they had only done one side of his throat. It would be finished – sometime – when the Drs could come, they would let me know. His cold got worse and I kept a fire 2 nights and days and kept him in bed last Tuesday. Then he got well again and it is lovely to hear him sleep so quietly.

Have just had to stop this and get Dora to bed. She has some cocoa and a crust so I have mine too with her; this is every night about 8. I fill the bottles with hot water for them now it is so cold and I go to bed about 9.30 and we all sleep till 7. Morris generally crawls into my bed for a cuddle. Kays sent me an eiderdown for a sample; of course I use it and think I must buy it. It is rather dark, green border, covers our big bed, 27/6. They recommend them in place of blankets as wool is such a price and almost impossible to get soon [...] I got Swanson's [commission] 25/- last week so I paid up your Ideal, paid for oatmeal and rice from Palmer, 14lbs each, also 2lb jars Marmite and 3lbs Nutter[72] from Tickle. You know how it worries me not to be in debt. I also bought something warm for myself I needed; something else I looked at and didn't get. But on Friday afternoon Mrs Middleton came up and took out of her bag a stone hot water bottle for a present. She said a little bird told her I was looking at some in the window one day. Now what do you think of that – 'ask and ye shall receive' which reminds me that when I ask the children what Santa Claus shall bring them for Christmas they answer 'Daddy'. That is what they want most.

Now about Chrissie, she is as fat as butter and keeps so well. This morning she got over me properly: said she wasn't feeling well - pain in her chest and stomach, wanted to stay in bed. I let her and wrote a note to Mrs Price. However, she ate her breakfast, 2 slices of bread and butter and a good helping of stewed apple and a cup of warm milk. After 9 she got up and later went up to the post for me and ate her dinner and thought she would go to school when she found I would not take her out with me. After tea I hear that they had exams this morning, Arithmetic and Reading, her two worst subjects; now how about that for a dodger? [...]

I will gladly do what you suggest about Dora's birthday; she will be pleased. I am going to get her a pencil box and she is asking 3 girls for tea; that is the most I can do for her this time. No cake, cannot buy

---

72 A nut butter, high in protein and fat.

currants or icing sugar or chocolate and oranges 4d each. I am glad I have some apples [...] Tickle ordered 28lbs of Nutter from Mapleton, and Palmer too, and they sent <u>50</u> each so I can have all I need from Tickle cost price so the children won't run short of fat unless everyone is short; then it will have to be shared out [...]

I must tell you about Morris. I always clean all through [the house] on Fridays. Last week he wanted to help so I set him to clean the flue and black the kitchen grate. I tied on him your snobbing apron.[73] After he had finished he looked a picture – nose, ears, hands and apron, oh dear. I told him to wash and he dried or rather wiped off the black on a clean bathroom towel. I am sure it would have been better for me if I had done the job myself but I suppose he is learning to be a useful man some day. I always said boys should be taught the same things as girls; he can do more now than Dora [...]

The children send best love to you and I am as always your loving wife

Lucy

---

32 North Avenue, Letchworth, Herts
Nov 16th. 1917

My dear Frank

Once more I gladly write to you and I hope you will enjoy the reading. First to ease your mind, I am quite well also, Morris is <u>much</u> better, and the girls are well too. I will let you know when Morris has had his throat operated on and how he is. I feel sure he will be quite alright, and please you must <u>not</u> worry about him. I took him to the Dr last Tuesday and he said it would make a wonderful difference to him and he never knew a boy who needed it done more. They will probably keep him in a day or two, if a bed is vacant, in the meantime I have to keep him home from school and free from catching cold. [...]

Do not think that Morris is in any way ill, he feeds and sleeps and runs about gardening etc as usual, has more colour and a little fatter than

---

73   Snobbing is a process in shoe-making, when mending the uppers.

3. 'I NEVER WANTED YOUR PRESENCE MORE THAN NOW'

he was in the summer, he teases the girls and we have occasional scrappings too, but on the whole they are very good, and very pleased I do not go out so much. I could not very well have left Morris so much as I did last winter so it was a good thing I gave up the Brittannia. [...]

When we got back Mr Palmer thought it looked like a probable air raid and did not want to come up here with us and go back, so we all stayed the night. It was such a change, I felt ever so much better after, and we have had no more raids (touch wood), of course the children enjoyed themselves immensely, they get all sorts of experiences too [...] Katie came last Wednesday and stayed till Monday. She could not be spared any longer, something will certainly happen there. It is rather rough for both of them; he is living unhappily with his sister and she is living at home, also not very happy, nothing to stop them from marriage but the law, they were hoping something would be done to make new divorce laws, but it has been put on one side. However I told her, I think it will have to come soon, for one thing, to raise the birth rate.

I have been doing some needlework this week for Mrs Worsley and this morning went to Miss Reynolds and am going for the day next Wednesday. Katie made Morris a fine overcoat and hat and Dora a nice warm coat out of that green one I wore, we lined it with plaid and put a hood on, and it looks so nice and cosy [...]

Palmer sent Eastman 2 bushels of apples and one of pears 33/-. Tickle has got me another ½ bushel for 5/-, hoping they will keep. We are getting ready for the famine that is coming. I quite expect we shall be rationed, but will no doubt fare just as well as we have ever done, we have always had to go a bit short, so don't really expect to suffer much if at all. We are now getting tea and sugar according to sugar cards at the Co-op, quite sufficient for our needs [...][74]

I am asked to be Secretary of our [adult] school: annual meeting next

---

74 The Co-op was (and is) a grocery shop run by the Co-operative Movement. In the early twentieth century it was used by the working classes, and by those who supported its co-operative ethos, and paid its customers proportionately with a dividend each year. More wealthy customers would buy their goods on account at preferred shops, and pay their bills quarterly.

Tuesday, and believe I am to be proposed. I wonder if I am capable, in place of Mrs Wiltshire you know. (Don't breathe a word.) I don't like popularity, you know, but when an important position is thrust upon one, what can one do: anyway I might not be elected, but if I do take it on I shall try to make it go, it is at a standstill now, or worse. Only 4 turned up last Tuesday, such a pity where so much can be done.

About leaving the bungalow,[75] there is nowhere else to go at present and I don't really want to move without you here.

The chickens are still doing their duty, 9 or 10 a week, and now eggs are 5d each and will be 6d soon. Milk has gone up to 7d, 8d in London and fresh butter almost unobtainable. I still have my Irish, so am very fortunate I think. I shall not let the children suffer if I can help it. They have got to keep well and fit to do their share in the Reconstruction [...][76]

I suppose you know that the Lord Mayor's Show was held as usual and the banquet too. It has caused rather a stir that such an example should have been set, when we are to practice such strict economy. The remains were given to the poor and according to all accounts there was a quantity.

The different 7 of them peace organisations had their premises raided last week and a lot of literature taken, and a stricter Defence of the Realm Act is to be enforced. Peace must not be mentioned, but I suppose it will come some time [...]

Your ever loving wife Lucy

---

75 Frank and Lucy had evidently been discussing whether they should renew the lease of their cottage when it was up for renewal, or move elsewhere in Letchworth.

76 The Reconstruction was a much-anticipated (peaceful) post-war reorganisation of society much desired by utopian and other groups wishing to reform social ills with greater equality for all.

3. 'I NEVER WANTED YOUR PRESENCE MORE THAN NOW'

32 North Avenue, Letchworth, Herts
December 1st 1917

My dear Frank,

I am so glad to be writing to you again just now, because I have good news for you. Morris has had his throat done this morning and is alright. The Matron sent for him on Wednesday morning and the operation was on Thursday. I went up late in the afternoon and the nurse told me he was quite alright, however I wanted to feel sure, so asked to see the matron and she told me it was quite successful and he would stay till Sun. afternoon. There were several other children done and were to be fetched away at 5 o'clock. I felt so thankful he was staying. I think it very kind of Dr Macfadyen to arrange it for me, as he has evidently done. The charge the Matron told me would be 2/6. as you were not working at a factory. I shall keep him home from school till the New Year I think and then I hope we shall have no further trouble with him. No mistake, our children have been a great anxiety haven't they? I wonder what future they will have. I could not help feeling a little anxious about Morris and felt it more not having you here to share it, but that is over now, so we go on step by step. I shall be glad to have him under my care again.

I do not feel that I can write you a long letter this time, but I know you will understand.

No! I did not get indigestion of the brain after your last letter, do you think it so weak? libel; after the way I am reading, talking and attending lectures. I went last Sat afternoon to hear Mr Zimmon and as you say, he is a fine chap. I took notes and will try to give you a good report [...]

I went to the town this morning and found no tea or butter or margarine.[77] Was told the Home and Colonial sold 200 lb of marge before 9 o'clock. Co-op were short of most things too, this is the first week I have not got my usual order. I was not quite out, so am still

---

77   Evidently food shortages were beginning to be noticeable, but formal food rationing would not begin until February 1918 (see Lucy's letter of 24 February 1918).

smiling, but really things are very serious. I was told people were going to raid a certain shop in the town they were so mad. London is worse, I believe. The price is very heavy isn't it, and it will take so many long years I suppose to recover ourselves [...]

You will be interested to know that I am expecting to take up an Insurance with Mr Palmer for buying Redcroft and I wrote and told Eastman he had not sent me Swanson's receipt and it was now due and I expected the [commission]. I should have it this time, he has got it and I have deducted it on my sheet. I had your box of clothes all out yesterday and well aired and brushed and Morris has done your boots and shoes, so we are taking care of your belongings.

I have been made Sec[retary] of our Adult School, and we started last Tues with a social which was well attended. Mrs Myles is Pres[ident] and Mrs Kearney Treas[urer] so now we shall see. Mrs Matthews has promised to give a first half hour next Tues. So as I can't do anything myself I must find those who can and will [...]

Love from the girls and lots of love from your ever loving wife

Lucy

3rd Dec 1917

My Dear Wife

Your letter arrived with the usual promptness and I am pleased with its contents. I am glad to know that Morris has come safely through his ordeal and trust he will now give no more trouble but grow into a sturdy boy and develop his intelligence and learn to use his gifts for the good of others. You say nothing of Chrissie so I presume she is bright and happy as ever. The [photograph of the] garden group [see Figure 7] still continues to give me great enjoyment. Your smiling faces are like a tonic to me. As you know, I live a great deal in the past here and it is surprising what varied experiences I have passed through. The other day I thought myself down at Clacton and again helping to get in the Life-boat which had been out all night in a storm and had on board eight men whom the crew had saved from a schooner which had been sunk. The weather was bitterly cold and the poor chaps were nearly frozen but hot drinks and wool blankets soon brought them round. You can use your imaginative powers and tell the children this little bit of Daddy's history. It will be fresh as I don't think I have told them this. I had a good time there and often wish to see the sea again, watching the clouds so often reminds me of it […]

I am sorry to hear of your food shortage but I think it is mainly due to transport difficulties. I wish to be remembered to all friends and tell them we are keeping our end up but it is monotonous work and only the knowledge of the faithful band of friends can help us so we rely on you and you gain strength from us and the bond of union is complete.

Forgive me if my letter is not personal enough but I trust you to tell me all home news and I know you are doing your best. Kiss all the bairns from Daddy and in your next letter tell me all about what you are all doing etc.

Lots of Love to my own sweet Wife from yours ever

Frank

If I have not put in what I wanted to say you must take it as it is

Dec 10 1917

Dearest Lucy

You were doubtless surprised to receive a little buff envelope this morning, and I imagine your surprise rather increased than decreased when you opened it and recognised the familiar handwriting. Now for the explanation. All men in the (won't fight battalion) who have served twelve months with good conduct have been granted special privileges amongst which is the being allowed to write and receive one letter a fortnight and a special visit once a month, in addition to the privileges already in force. As I am not yet having a visit from you I shall be able to write every week and you can reply and I shall have one letter a month left in lieu of the Special Visit. Now I hope it is all clear to you, and that you have recovered your usual calmness of spirit. If so I will commence the letter and to tell you I have no news, for of course that is how to start a letter isn't it. Also hoping you are well as it leaves me at present and so on.

Your last letter was delightful and I'm quite looking forward to the account of Saturday's lecture. I was with you in Spirit and saw the dear old hall crowded with the sedate and sober M.C.[78] people who take life so seriously [...]

I have written Dora's letter, it is rather prosy but you must explain it to her. She is impressionable and it may help to strengthen her in serious thought and effort. One privilege I neglected to mention and that is we can have books sent in to us. I will let you know what I wish next time I write. Now I must close eagerly awaiting your reply and sending you all my best love and lots of kisses

Yours still optimistic and endeavouring to be cheerful

Frank

Dec 18th 1917

My dear Frank

Your letter did not reach me till afternoon post yesterday, but glad to have it. I look forward to yours as you do to mine. We are all well and Morris has been to school since last Thursday. He seemed well enough and I wanted him to be in the breaking up. He has taken no harm and enjoys the frost and snow. We have had a little. I wonder if you are as cold as we are. I could not sleep at all the night before last, because I was so cold. Dora was awfully pleased with her letter and book. I did as you asked me about it and she took it and showed Miss Amor. She did not have a real party but Ida Price, Lily Wheeler and a little Russian Jew girl Fanny Sepiro came to tea and stayed till 7.30. They enjoyed

---

78   Possibly 'middle class'?

themselves of course. I had to put on my best frock and company manners of course and joined their games.

The girls went to Fanny for tea on Sat. These people came from Highbury from the raids. The father is a Russian, also the mother, and they have a French nurse. The children like ours were born in England but have travelled about a lot. Chrissie and Dora seem very taken up with them. They have a furnished house in Norton Road. I expect to meet the mother this afternoon at school. Dora is 9th in class and [had] a very good report. I think of asking Miss Amor about her chance for a scholarship for next March. What do you think about it? Chrissie is 32nd out of 46. She is a little ashamed, I think, and wishes she were nearer top. I was glad to hear her say that. I believe she will make an effort next term. Mrs Price says she don't bother to think and I am sure she could do better if she liked to try. Morris will be only one more half term in the Infant School. He gets quite a big boy. Since he came home from the hospital (Isolation) he had a grey jersey and those grey flannel knickers […]

I have had a note from your mother, they are all well and sent Dora a birthday card and 1/6 for Christmas. They are going to divide the money in the box. About 2/- each and do their own shopping this year. I will let you know what they buy. It is something fresh for them. Everything is of course very dear, oranges 4d each and so on. I shall not buy a turkey. You might like to know that I have got into Dora's blue jersey, I was so cold. I feel like a fisherman and Morris wears that blue scarf your mother sent me round his body and the ends over his shoulders and tucked in front. The ribbed part round him he thinks looks like a cork belt. We have got some sprats for dinner today, a whole ½lb between us for 4d […]

Now I must stop writing but ever thinking of you and all love to you.

Your loving wife Lucy.

>   Number 125, Bedford Prison
>   22.12 1917

Dearest Lucy

As circumstances over which I have no control will prevent me from being with you all on the 25th I am writing you a Christmas letter. I wish you all a Happy Christmas, and am very glad to be able to say that I myself shall not be unhappy even though separated from you all. I shall look back upon all the happy times we have spent together and you know memory can carry us far away from our surroundings. I shall also have a book to read and you are well aware what a source of enjoyment a book is to me, and I shall also use my imagination and picture you all at Mrs Ironside's. I'm glad I paid her a visit as I shall be able to visualize your surroundings. So please go the party with a contented mind as regards myself for no news could have given me greater satisfaction […]

As to the cold weather I'm glad to say that although it is cold, we do not feel it so badly here as at Wandsworth and I can sleep alright. I hope the youngsters have not got chilblains this year, and that they will be free from it in this winter. Dora's report was good but Chrissie's just shows that she has been lazy. Tell her I am sorry to hear she has not been 'playing the game'. Tell Dora that she is a good girl to have tried hard and that Daddy is pleased with her. As to her trying for a Scholarship, I do not mind in the least so you can go ahead. I shall not startle you by coming home unexpectedly this year, eh.

Now as to the privileges. We have permission to wear our own clothes, but we must have clean linen sent in every week, which would mean a lot more work for the already overworked officials and entail of trouble for our friends. As we could not shine or clean our boots etc I can see no sense in this. We can have someone to clean our cells by payment of 6d a day. COs are millionaires, or the people who form such rules are. We get an extra exercise in the afternoon and are permitted to converse at exercise.

You know as to letters and visit, now as to books. We can have any books sent in to us and they are our own property, the only stipulation being, that the books must not be of a political nature. This is a boon especially to those who want to study languages. The only language I feel inclined to study is Billingsgate.[79] I should like a book upon general subjects, such as the handy man at home or work; if you go to [W H] Smith's and ask for Catalogue you might find [the] one I mean [...]

With best wishes to all and all my love to you

yours ever Frank

---

32 North Avenue Letchworth
Dec 26th 1917

My dear Frank

I got your letter on Christmas Eve and was so glad to have it. Well the 25th has gone into the past. Did you recall all the 20 that we have passed since we first met? I hope you got a nice book to read and dwelt more on the future. I am afraid I had no time for the past, as you say children dwell in the present and ours did and lived in every moment. You will be glad to know that they had a happy day and will remember it. They decided not to hang up stockings but to have their presents at breakfast. After, I said, or there would be none eaten. They did not go to bed very early on Christmas Eve as we had lighted candles and a little tree chiefly for the dolls, etc. so they did not wake up till nearly eight. Of course Chrissie could not resist having a look at the parcels which were in my room so I allowed them to open a box which Mrs Middleton had brought for them while I lit the fire, it was so cold. In the box was some animals made by interned Germans, also a box of interlocking bricks and a book each for the girls.

We had breakfast at 9 and just as it was ready Mr Stacey brought over a large wooden box which had come last Sat from 39, but I didn't want

---

79   Billingsgate was the famous London fish market, here used as a metaphor for 'swearing like a fishwife', ie Frank feels like learning new bad language.

the children to know. He opened it for me and found Dad had made a wooden bedstead big enough for the big dolls and Katie had made bedclothes for it. They were delighted. Morris had a box of pencils etc. Miss Blackbourn had brought a pair of slippers for Morris and handkerchiefs and gloves for the girls, and I gave Dora a silver thimble, Chrissie a brooch and Morris a mechanical motor car. Your mother sent 1/6 so I bought a box of crackers and then what they bought each other. I am afraid I had to help them choose, but they will do better next year. Dora bought for Chrissie some Plasticine, Morris a pencil case like he had last year (he wanted that). Chrissie bought Dora a note book with pencil and Morris a ball, and Morris Chrissie a silver thimble and Dora a game, Halma. Between them they got me a butter dish and you 2 handkerchiefs. They seemed very satisfied with their purchases and enjoyed the shopping. Miss Bigsby came in the morning with a book each for Dora and Morris and [a] painting book with tubes of paint for Chrissie, also a lot of walnuts and apples and chocolates. Wasn't it kind of her? We had a nice chat.

So you see Santa Claus did not forget our house this year. Mrs Middleton also gave me a tin, 2lb of honey and a ¼lb of tea, most acceptable: do you ever have tea? We had a very simple dinner, with a Christmas pudding. No pork or turkey. Mrs Stacey paid 8/6 for a fowl! I am afraid Mother would be horrified at our dinner. Tickles had eggs for a change. She came to see me too in the morning. It was a lovely day, like spring. I thought how you would have enjoyed a walk with the children.

We went to Mrs Ironside's at 3.30. There were 13 grown-ups and 12 children and we had really a jolly time. We got home soon after 9 and I soon got the children to bed and had my cup of cocoa as usual and took the hot water bottle to bed (that is a comfort to me) about 10 so that I should not feel lonely. I soon went to sleep to my surprise, so cannot say I passed a miserable day. Morris was not <u>very</u> well but joined all the games. He is not very well today. I think it is only a little cold. He feels the cold very much and it is awfully cold again. The children are already looking forward to spring coming. I don't think London people are because of expected air raids: they simply live in constant dread and fear, what a terrible life. They can never forget there is a war on […]

3. 'I NEVER WANTED YOUR PRESENCE MORE THAN NOW'

Now I must stop, am going to try and go to the ILP social next Sunday evening at the Skittles, so will have a lot to tell you next week, I hope. Did you know the North Herts Labour Party now is over a thousand members? Keep up hope and spirits and keep well. Am thinking of coming to see you in the New Year with Bertha Wells or Mrs Bowry: would you like me to come?

Love from Dora, Chrissie and Morris and

Your loving wife,

Lucy

31 12 1917

Dearest Wife

Your letter to hand. The descriptions of the visit of Santa Claus was very vivid, and I filled in the gaps which you left [...] I'm glad that the sins of the Father have not been visited on the children and that they all had such a happy time and that so many kind and good friends are around you [...]

I received your book and Mr T's, also Myles' photo on Monday, and as I was eating and enjoying my dinner I had given to me the group [photograph] Miss Lawes sent. I was surprised, as you may well imagine when I describe it to you. It is a group of ILP-ers and others who have been taken outside the Skittles Inn and Miss Lawes and a comrade are holding up the Letchworth banner. In the background stands Reggie Stamp and Nickels and several others from London, and in the front row I espied Millie's smiling face. It was like seeing them all again and I thought of the times we had all spent together. In the classroom and at the College, lectures and parties etc all rolled before my vision; and now some are dead in Flanders, some still fighting, for what, and others are in prison (it's a mad world after all). Ray Cree is in the group too.

Friend Machin gave us all a book for Xmas. Mine is *A Soul of a Bishop* by Wells.[80] I thought that by the time a man got to gaiters and an apron his soul was buried in Sacerdotalism but Wells, in his usual way and excellent manner, shows how in spite of all the counter influences a Bishop may find his Soul. It leads him to renounce all dogma and doctrine, and to leave the church and at last to discover that he must not preach but live his own life and let each man create his own theology for himself. There is nothing new in the book for me, but to the ordinary man who cannot square things now going on, with his notions of right and wrong, it would be a great help and stimulant to thought.

I envy you your honey but as to the tea, well after so long without, I think I could say no to a cup. I have not mentioned all my Xmas presents. I had two cards, one from Jordan's Meeting and the other from the Friend's Chaplin Committee.[81] I will quote you from one of these as the words are so good. 'Be still and cool in thy own mind and spirit from thy own thoughts, and then thou wilt feel the principle of God to turn thy mind to the Lord, from whom life comes; whereby thou mayest receive his strength and power to allay all storms and tempests. That ye may feel the power of an endless life, the power of God which is immortal, which brings the immortal soul up to the immortal God in whom it doth rejoice'. George Fox [...][82]

I've left out all you wanted me to say and filled my letter up with scraps

---

80 A 'pendant' to Wells's earlier work *God the Invisible King* (1917), which was 'amateur theological speculation', this novel reworks Wells's own religious experience as a 'condition-of-the-war' novel, with a utopian ending. http://wellsattheworldsend.blogspot.co.uk/2017/10/the-soul-of-bishop-1917.html accessed 13 February 2018.

81 Jordans Meeting was the Local Meeting of the Jordans Quaker community, equivalent to a church congregation. Chaplin Committee is probably a misspelling of Chaplains, the group of Quakers (Religious Society of Friends) who worked as prison chaplains.

82 George Fox was one of the most influential founders of Quakerism.

as usual so will close by sending you all my best love and wishes for a Happy New Year.

Frank

PS I will write re visiting next time as there is no hurry about it. I like your so called trivial home talk and cannot get too much of it. I can take up the worldly affairs when I get free again.

Yours still hoping and trusting

Hubby

✍

32 North Avenue Letchworth
Jan 7th 1918

My dear Frank

Please excuse pencil, but I can write more quickly with it. This is Monday evening and of course I have not yet had your letter, but thought if I started now, I could finish it tomorrow. Dora has been to spend the afternoon with Nellie Gregory and I went to fetch her at 7 o'clock. The stars shone beautifully and it was frosty, quite pleasant for walking. I thought of our winter evening walks years ago, and we should still enjoy it, given the opportunity. I am a much better walker than ever I was, only I am not fond of being out at night as you know.

You will be glad to know that the children are much better. They still have a cough and I shall not let Chrissie start school tomorrow with Dora. Morris does not go till next Monday and she can stay at home till then. She does such silly things. I sent her out for a little while this morning, it was so bright, and she came back in about ¼ of an hour, had put her foot through the ice on the pond at Norton, of course her boot and stocking was soaked and must have felt cold. The weather is still very cold and yesterday was wet [...]

I had your letter by the afternoon post, and fancy you are not very well. I do hope I am mistaken, but you do not say. Sorry my letter was so late reaching you and I can imagine how impatient you are to hear from me. I will try in future to write on Sundays, then you should get it by Tuesday. It is too bad of me to <u>seem</u> to neglect you and I am very sorry. I think it is time we saw each other if possible to manage it perhaps not before the end of the month [...]

I am sending the Adult School Hand Book as the Lesson Sheets are not yet in, not got them from Printers yet. I hope you can have this and will enjoy it, also give me a few notes each week. I shall be glad to use them - if we continue [...] The children are still improving and I am much better again now, only cold and tired of trailing round in the snow all the morning. I had to get the chisel and take some [ ] off the front door this afternoon when I came home, it would not shut to fasten. I am getting very handy, I can tell you. Morris will be pleased to have the book, but his birthday is not till the 28th [...] Miss Wale lives in Norton Road at the back here, and she and her sister have children of Interned Germans with English mothers who have to work,[83] and a committee look after and send some of them down here when they need it. They also provide the Christmas Tree. Next door has had 7 under 7 years and one girl of 12 who is very useful. They are all going back soon when she will have 3 or 4 older boys. Rather an undertaking but they seem to manage alright and like it [...]

I must stop now. Hope this was worth waiting for. The children all send love to Daddy and I as ever my best love and constant thoughts.

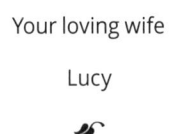

Your loving wife

Lucy

---

[83] German citizens living in the UK were interned at the beginning of the war, even if they had been resident for many years.

3. 'I NEVER WANTED YOUR PRESENCE MORE THAN NOW'

Number 125 Bedford Prison
7.1.1918

Dearest Lucy

I received your last letter on Friday morning. Am sorry to hear you are all suffering from colds etc, and that your old enemy has returned. You must keep yourself warmly clad, and take plenty of exercise. If you can't get out, try skipping, as it is splendid for the circulation, and invigorating too. I am glad that Chrissie had her party and that you all enjoyed yourselves [...] As to my eyes, do not worry about them as I do not strain them, and although everything here is at such close range I think it will only have a temporary effect on them. Whatever we suffer, it is part of the trial so I for one, shall not complain. All this has its compensation and from one point of view is extremely funny and we shall all look back on this phase in our history with mixed feelings [...] I shall not be writing again before Morris's birthday, so please wish him many happy returns of the day and let him have the book on Natural History as a present from Daddy. He can get Dora to read about the Elephant etc. As to visit I will send you the Special Order and you can come or not, as you think best.

Do not make up your mind that I am coming home suddenly, as I am sure it will <u>not</u> come off. I can accept no condition for release. I am determined to see this through. As you know I was quite willing to do anything in the way of work but this being denied me, I should now take it as adding insult to injury to be offered conditional release. I have managed to write a long letter after all, but find it difficult to do so unless you send along a subject for me to exercise my thinking powers upon [...] I will write you every Monday so you need not wait until you get my letter, but let next week's cross so that I do not wait reply as I don't like waiting to hear from you. Kiss our bairns and give them Daddie's love and accept all my love for your Dear Self from

yours ever

Frank

PS I should like to hear if you have got those specifications from Reg. I hear he is moving. How would his cottage suit you?

32 North Avenue Letchworth
[Saturday] Jan 12. 1918

My Dear Frank

I hope you approve of your son's handwriting, he takes up rather a lot of room to write a very little but it was his own composition. Dora has drawn and painted a fine picture of 'Ginger, she calls her 'Kitty'. She wanted me to send it you but I thought you would not care for it, as a photograph. We will save it for you. I went to see Reg G. but found no one at home, so sent a note and he will let me have what you want. We do not think we would like the cottage. Too small for our needs and they have rats.

It has been so cold here this week, it is reported in the *Citizen* that a rent collector found the ink frozen in his fountain pen going from one block of houses to another on Tuesday, and Mr Brunt said it was 19 degrees below freezing on Tuesday night, the lowest known here.[84] The children are all much better, almost well. I am finding the food problem a teaser now. No more Nutley or Mapleton's butters to be made. Fat seems the hardest to get of anything, and people are having a great difficulty to get meat. When we are rationed (as we expect very soon) I shall put in for our meat ration on account of the fat. I might take it out in bacon (perhaps). I have registered for Marg. at the Home and Colonial, but I shall not stand in queues for it, I thought probably they would have a bigger supply than the Co-op. The registration won't come into force yet for a few weeks and I have had none from H and C for a long time, but I only get ¼lb per week from Co-op. Pearce says we can't have it if he can't get it, so what is to be done. Are these troubles of any interest to you? I think of course we shall put along somehow alright and I do not worry.

Mrs Myles tells me she is feeling it difficult now, she has Mr Garside and Morrison lodging there so it makes more to feed.

---

84   The *Letchworth and Baldock Citizen* was the local paper http://www.hertsatwar.co.uk/hertfordshirenewspapers, accessed 10 April 2018.

3. 'I NEVER WANTED YOUR PRESENCE MORE THAN NOW'

I have turned another overcoat this week.[85] It is a rare job, real hard work too. I can do it pretty quick and charge 10/- so it pays well, but it is tiring. I am going to help Miss Reynolds again next Tuesday afternoon and the children are to call in for me [...] The book I got for you is a series published by Crosby Lockwood and Son. There is a *The Cabinet Worker's Handybook A Practical Manual on the Tools, Materials, Appliances and Processes employed in Cabinet Work*. Also *The Woodworker's Handybook*. Would you like either or both of these? [...]

I have had to assert myself once more, like this. I noticed a very unpleasant smell here last week and after one day decided it was drains. I went to Mr Palmer but it got much worse; I went myself to Mrs Marshall.[86] She suggested it was green water — however this was Thursday and Mr Marshall called on Saturday. He said it was something under the bath, but on searching everywhere discovered nothing, and I still persisted it was sewer gas. So he next tried to find the manhole. I told him there was not one but he dugged and poked about all round, till he gave it up and went to the old ladies next door. There he found one and found that ours runs into it. He opened it and found it full up. He suggested they should share the cost of cleaning up and they said no, it was ours. So he said well leave it and walked off. I heard all this and told them I considered the children's health was the first thing and it must be done at once. However the smell was so awful again in the evening I went up to Mr Palmer yesterday morning and we called on Donelly the Sanitary Inspector. I was not going to let a thing like that go on while they quibbled about the cost. Of course the Hitchin Rural Inspector 'Hill' came this morning (Monday) and told them it was on their premises (the old ladies) and he would serve a notice if it was not done at once. He went in the house so I did not hear what was said, but she said they would cut us off and have their own trap. (At their own expense of course.) When he went to the door [and] introduced

---

85 A way of extending the life of a garment by unpicking its seams and reconstructing it with the worn side of the fabric on the inside. It was an indication of genteel poverty in Victorian novels if a woman wore a 'turned' dress.

86 Marshall was the Sunderlands' landlord.

himself she said, who sent for you? I called out 'I did'. However it is still not done: if it is not done by tomorrow morning I shall call on Dr Macfadyen. We'll see who's who.

I am really enjoying myself over it and don't think we shall take harm. I am using plenty of carbolic. But just think of such a thing, and I met the old dear coming out of church yesterday morning. May they be forgiven, but they know now I will not stand too much if I <u>am</u> on my own. Marshall has not troubled any further, all he wants is his rent. I call it scandalous, don't you? I am glad our time is nearly up to leave. This is the limit. She sent for Mr Smith up the road and I heard him say if she could prove it was our fault, she could get out of paying. I don't think it is, we don't play games of that sort and the children are too sensible to be putting things down drains, although an accident might happen. Anyway, we shall see what happens. I thought you might enjoy the reading of this little tale and speculate on the concluding chapter.

Now I must stop if this is to be posted today, so will send you all my love and the children's. Hoping you are well.

Your loving wife Lucy.

The women's vote passed the Lords last week.[87]

✍

32 North Avenue
January 20th 1918

My dear Frank

[...] Morris has had a second and I hope final operation on his throat

---

87   On 11 January 1918 the House of Lords voted by a majority of 63 (134 votes to 71) to extend the suffrage to women under certain conditions (age, and ownership of property). This made it possible to proceed with overhauling the voting system to allow the expected addition of some 6 million women to the electoral register after a later vote, which took place on 6 February 1918, bringing the Representation of the People Act into law.

and is quite alright. He was sent for to go on Wednesday morning, but there was so much snow about I kept them all home from school. About 10 o'clock I let them out to help me dig paths to the chickens and coal cellar and told off Morris for the front gate. However they soon got to enjoying themselves snowballing and building a snowman and had a fine time till dinner time. The snow was quite a spade depth, so you can guess there was plenty of it. Then I took him up to the hospital about 4 o'clock in the afternoon and he had the operation on Thursday and I have been to visit him this afternoon (Mr Palmer also called in to see him). They are keeping him until Wednesday, so he will not be so likely to take cold this time. He was in bed but looks quite himself, and I looked at his throat which seems all clear now. His temp and pulse is just as it was on Wednesday, normal. He wanted to come home but I left him happily having his tea. So he will give into the inevitable. I am sure you will be pleased to hear this job is now over, we have dreaded it for so long, haven't we, but strange to say I have felt no anxiety at all this week. I seemed to know it was the right thing and so must be perfectly safe[...]

Now about the drain, I had a word with the old lady and tried to be pleasant but very firm. She said it is in the hands of Ray and so they had been to the estate office and I had no right to have sent for the Sanitary Inspector. Of course I insisted I had every right to use what protests I could in the interests of my children and so on etc. I think they were really frightened at what might result. On Thursday afternoon the work was done, took the man about half an hour. I heard her ask if it was from next door and he answered, 'Can't say, mum, but it's gone', so they did not get the satisfaction they expected and I have not seen them since. I think I had a victory, and did not lose my temper.

Bedford Prison
21.1.1918

Dearest Lucy

Your last letter was a thunderbolt. I have been cogitating upon the Drain puzzle but can form no definite conclusions. I should think perhaps that a heavy motor may have caused a pipe to break or some bad workmanship in the drain itself. As to the attitude of the property owners, I am not a bit surprised [...]

Am sorry to hear that you are having a difficulty in getting fats etc. You must get all the oil you can: olive or cod or Scott's Emulsion etc. The idea that women and children are non-combatants should now be exploded, seeing that the shortage of fats is largely due to the need of them in the manufacture of high explosives. To deprive women and children of the necessities of life is to make them participants in the warfare as the[y] are directly assisting in the efficiency of the fighting units [...]

As to the books. I do not want the Mechanics Handbook or any of that series as they do not deal with the subjects I want. Perhaps you had better leave it as I seem to have given you a Chinese puzzle to solve. I am sending back the invoice you inadvertently left in the handbook you sent. Also enclosed please find visiting order. If you are coming to see me with Bertha Wells and she is also going to see Fineburg you had better be prepared to stay all day in Bedford, and have one visit in the morning and the other in the afternoon, as space here is limited.

I am glad you have heard from Mother and that she is well. I trust you will have had a good time at the Co-op Social and that the lecture was a success. I look forward with great interest to your account of it and of course shall criticise it if necessary. As I write the sun is shining and the birds are singing and the atmosphere is quite warm. One almost forgets the heavy snow fall we had back three days ago, and thinks that Spring has come at last.

I have been reading Dickens' *Tale of Two Cities* and his Italian tour [...] [George] Fox's *Journal* also has claimed my attention and the wonderful events which happened to him make me feel how commonplace and

3. 'I NEVER WANTED YOUR PRESENCE MORE THAN NOW'

unexciting our lives are. Now I have used up all my space so must stop my rambling. Kiss our bairns from Daddy and tell them he sends his love and prayers to them. Also accept some for your own dear self.

Yours Lovingly

Best wishes to all enquiring friends

Frank

*

32 North Avenue, Letchworth Herts
Jan 27th 1918

My dear Frank

I hope you enjoyed my visit as much as I did, but what a lot we left unsaid, and I long more than ever for your freedom. I reach home at 1/4 to 4, having met Mrs Tickle in Station Road and Mrs Bowry in Norton Way [...] I did not go in anywhere at Bedford, but ate a few Marmite sandwiches at the Station. I enjoyed the journey to you very much but was rather tired on the return, but I overheard a very interesting conversation between 2 young soldiers on the train to Hitchin and some women from Hitchin to Letchworth. I was very much surprised to see what a great place they are making at Henlow Airdrome: these soldiers said 'that is to be ready for the next war'.[88]

You will be interested to hear there was a protest meeting yesterday morning at 10.30, and they had a great crowd and finished up with a Socialist meeting with Kidd and Moss speaking: we did not organise the meeting, I don't know who did. It was like this — the trades council met the tradesmen on Tuesday evening last, and decided that all the marg. that could be allowed per head was one ounce (Moss held one up, one weeks ration) and ½ lb of meat for the week. Ball was in the chair, and the women seem to think it is his fault and want to limb him, he was to explain at the meeting why more could not be got into Letchworth, however he did <u>not</u> turn up. It was said too, last Tuesday,

---

88   Built in 1918, now RAF Henlow.

that the [refugee] Belgians worked very hard and were big meat eaters and must be supported, meaning they would not be allowanced: you can guess how that was received by the English women.[89] Well they appointed 8 women from the crowd as a Food Vigilance Committee to overlook the food control and see if enough cannot be got, to be distributed fairly. You would have enjoyed yourself.

The munition workers too want to know why soldiers on Home Service are allowed 12 ounces of meat a day and 4 oz bacon [and] those at the front 1 lb, and they who work much harder are only to have ½ lb per week. They don't mind going short but know so much is wasted in the Army. There are 200 or 300 airmen billeted in Smith's factory and Dean is supplying them with meat, so he has none for the people. Longley and Waite pool their stores (do you remember these butchers?)

I did not intend to mention food this time, but know you would be interested in the people waking up. You will be glad to know I took Morris to the Dr and got a certificate for a qt. milk a day for 6 weeks and can have another again if necessary: certainly the children need it and he wishes he could order me more, but they might make a fuss as they are over 5. He suggested I got some Scott's Emulsion for Morris if I could afford it, or made one of mutton fat and milk, if I could get the fat: he told me how to do it. I am glad they consider the children need looking after [even] if the gov. don't.

I did not go to the Adult School today, in fact have not been out at all;

---

89 'Over the course of the war Letchworth became one of the key centres for refugees in Hertfordshire and the county as a whole. This was largely due to the influence of three refugees who arrived in Letchworth in 1914. They were Jacque[s] Kryn, a diamond merchant, his brother, George and a colleague, Raoul Lahy. They subsequently formed the Kryn and Lahy Metal Works in Dunhams Lane, Letchworth in March 1915. By the end of August, 1915, more Belgian refugees were welcomed into the town to work in the factory producing weapons and munitions for the war effort. By the end of 1916 they made up a quarter of the population of Letchworth—there were around 2,000 in the town.' http://www.hertsatwar.co.uk/belgian-refugees accessed 9 February 2018.

had and still got a nasty toothache. Dora and Chrissie went for a walk this morning and to Sunday School this afternoon.

Mr Myles sent me a letter that he had received from Catherine Marshall[90] saying your case is on record and would he give an enclosed letter to nearest relative or friend who will take the necessary action. The letter contains a quotation from Lord Curzon in the House of Lords in Dec when he said 'A letter should be written by the War Office to the Local Gov. Board on the following lines. "It having been represented that there are at present moment serving in the army a certain number of men who would have been given absolute exemption had such tribunals been aware that they had power to give it, the Army Council would be grateful if the Local Gov. Bd. could see their way to circularizing tribunals asking whether such had been the case and if so that the names of any men who would have received absolute exemption may be forwarded to the War Office for their consideration". Lord Curzon said "He believed that the cases where exemption was refused owing to the misunderstanding of the law were very few in number and that the tribunals would have to look up all their records to reply to these queries." Unless some concerted action is taken the investigation by the tribunals will be of a very perfunctory character and it is therefore very necessary that every attempt should be made to place again before tribunals by those conscientious objectors who demand absolute exemption from the Act, a clear statement as to why they are still in prison. It is now possible for you to address from Prison to your Local Tribunal an application for your name to be forwarded to the Local Government Board as being legitimately entitled to absolute exemption, if you do this you must give reasons why they should give you exemption and a reference made to the application formerly made to the Tribunal.'

If you do write let it be brief and to the point. Yours is a peculiar case having been released once and then taken up again and the reason for that has never been understood by anyone, especially being a C3

---

90   Catherine Marshall was a prominent suffragist and organizer for the No Conscription Fellowship with Clifford Allen.

man: you certainly are no younger and no stronger now than you were.

My mind is very full of you and I do not feel I can write much more. When I think of this matter and the Slaughter and struggle of the world and the sickness and semi starvation, my home affairs seem so very trivial, so you must forgive me this time [...]

I will try to get McCabe's book, would you like it? Also would you like to learn Esperanto?[91] I can get the books for you, Miss Bartholomew is taking a class one evening a week and would like Dora to learn, she says it is quite the thing to study now. I forgot to ask you and I wanted to know what work you were doing. I could not learn Esperanto myself just now as I have so much on my mind and in my hands, but I believe I'll have a go when you come home. Morris wants to have 2 little boys to tea tomorrow as it is his birthday: I have got a jelly for him, you know how he likes that. He is awfully pleased with his book you said he was to have and I am giving him *Heads without Heart*, my first prize at school when I was 7 [...]

I don't think I have any more to say now, anyway, I'll close up for tonight and go to bed, lots of love to you from us all

       Lucy.

Morris will come next time I come.

<u>Monday</u>. Have just heard from Eastman and he says my position will remain the same, and they would be prepared to give you a full time appointment when you come out of prison, on a salary and commission providing the business done justified it. Now I consider that very good: he writes very decent to me this time, so I suppose my book gave satisfaction, he never complains about anything now.

---

91 Esperanto was invented in the 1880s as a constructed international language, and its first instruction books were published in 1887.

3. 'I NEVER WANTED YOUR PRESENCE MORE THAN NOW'

Bedford Prison
28.1.1918

Dearest Lucy,

I now sit down to say all the things I neglected to say when you were here on Friday. I hope you had a pleasant journey home and that the visit gave you as much enjoyment as I derived from it. I have had my drooping spirits revived and received fresh inspiration to go forward, feeling secure in your Love and in the love of Him who is the source of all love and from where we draw our supplies [...]

Seeing you and hearing your voice has stirred me up and I am again the Lover, Husband, and Father and not just the <u>prisoner</u>. I shall have a new perspective in here too, for the ground over which you have walked will be hallowed to me with memories and cannot look the same again. My cold is better I am glad to say, and I have not had the headache so badly [...] I want you if you can to let me know your impressions of the visit. As I did not expect you quite so soon, I did not have the waiting period and all my feelings were of joy. It was good to see your dear face once again, so brave and calm as it is, I always gather strength from you. I do not think it is unseemly to acknowledge this as I am sure the influence of women is far greater than generally credited. I hope you had a good time at school yesterday. I thought of you. Let me know about it. Remember me to Mr Cobbold and tell him I advise him not to try prison but to take the experience second hand. About books, I should like you to get the following, at varying intervals of course, and send along

Darwin's *Voyage of the Beagle* Collins Clear Type 1/-

Lord Macaulay's *Historical Essays* " " " 1/-

Matthew Arnold *Poems* " " " 1/-

Ed[ward] Carpenter *Civilization Its Cause and Cure* Allen & Unwin 1/-

" " *Englands Ideal* " " 1/-

Jack's *Embryology* 7d (Heredity) Liberty 1/-

Mazzini *Duties of Man* Dents 1/3

THE CONSCIENTIOUS OBJECTOR'S WIFE

I should also like *Inquiries into Human Faculty* Everyman 1/3 and if possible you might borrow *The Bible of Nature* [...]

I send you all my love and Sincere wishes for your Welfare

Your Affect. Hubby, Frank

PS No letter next week as you had the visit

&

32 North Avenue Letchworth Herts
Sunday Eve Feb 10. 1918

My dear Frank,

What a long time it has seemed to wait for your letter, and I am sure you feel the same. I never know just where to start, not that I have any particular news [...]

The rumour of Fenner Brockway's release is not true; nothing doing yet anywhere, that I know of.[92] I saw Mrs Harvey Smith last week and asked her. Mrs Williams is not back yet, but expected any day.

Ray Cree has got six months, just gone to [Wormwood Scrubs], also Bertrand Russell has got six months.[93]

Mother wrote yesterday and said you would be walking in some day. I wish it might be soon [...]

There is now a prospectus out for the New Town but I have not got hold of one yet. Has Dr Crowley sent you the book yet? I went to his lecture yesterday on 'Child Welfare in the County School'. You know and agree on all his points, I am sure, he is so breezy and enthusiastic, it does

---

92 The anti-war activist, editor and politician Fenner Brockway had been arrested in 1916 and served various sentences for his refusal to be conscripted and for his anti-war activities until 1919.

93 The prominent philosopher and anti-war activist Bertrand Russell was imprisoned for speaking against the invitation to the US to enter the war on the Allied side, and served his sentence in Brixton prison.

one good to hear him speak. Bond Holding was the Chairman, quite a contrast I thought [...]

Katie talks of coming down to Letchworth for her 'honeymoon' in the Spring. I suppose I shall get blamed for that business as I was for taking her to Oxendon; I don't know if Mother knows I write to her privately to his address sometimes. She seems very grateful for my sympathetic attitude, but how could they do otherwise, and she is nearly over 'military' age. Mother will miss her very much, she depends on her to get the supplies of food they can get, they have more trouble than we have. I don't know how they exist without a Sunday joint, last Sunday she told me they had sausage! They have laughed at us, now it is our turn. Mrs Thomas tells me she is so glad she stayed here and learned some of my cooking [...] Now I must stop, don't forget to let me know about Esperanto. Mrs Myles can let you have the books and says it is quite simple to learn by yourself.

We all send you our very best love and constant thought

Your loving wife

Lucy

11.2.1918 Bedford Prison

Dearest Wife

Once again I sit to put my thoughts on paper to you. My dearest thought is to picture you all busy in your several ways after school hours are over, and the energetic runnings to and fro have simmered down into the quiet of evening. I conjure you up in my mind and can hear one of the children say 'tell us a story Daddy' [...]

I have been reading Tickle's book on Bees and it is a most fascinating subject. You really must keep bees. Get a good book from the library, read up about them. I am sure you will be drawn to them. Give my thanks to the Dr for the book he sent, when you see him and say I have found it interesting. As to the Handyman's book, there is a copy at Romany so if you could get up there one day and get the publisher you must then get me a copy, if it is not too expensive.

I shall be pleased to try and learn Esperanto as I am sure it will be useful to be able to express myself in another language when English fails me, so just send along the necessary books.

Is Dora learning? If so I might keep up a correspondence with her, that is if you will permit a space to be allotted for that purpose. You will be glad to hear that I have written to the Tribunal but I do not expect anything from them myself. However we shall see.

You must let me know when you want to come again and see me, so that I can make arrangements for the visiting order to be sent you and while I think of it. You must condense your letters into four pages as that is the regulation, to be the same size as this letter is.

We had a temperance lecture here the other day. It was interesting and reminded me of my temperance lecture days. I wonder, was it any good or was it just all talk? My theories of reform have undergone some modification. The lecturer talked of the power of Alcohol to paralyze the brain and disturb its proper working etc. I suspected him of swallowing Sturge's and Victor Horsley's book and regurgitating it piecemeal [...][94]

We are a funny people, aren't we? With loud acclamation we laud temperance and morality, and silently we let the great liquor trust assist to make our laws and mould our social labels to their dirty ends. Beer is cheaper in a soldiers' canteen than it is outside, and to be drunk in the army is not a crime if you can get to bed.

[...] I'm afraid it is sending coals to Newcastle to give you a temperance

---

94 *Alcohol and the Human Body* (Macmillan 1909) by Sir Victor Horsley and Mary D Sturge, sold over 85,000 copies in the UK and the USA, and was a leading work on alcoholism (*Oxford Dictionary of National Biography*). Sturge was one of the first British women doctors and a prominent Quaker, and Horsley, also a Temperance advocate, was a brilliant experimental surgeon and social reformer.

3. 'I NEVER WANTED YOUR PRESENCE MORE THAN NOW'

lecture, but it will do for Chrissie as she is a good Templar:[95] she may make use of it at the lodge [...] I send all my Love to you Darling and I feel we are all in the arms of the Source of Love so we need fear nothing.

Yours always Frank

RSVP!!

🐦

32 North Avenue Letchworth Herts
Feb 18th 1918

My dear Frank

You see our son has done a bit of decorating to start my letter. I will remember you told me to limit it to 4 pages. I have very little news this time. We are all well and always thinking of you and wishing for your return home. You will be interested to know that your letter was read at the Tribunal last Friday and sent on to Hertford for them to decide. I met Mr Furmston on Sat and he was there.

Your mental picture of home is correct, only instead of 'Tell us a story daddy' it is 'Read to us, mother', and I do, nearly every evening. Last Saturday afternoon we all went to a concert at the Church Room at the bottom of Common View. Miss Amy Reynolds, the little one, arranges them. Classy things of course, first one was violin, 'cello and piano; they could play though, the girls sat very still and behaved very nicely. Morris fidgeted a bit and wanted to talk, question, of course: he will know better next time, he has not been to that sort of thing before [...]

Dora is not learning Esperanto yet, you shall have the books as soon as I get them. Mr Myles says their's are out of date so I shall see what Miss Reynolds says, as she suggested it, also about Dora. Yes, I would spare a small space each week. Let me have the visiting order next week, then I will come as soon as I can after. I did not get your letter last week till Wednesday evening, but I find the postal arrangements have been altered and that was the reason. I was terribly anxious about you,

---

95   The Templars was a children's Temperance movement.

thought you must be ill. I hope you have got the books Mrs Matthews has lent you, and hope you were allowed the pamphlet about the New Town [...]

I did not intend to mention food at all this time, but I must tell you I have just got our Ration Cards, 2 each, that is 8½ the size of this paper, one for meat and the other for margarine (and other things presently). I have also got 4 sugar cards and one to tear off each week also a milk card and meat card making 15 cards to carry about. I am glad I haven't ten children and 2 or 3 lodgers; I might do a trade in small attaché cases to put them in? The West End shops are already selling Ration Bags for ladies to carry bread and sugar, etc, in when they go visiting. This is a funny world now, I often think it must be a dream or nightmare, and I shall wake up in my old workroom. What tales the children will have to tell their grandchildren, if they survive; it will be the 'survival of the fittest' for the next few years I think, so keep a good heart and a strong mind and clear brain to help in the wonderful world you are going to Reconstruct after this dreadful time is past and over. We will have a good rest (if possible) and then brace ourselves for a good 20 years hard work: what a future? Do you feel ready? I have just thought 'Be strong in the Lord and the Power of His Might'.

It is very cold again, such a sharp frost.

My chickens have not laid since Christmas, but started again on Saturday (and one pickled egg left: they must have known) so I shall not have to kill them off yet. Eggs are 5d each so a few even a week will pay me and be nicer than meat.

Now my paper is used up so I must stop.

love from Dora, Chrissie and Morris

and best love and constant thought from

your loving wife Lucy

3. 'I NEVER WANTED YOUR PRESENCE MORE THAN NOW'

Bedford Prison 18.2.18

Dear Lucy

Your letter gave me great delight. As you say, it did seem a long time since the last one but the interview we had together was worth it. I should like very much to see Jones so bring him along by all means. I like Chrissie's optimism. She is sure she is coming next time. Well, I suppose there will be a next time, as I see no likelihood of release yet, for the question of Peace gets more complicated than ever [...]

Imagine a calm grey sky, no clouds yet no blue, just a dull grey everywhere. As you gaze a streak of pink is seen emerging and pushing its way through the grey, makes a rift. Then a silvery gold bank arises and great bands of flaming red appear, to become suffused into a golden haze, a great Mosque, its dome shining in the sun like gold and all around the palms are waving, whilst the worshippers are bowing to the ground. The twitter of birds sounds in the ear like the tinkle of silver bells as a glorious cavalcade of white-robed Arabs ride up to the mosque and are lost in the multitude surrounding it. All is a mass of splendour each as has been described by travellers in the east, and one remembers that beneath the splendour is the poverty and degradation of the mass to maintain a great Sultan's power. As we gaze the scene changes, the golden haze departs and the multitudes evolve into flocks of sheep peacefully grazing on the mountain side and a calm comes over one in harmony with the scene. Hay ricks appear and then a farm house and buildings nestling in the wooded mountain side. All is beautiful, but one remembers the cottager and sees him toiling in the fields for a base pittance. Comfort is denied to such as he, toil is his portion whilst the master bargains for high prices for his crops and makes fortunes through the people's necessity. One thinks of these things as he looks at the laden wain wending its way down the mountain side and wonders how long such things will continue. Even as we look the scene changes: what was once a farmhouse is now a huge rock standing out in a quiet bay and all around are jutting headlands over which the surf is breaking [...] The sea is a beautiful greeny blue and the sky is a mass of diffused green and pink and golds and one can hear the gentle swish and fall of the waves as they roll along the broad stretch of sands now in view. A distant church clock strikes the hour and a strident siren emits its shriek, the dreamer is awakened, red walls and dull state roofs together with ugly telegraph poles and factory chimney stacks force themselves into view, and another day has begun. So you see Joy can be found even in a prison.

I have not left much room for the replies to all the letters I received, but must say how glad I was to get them [...]

> Just room to send you my fondest Love and dearest wishes
>
> Yours Ever Frank

PS Many thanks for books

✦

> 32 North Avenue, Letchworth, Herts
> Feb 24th 1918

My dear Frank

Your letter last week was particularly enjoyable, the children too were pleased to have their little bit. As usual I have no news. We are all well and Morris and I are looking forward to visiting you one day this week.

Our meeting at the Skittles last Monday was almost a failure, as no mothers turned up, some of our [Adult] school did and the girls had a very good time. When we came out at about 9.30, the guns were going. I ran home with Dora, afraid the other two would wake up and hear. However we only heard them a little while and I got Dora to bed at once, but I stayed up till 12. Nothing happened so I soon went to sleep. It has been quite alright since.

I had a letter from Katie and they had 3 awful nights up there and Mother came down on Sat. I think Dad and Katie are glad for her to be here. Of course, I am constantly trying to bring her to see my view of things, but she has no power of thinking for herself. It is really quite peculiar. I think the matter is, it seems to me she lives in a little narrow world of her own and her mind is so full of her own ideas, there is no

3. 'I NEVER WANTED YOUR PRESENCE MORE THAN NOW'

room for anything else. I don't know how long she is staying. I can put up with her and shall no doubt find her useful.

I went out sewing on Tuesday afternoon to a house in Broadwater Avenue. We had our school on Thursday and had quite a good time. Mrs Myles was quite cheered, I got an inspiration and wrote the questions out for this week and gave them to three good members to answer, I thought this would bring them. We had 10 there, we hope to go on now and do well. Mrs Wiltshire has gone on a visit to her husband for a few weeks, I believe.

You will be glad to know that my chickens are going on laying again. The difficulty is getting food for them now, so I don't know how long I shall be able to keep them, they may be commandeered yet. Well, the rationing comes into force tomorrow, and I wonder how it will answer. Mother will be able to use my meat ticket mostly and it will leave a little more for Dad and Katie.

We are going on with the garden. I have given Dora a patch and will put the front borders in charge of Chrissie and Morris, if they will attend to it. They would rather grow vegetables, but I shall let them put in some radishes for a border. I forgot to tell you that the bulbs have survived and are coming up well, I do hope they will bloom this year. I also forgot to tell you that I have made my wretched oven bake at last. I found a loose fire brick about 3 in thick [on] the oven side of the gate which I moved and now have nothing to complain of. Now I am able to use the fire I use the kitchen more and only use the front room in the evenings.

[...] *The Citizen* had your name in Tribunal news this week. You see you are such a well-known Character in Letchworth [...] Mrs Matthews has lent me a copy of *The Friend* this week, as it has the report of the meetings.[96] It was chiefly concerning the schools attended by their children. I like a passage by Dr Mary O'Brien Harris, (her husband is coming to our Adult School on Sunday) [...]

Percy Alder has an article called 'New England', in which he brings in

---

96   *The Friend* was and is an independent weekly Quaker magazine.

the 'New Town' and finishes up like this: 'If such a town be established it would develop among its citizens a social life based on mutual aid and goodwill with which I fear we are for the most part unacquainted today, and all who have the courage even during this calamition was to work for Shelley's ideal of "joyous widest commonalty spread" deserve the admiration and I trust will win the support of all right thinking citizens.' This paper also tells that 100 acres opposite the Hostel and Meeting House at Old Jordans have been bought to establish a village community.[97] It also says the invitation to an International Christian Conference has been received by various regions [and] bodies in England, the date suggested April 14th.

If Dora enters for the scholarship examination it will be in May: she is quite keen. Even if she does not win it will be an extra effort to gain knowledge. I hope I have left no question unanswered, if I have ask when you see me in a few days. Now my space is gone so I must stop,

love from us all, and looking forward to the merry time you have promised us,

Yours ever

Lucy

Bedford Prison
25-2-1918

Dearest Lucy

[...] I had a reply from the Local Tribunal and it states 'that they do not see their way to take any action in the matter'. I think Furmston must be mistaken. The reply is no more than I expected. Leopards do not change their spots and such men as E Harrison etc, who are do[ing] so

---

97   The 'Jordans Scheme' referred to throughout these letters was a plan of both the local Quakers and the garden city movement to build a new village next to the village of Jordans in Buckinghamshire.

3. 'I NEVER WANTED YOUR PRESENCE MORE THAN NOW'

well out of the war, are least likely to understand our point of view. My remaining here will not affect his shipping shares, but my being free might. I trust you are now satisfied and will not call on me to ask Pilate to wash his hands again.

I am glad you are reading *The Valley of the Moon* again. It is a lovely story and I often think of it. In reading the *Love of the Honey Bee* I came across the description of a little bee Tom. It was owned by a man who had been a city clerk in London. One day he bought a book on Bees for threepence. It attracted his attention and he studied it well. He resolved to try the experiment, so saved a few pounds and took a little cottage, with half an acre of land attached, in Sussex and he together with two sisters started in a very small way. Had some half dozen hives at first and grew his own vegetables etc. He got the honey from the hives of other people round about without using sulphur and they let him have their bees for doing so. He made a market for his honey in the neighbouring town and had a donkey and cart which one of his sisters used to drive. They all lived happily and healthily and thus found their Valley of the Moon.

Can we do something like this in new town which is coming? You must think this out, for I want to hear your side of the question. Also get the children to think of it, and see what conclusion they arrive at. I am sure Dora will think of something original to do.

Your description of the Ration tickets amused me and I've been trying to imagine the feelings of the small shopkeeper who supplies [the] wants of the very poor and only deals in pennyworths. Will he have to stamp every card for a pennyworth of jam or an ounce of tea and so on? Can you lend your cards to your neighbor, or must you do your shopping yourself? If so, who identifies you? Should you lose your cards, do you starve until you get some more, or can you go on the parish for relief? Who is responsible for loss, the Housewife or the husbands and does each lodger have to get his own allowance? Do the officials come and count the lodgers and children? If you go for a holiday from home, do you have to take your food with you or do you report to the food controllers etc? I don't want you to answer all these questions, but have just quoted them to show how it looks from an outsider's point of view. For, of course, we here are outsiders, or rather insiders I should say [...]

I am sending you [a] visiting order with this letter and look forward with joy to seeing you again. You cannot understand how detached one gets and feels in here. It is quite an effort sometimes to even think of the outside world, and I'm sure my letter must betray the same things.

Do not think because I have written this that you and the children are not always in my thoughts. You are, but it is with a sense of unreality, as it were, and so I want you all to send along as many thought waves as you can. Tell the children I always keep my window open so a gentle breeze may waft a song from Chrissie or a shout from Morris, or a piece of poetry from Dora and a prayer from Mother.

I send you all my Love and lots of Kisses to her paid when home I come and am eagerly expecting to see your Dear sweet face again

Yours loving Husband and Father

Frank

୬

March 11th 1918

Dearest Lucy

You are doubtless looking forward to receiving this letter and I trust will get as much enjoyment from its contents as I do in writing it. To set your mind at ease, I must say that I am well and have had no recurrence of the Lumbago I told you of. We are all well and the only thing which seems to be prevalent amongst us is an undue <u>optimism</u> which sustains us. The news we get from outside usually only amuses us, because being so completely cut off from the world and its doings, we do not fully grasp the reality of it and think it all foolish. You remember the story of the Lunatic, who seeing a man toiling with a loaded barrow, asked 'why he did it' and on being told 'for a living', laughed and said 'Man, you're the wrong side of the fence, come in here'. We are like the lunatic inasmuch as our peculiar circumstances cause us to see things

3. 'I NEVER WANTED YOUR PRESENCE MORE THAN NOW'

according to the relation to our surroundings and not to their true perspective.

[...] It was so nice to see our Morris once again and I have rebuilt home to myself many times since. His sweet innocent face and open truthfulness in such a place as this were like rare lilies growing in a garden filled with weeds [...]

I hope you were not upset by the air raid and that the guest you have with you behaved as little like a lunatic as possible and gave no trouble, for I am sure you have quite enough to manage in the children, and I do not thank the patriotic friends for foisting such a splendid example of Christian endurance upon you. I heard nothing of it and feel ashamed of myself for being out of all the anxiety through which you are passing, and unable to help you in any way.

Have you sold your bicycle yet? If you have not, perhaps you could get Matthews to put Dora's in order in exchange for yours. It would be nice if she could have the little one to ride on. Forgive me if my suggestions seem wild and impracticable. I have imagined you in the Dentist's chair and have sent my sympathies out to you and hope the job is well over by this time and that you have not suffered much. I expect I shall have to undergo some Dental treatment when I get free as some of my teeth are getting bad but they do not trouble me in any way.

The weather is so nice again now that one feels the winter is over: spring is here. I can see the buds coming on the trees and the birds are mating and busy with nest building and love making. Fulfilling the design of their creation and giving him the praise. When I get free once more I do not think town life will attract me. Space and air and a sense of roominess will alone satisfy. Bedford is a town of clashes. Yesterday afternoon I listened to the Salvation Army band in competition with a drum and fife band, a military band, church bells ringing, cocks crowing, hens cackling, dogs barking, carts rumbling, motor sirens, and a congregation singing in chapel, together with various other noises too numerous to mention. It put me in mind of the song 'I'm glad I had a nice quiet day'. So much for the good old English Sunday as exemplified in a country town. You can easily see it is conducive to ease and quiet contemplation [...]

I'm interested in the Jordans scheme,[98] so if you can, send along all the information you can get. Will you get me the *Life* of W[illiam] Morris? You will be able to borrow it, probably. I have been studying the *Carpenter and Builder* and making plans for our next bungalow in [the] 'New Town'. It is an interesting occupation for an idle man, and castles in the air are very easy to build. If one forgets the staircase it doesn't matter as imagination needs no such aid.

When you see Dr Crowley tell him I want a niche in the scheme and am quite content to play a very minor part [...]

Best wishes to all enquiring friends, tell them to cheer up, the war won't last for ever and if it does we'll all meet elsewhere. Sweet thoughts be with you

Yours lovingly

Frank

32 North Avenue, Letchworth, Herts
Mar 12. 1918

My dear Frank,

I was glad to get your letter this morning, and was so glad to feel the human touch in it. I felt your love and sympathy going out to me, and it was a comfort to know you felt I needed it, not knowing how much. I never wanted your presence more than now, and as I cannot have it in the flesh must be content with the spirit.

The raid last week was rather upsetting to Mrs Gardner[99] and I: the children did not wake up and the noise of the guns was terrific. Mother was not very well and did not get off the bed; she said it was nothing

---

98 See Lucy's letter of 24 February 1918.

99 Lucy's new lodger.

3. 'I NEVER WANTED YOUR PRESENCE MORE THAN NOW'

to hear after London. On Thursday I felt rather anxious about her and sent for Dr Macfadyen. He said she was rather bad, bronchitis; of course I wrote to Katie and she wanted to come and fetch her home. I replied she could not be moved.

On Friday night I was up nearly all night trying to ease her chest. On Sat morning, Dr said it would be as well to let my father know, as he saw no improvement in her condition, so of course I wired. That was one o'clock, but it did not go till 2. She had her dinner and Mrs Gardner went out shopping. I sent Morris and Chrissie to the Station and Dora was out in the garden, when I saw the change and [Mother] did not know me. I called Dora to run over for Mrs Stacy, and just as she came in [Mother] stopped breathing, nothing more. I had an awful shock, but simply had to pull myself together and act. I of course wired again to Dad and they came on Sunday morning, went back yesterday, coming again on Wed. eve for Thursday.

I sent for Roy and just managed it all. Poor father is dreadfully cut up, it was such a shock to them both. You will be glad to know there is no influence on the children; they are exactly as usual, and it keeps me up too. I feel I am being strengthened. 'As thy days, thy strength shall be'.

I feel I must have a change and holiday; I have had so much to bear this last 12 months. Now I have had an offer to let the house for the summer, 25/- weekly, and Mrs Gardner can arrange with her uncle, Mr Fox, for us to have his caravan at Wollscombe, Devonshire for next to nothing (or could get a room very easily). [...] What do you think about me taking the opportunity (after my teeth are done)? No raids there.

Am glad Mrs Gardner is here, she is company, do not worry about me. I shall be quite alright again after this week.

You will understand that I cannot write a long letter to you, I cannot write what I should like to say to you, but will try to write a nice letter to you next week. I hope you won't be vexed at this happening here: she was at her best here with me, and happy, and I am glad to have been used to give her peace at the last. Poor mother, she missed the joy of life somehow, but she understands now. Dad and Katie are very glad she was here, as [the bombing] last week, [they] said, would have finished her. It was very dreadful. 4 houses down in Lyndhurst Road, and her end would not have been peace.

Now I will stop, so glad to know you are really well, and enjoyed our visit. Morris will never forget it, the children all send love to you and everyone I speak to wishes to be remembered to you.

Perhaps you would be allowed to write a special letter with a message for Dad. We must let bygones be bygones, you know.

Lots of love from your ever loving wife

Lucy

18.3.1918

Lucy Darling

Your last letter 'struck me all of a heap', as the saying is. However I am recovered and my thoughts have been with you all the time. You have had a lot to bear since I have been away from home, and you are so brave and strong with it all that you send me strength. You know, and have had experience, as to how weak I am. I long to be able to hold you in my arms and comfort you, and it is when I most keenly feel your needs that I chafe most at my confinement.

We are learning to put our trust more and more in the Source of Love, as we feel the need for Love and cannot express it in action for each other. I agree with you with regard to the holiday, and am rejoiced at the opportunity which seems to have opened for you. Go by all means, and enjoy new scenes and occupations. It will fit you for the twenty years work you talk of. Of course, there is a lot for you to do before you can get away, but I suppose you can get over all the difficulties. As to the Planet, I should get into touch with Pound. He lives in the Prize Cottage, Icknield Way. He ought to be willing to do it for the Com[ission]. Palmer might manage Kays. As to boxes with locks and keys, my big box has a lock and also my tool box: get Stone to put some screws in the hinges and if you can find the keys all will be well. Make sure that your proposed tenant <u>is</u> a good one and not likely to chop up the bedstead for firewood as some of them have done.

It is so easy to sit and give orders that my pen speeds along at quite a rapid rate, but of course it will be just as easy for you to <u>disobey</u> if the orders do not fit in with your own desires. I tried to write to your Father but found I could frame no words to suit my real thoughts, and as I had no wish to be hypocritical I thought it best for them to be left unsaid.

[...] I should like to get a share in the Town if you can manage it. Did you manage to get the fruit trees pruned this year? Devonshire is a great bee-keeping county, so if you go you must learn all you can about them whilst you are there. Do the children know of this project yet? It will be a source of great joy to them. [...]

I suppose you will go on cropping the garden just the same so that it will yield you the crop in the autumn. You will certainly have to pension the hens off, they have done so well by you. I suppose they are doing work of national importance. Just fancy a hen being more useful than a man and yet I feel that they are more useful in a sense than I am at the present time. It is a topsy-turvy world and must afford great amusement to the Gods.

I am reading Walt Whitman now. He is splendid and expresses some fine thoughts [...] When one thinks of the times in which he lived it is easy to see he was a true seer, and all through his poems he strikes the democratic note. I came across a book in the Advert Columns of the *Carpenter Builder* called Spon's Workshop Receipts: you might make enquiries at Smith's regarding it for me and let me know all about it, for I think it will suit my requirements [...]

My space is nearly done Dear, and I have not said what I want to say to you but I send you all my Love and Sympathy. My heart yearns for you and will not be satisfied. You must read my thoughts by your own, for we are one and our joy and suffering is one and no matter what comes we shall not be divided for we belong to Love and Love is all encircling.

Your Loving Husband

Frank

PS I will send the visiting order next week as I feel sure you would like to talk things over with me. If not, let me know by reply.

---

32 North Avenue, Letchworth, Herts
March 19. 1918

My dear Frank,

I was so glad to have your letter this morning. It was just what I needed. I can think your thoughts for you, we are so united I am sure, and nothing can part us really, or come between us.

I am sorry you could not manage to write a few lines to Dad or to me, but I can quite understand even your feelings in that. I am recovering a little from the shock I had, but have not yet been to the dentist. I have arranged for an interview with Clapham for Friday morning, and am prepared to have them out next week. Mrs Middleton will go with me as she wants me to have gas. I shall be glad to have the job over.

The children are quite well and excited over the proposed holiday. I am still thinking of it and am glad you are willing we should take the opportunity. Mr Marshall is quite willing we should stay on, in fact [he'd] forgotten the lease was out and never thought of anything else. He is also willing for me to sublet furnished, providing he knows who the proposed tenant is. I have had offers for the house.

Mrs Gardner's sister Claudia has come to Letchworth for a couple of days; she is going to find some accommodation for me and let me know all about it as soon as she gets back, that is at Barnstaple. I did not tell you that I am taking up some new business through Picton, £500 life for a house mortgage. I hope it comes off, that will pay our fares down. I should like to talk things over with you if you will send me the order; I shall not be able to come till after Easter. Shall I bring both the girls then? [...] Yes, of course this will put a stop (for a time) to Katie's 'honeymoon'. I am sorry for them, but perhaps it is just as well. I believe they are both coming down for Easter with Dad, if he can get off.

They will feel more than ever drawn to Letchworth. Katie wants a change of life, she looks very seedy and is getting so thin and old looking, I am afraid like Mother. Macfadyen said Mother had been really ill for years. You will be glad to know that I sent to the Sanitary Inspector and had the room fumigated. Mrs Gardner is going in there tonight for the first time, and does not mind at all.

I want to talk such a lot to you but do not feel able to write. I, like you, feel the separation very much just now, the actual presence and touch of one we love, makes the comfort we so much need at these times. There are quite a lot of flowers out now, violets and primroses in the garden and crocuses and daffodils next door, but even they make me feel sad because they fade and die, I try to remember that they rise again.

I arranged for Rev Crowle Smith to take the service for Mother and he came to see me the day before and was exceedingly nice; he wishes me to send you his regards. We have his entire sympathy, and he is very sorry for me and is coming to see me, to know if there is anything he can do. Annie wished to hear him preach so we went on Sunday morning to the Wesleyan church. He is very unconventional and says what he thinks, not minding what the members like. He preached on Immortality and Judgement, which he thinks is passed directly a soul passes and that soul has a second chance. He also admitted that we cannot be sure that parts of the Bible are really true: that struck me as rather advanced [...]

Yes I do remember the lovely Easter we spent together, although I have so little time for quiet moments, and that is what I feel to need, my brain is one constant whirl, first one thing then another. Perhaps you cannot understand, you see I am still mother as well as a worker, and the children want a good deal of love and attention. I will see what I can do at Smith's for you.

Mrs Gardner sends her kind regards, and Reg is working at Wales' and doing up some furniture for Rine Williams. Now I must stop longing for the next letter; sorry you will not get this as soon as you would like. I shall be glad to see you again and let me know about the girls coming. We are going to see Miss Gay to have our photos on Saturday. Now goodbye

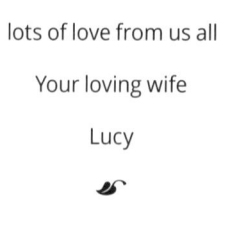

lots of love from us all

Your loving wife

Lucy

✌

Bedford Prison
March 25 1918

Lucy Dearest

Your long looked-for reply received at last. As I perused it I felt that you are not your usual self and that it was a great effort on your part to write. I am glad my letter cheered you for it is quite a new departure for me to be able to cheer one as I am usually a Job's comforter.

Now that you have got your house cleared of the <u>necessary</u> visitors, you must concentrate your thoughts on the coming holiday. I think the idea a splendid one. Do you remember seeing a fine caravan whilst we were staying at Folkestone? It was fitted up with silver fittings, bevelled glass and built of oak, fit for a prince or even a Socialist. I don't suppose you will get one like that, although you deserve it, but I am sure you will be comfortable and the very novelty will ensure pleasure. How do you manage to control the children? They must be just mad with delight, and I can imagine them full of plans and ideas as to what they will do etc. What does Katie think of the scheme? Is it classified with the rest of our lives as <u>Mad</u>? Did you discuss 'New Town' with them, or will it form a topic for Easter?

Re Crowle Smith, I have wondered who conducted the service and thought perhaps it was the irony of fate to be buried by a C of E man as she disliked them so, but you settled the difficulty very well for them all [...]

3. 'I NEVER WANTED YOUR PRESENCE MORE THAN NOW'

You did not mention the Esperanto book, but I am not keen, as it does not seem to be very urgent. [...] If you cannot borrow W. Morris you can get it at Smith's. It is pub[lished] by the Home University Library at 1/3. I also want some more books as per list below and if you ask Allen, perhaps he can get them trade price, or failing him try Simmons through the ILP. No. 33 *The Bible in Spain* by Borrow and no. 60 *Sartor Resartus* by Carlyle are from Cassell's The People's Library 8d. 224 Mazzini's *Duties of Man* and no. 281 Thoreau's *Walden* are from Everyman 1/3. I also want Carpenter's *Toward Democracy* which I know is published in a cheap edition but I can't think of the publisher. You need not send them <u>all</u> at once; but spread them over some <u>months</u> to come.

[...] If you let the house put my bicycle in the care of Matthews or Palmer, it will then be out of harm's way and handy for me if the unforeseen happens at any time. Have you heard from Alf lately as I am anxious about Mother? [...]

I should indeed be pleased to see Dora and Chrissie and eagerly look forward to your visit. Remember me to Dad but don't defend me [...]

My space is nearly gone so I wish you a happy Easter and a nice rest soon. I hope you will not suffer under the Dentist. Kiss the children from Daddy and accept all my Love and Sympathy and sweetest thoughts

Yours Ever

Frank

PS Have enclosed visiting order.

---

32 North Avenue Letchworth Herts
March 25th

My dear Frank

I am starting your letter this evening as I might not have much leisure tomorrow and I do not like to keep you waiting so long. Does the time seem long to you, I mean all the days and weeks?

You will be glad to know that I am feeling rather better, and also glad to know that I have at last had 5 of my teeth out, 1/4 past 9 this morning under gas, and I got over it splendidly although the Dr said 'Well, you were a nervous one'. I have been resting all day and shall be quite alright soon. I am going again next Tuesday for stopping. I really did not feel one twinge of pain, it is very wonderful what can be done. I asked how long it took and Dr Clapham said 2 minutes to send me off and one to do the job. Mrs Middleton had promised to go with me, but on calling for her, found her out, so wondered how I should get on alone. Well, about outside her gate I came across Mrs Price who at once said, I'll come and see you home. As it happened I did not need any assistance, but it was very nice of her all the same. I only kept her waiting about 10 minutes and surprised the children and Mrs Gardner by returning so soon and smiling.

Mrs Price told me a movement is afoot on your behalf, also Arthur Francis. I like to keep a spark of hope burning, it helps to give me courage to live through this separation. Miss Middleton called this afternoon apologizing for having forsaken me, but she had the weekend in London. (She is the same age Mother was.)

Tuesday.

I had your letter this afternoon, and felt ashamed to have troubled you (unconsciously) with my sadness, but I think and hope you understand what I have been going through, after all she was my mother.

[...] Carrie sent her photograph for you which I am enclosing. We had ours taken on Sat. What a lovely day it was and Sunday too, but this morning it was a white frost again. I will send you one as soon as I get it, but have not had the proof yet. Miss Gay is very jolly. I had quite a pleasant visit to her studio. She wanted me to have one as well with one of the girls. I refused as I could not possibly make a choice, she said 'no, the mother's sense of justice would not allow of it', but which one was your favourite? What a question! I announced neither, but I believed you perhaps thought most of the boy as the hope of the future, and she replied 'Silly man, it is the women of the future who will count', and I answered, Yes, but it rests with the mothers to make the boys men of the future: how was that? However, she took one of Morris with me, which will perhaps be useful to send you later on if it is successful. She quite enjoys herself, doesn't she, and seemed surprised at my big children, of course Chrissie giggled [...]

Now about our holiday. I am afraid I should be rather lonely in the caravan without you. I love the idea and so do the children, but do not think it quite wise to take it. Mrs Gardner's sister Claudia was here last week from Barnstaple, and has offered me a bedroom and sitting room with her. I am waiting now to hear from her before I definitely decide. It was 4 offers for the house, the first people are anxiously waiting my decision; they are Russians at present in Brighton, want to be quieter and have a gardener to do the garden as they want [...]

Now my space is used up so I must send love from all the children, they never forget Daddy, and all the best love from your ever loving wife

Lucy

4. 'The countryside is glorious', April to August 1918

Bedford Prison
April 8 1918

Lucy Darling

[...] I enjoyed your visit immensely, although I am sure you had quite a lot to say to me which remained unsaid. Perhaps it will form the basis of your next letter to me. Both you and the Girls are looking very well and Chrissie as grown very much. Dora too has grown not only in stature, but she seems more mature and I am sure she has a strong sense of humour. As to her music, I suppose she has mastered the drudgery stage and means that she does not want to make it her profession. Does she still practice or play at all, or has she jumped into some other craze? I was glad the weather was good to you this time and hope you were able to enjoy the waiting period and also the train journey. It must have been quite an event to the girls. Let me know if you had any adventures. Last time you whetted my appetite, by telling me you had an interesting conversation in the train but you omitted to say what it was all about. Such stimulation is not good for anyone in my position.

[...] I think you have acted <u>wisely</u> in your money affairs so should make no changes. If you still have *Daddy Longlegs* and the sequel,[100] will you put a wrapper round them, leaving the ends exposed for book post and send them on to me as I should like to read them again. [...] I propose you get an 'Esperanto lesson book', and start with one, but I do not want you to feel <u>bound</u> to this suggestion. I think confinement is making me super sensitive, as it seems like taking a liberty to offer you suggestion or advice, and I am sure advice was about the only thing

---

100   Jean Webster's hugely popular novel *Daddy Longlegs* (1912), about an orphan sponsored through college by a trustee of her orphanage, who secretly falls in love with her, was followed by *Dear Enemy* (1915), telling the growth to maturity of another orphanage girl.

I ever gave away before. I noticed that Chrissie's hair is growing and turning to quite a deep golden but I suppose it will get dark.

I hear that Wiltshire has taken a cottage at 1/3 per week and intends to settle in the heart of the country, so whilst you are away you had better see if you can find a nice place at about 2/- with orchard and pigsties thrown in where we can settle and be far from politics, strikes, and social reform etc, not to mention New Town, and where we can <u>end</u> our days in peace. I hope you like the picture. I will be nought but a digger and delver, content with a crust <u>without</u> marg and think of nothing but crops, and you will make butter and keep chicks and pick fruit etc and the children can help us in this 'Ideal Life', it would indeed be the end.

[...] Have Matthews left the Manor yet? remember me to them and thank them for books. I have been reading Whittier's *Poems*. He is the Quaker Poet of the Anti Slavery movement in America and he together with Woolman stand out as examples of what can be accomplished by pacifist action.[101] His poems are full of fire and zeal for liberty but he strikes a note of homeliness too. His 'Snowbound' is a picture of backwoods life superior to Longfellow's Miles Standish in its simplicity and rugged truthfulness. [...] I send you all my Love and sweet thoughts and know that nothing can separate ourselves

Your Loving

Hubby

---

32 North Avenue Letchworth, Herts
April 9th 1918

My dear Frank

I was of course very glad to have your letter yesterday afternoon. The children were pleased to have their bit. I am sorry they have not

---

101   John Woolman was an eighteenth-century Quaker and anti-slavery campaigner. The poet John Greenleaf Whittier was a generation younger, also a Quaker and an anti-slavery campaigner.

written one for you, but I want to get this posted as soon as possible, so don't think I can wait for them this time. We all very much enjoyed our visit to you on Friday, the girls did not think it nearly so bad as they had imagined it, and I thought you more like yourself than I had seen you, I hope the cheerfulness was real [...] I thought you were rather sarcastic about the country life 'Ideal', I hope you do not think I am running away from duty, and want to rusticate till the end: that certainly is not my idea of life. I like you want to spend my strength for humanity, but I feel that just now it has already spent itself and needs renewing. This letter has been delayed through my spare time being taken up with frantic neuralgia, directly I start to write or read, it commences. I am due at the dentist again tomorrow so hope to be relieved, if not must consult the Dr. Do not worry, I shall soon be alright, but wanted to justify my position with regard to holiday. I have seen the people who want the house, the lady (Mrs Winestein) got anxious and came from Brighton to hurry the arrangement, I believe, however she was quite satisfied and I have settled with her to have the house and part of the garden for 4 months from the end of April and 25/- per week, also to pay me £2 for the use of the fowls, and if killed the balance of market price, but she could not bear the thought of killing and eating birds they had fed. Mrs Palmer will collect the rent weekly, or as I like to decide, also make up an agreement for me, to be signed as soon as they come. There are the husband and wife, a little boy and baby, also a maid who has been with them 5 years, they have their own linen and silver, so don't you think this very satisfactory?

Of course I have a good lot to do to get ready for them as I must leave everything clean and in good order.

[...] I have sent you *The Bible in Spain*, Mrs Middleton has given you and I bought W. Morris. *Towards Democracy* was only in a 5/- edition, nothing cheaper: is it worth it? You can have it if you like. The others Allan will get me. Dora started Esperanto last evening and seemed to like it, I shall very likely go on with it when I have the spare time and free from pain.

4. 'THE COUNTRYSIDE IS GLORIOUS'

[...] A meeting was held at Howard Hall last Sat week organized by the Women's Freedom League. Miss Anna Munro was to speak but an accident prevented her from getting here. Mrs Harrison took her place and spoke of various things interesting to women on the use of the vote.[102] I feel that women have now a wonderful power to exercise for the world if used rightly, and more so, now so many more men are to be called up. 55 is now the age and so few are likely to return, it makes my brain reel to think of it all, and wondering where and when it can all end. I agree with you that the end is easier to meet in the whirl of excitement but don't please think of the end like that. I like to feel you are preparing for a future in this life, people will wake up to the horror of it all presently, I only hope it will not end in Civil War. Ireland is now to be conscripted, but that will not be without a struggle on their part.

I suppose when this new Man Power Bill comes into force,[103] we shall see a lot more men going to Prison for their conscience and a lot will be proved like Crowle Smith and that sort, there will be no half and half now it must be one side or the other [...]

Now my space is used up and I hope this letter is satisfactory to you. As you say, one cannot convey on paper what is in the mind but I am thankful for this weekly letter. The children all sent lots of love to you and kisses in imagination. You know my thoughts and heart is full of you always and for ever

Yours

Lucy

---

102   The Women's Freedom League rejected violent campaigning methods, and during the war became a pacifist organization. Anna Munro was a suffrage activist, socialist and temperance campaigner.

103   The fifth revision of the Military Service Act of April 1918 extended the military service age range to 17–51, and for the first time conscripted men from Ireland (though this was not enforced, in the event).

THE CONSCIENTIOUS OBJECTOR'S WIFE

Bedford Prison
15.4.1918

Lucy Dearest

[...] You ask me in your last letter as to whether times grow quickly here. Generally speaking, Yes. Having no objectives, such as a certain date when all this will be over, one gets into a way of not thinking about release. Of course it is at the back of one's mind as a sort of happy event which may happen someday, but it is quiescent. Then again our days are cut up into a certain formula which is repeated Ad Infinitum and if it were not for the difference in diet one would have a difficulty to tell a Monday from Tuesday etc. All this tends to make the past a blank and as our lives are really only measured by events; it therefore follows that the letters and visits which one gets are the determining factor which makes time. Last week has seemed an age to me because I have not yet received my letter from you.

I have conjectured all sorts of reasons for the delay but am not anxious, for I know were you in trouble either you or someone else would write at once. I will not weary you with all the reasons I have thought of, but please don't do it again as I have no other things to counteract the anxiety caused by waiting and my nerves are not in the pink of condition. Don't think that I am ill because I say this as really I am very well, as I trust both you and the children are.

I suppose the people outside are greatly concerned regarding the extension of the conscription act. Peter Myles and several other of our friends will be called upon to face the music now. Bond Holding and Ball are both under the age, let me know as to what action they take. Will it affect Noel and any of the ILPs? How will Katie's Pal stand? Some of these people who have just gone in in their own way and accepted the war, like a child accepts a rain storm, will now be forced to do a bit of thinking. [...]

I have been reading *Nicholas Nickleby* again and I must say I enjoyed it. Dickens certainly exaggerated his characters, makes them either too good or too bad, but most of them are lovable. The picture of Miss La Creevy the portrait painter is very good and recent events give it

4. 'THE COUNTRYSIDE IS GLORIOUS'

a more lifelike touch. As an instance of what I mean, she is going out for the day and before she goes she carefully locks the tea caddy and hides the key under the fender. Caddies with locks must have come into general use again now, with tea being so scarce and dear, and likely to be dearer if they raise the tax on it in the next budget […]

Write me full details of home affairs and you can leave all other affairs to take care of themselves. I hope I have left nothing out that I wished to say if I have you must forgive me. I send you all my Love and I know you can feel all my affection for you as my spirit is with you always.

Kiss the Bairns and accept some for self

Lovingly Yours

Frank

PS I suppose the next letter will have to be at a new address eh?

April 15th 1918
32 North Avenue Letchworth

My dear Frank

Your letter received today teatime Wed. I was just getting anxious about you. I cannot understand why you did not get my last week's letter sent with two books W. Morris and *The Bible in Spain* on Wed last. I hope they have not got lost and I know how you must have felt waiting for a letter that does not come, but I should of course always let you know if anything prevented me from writing.

My dear, I also feel all you feel, I felt just the same for you last Spring. I know how you long for freedom, and we long for your presence, perhaps we shall have it soon, who knows. I am ashamed to confess how depressed I have been feeling lately. I suppose the condition of things and news from all points is not conducive to joy. That is why I feel it will be good for us to go away for a change as we must keep the children happy as long as possible and the effect of mind on the body is great. I do want them to be strong and healthy. I find it very necessary to excuse the steps I am taking, although everyone I mention it to says 'the very thing, a grand idea, the best thing possible', and so of course you know the railway fare will be a great deal but I somehow think it will be worth it. I don't like to think how many miles we shall be separated, but we might as well be now as far apart as the poles and distance does not matter when our spirits meet [...]

I saw Miss Pass this morning and she says the War will end in July and her brother is awfully busy and <u>could</u> do with you. She says his foot will exempt him but I said he could do munitions or something more important than picture framing, we shall see. Allen is getting the books you want. Mrs Middleton is sending you two of them and paying for them. Miss Bartholomew has brought the other William Morris. I will let you have it and then you can give one of them to our Morris when you come home.

The children have each written you a little letter. I hope you may have them. You shall have the photographs as soon as I get them, next week I expect. I feel rather lonely evenings now Mrs G has gone, but of course we like the house to ourselves. It seems ages to me since Mother came down 7 weeks ago and such a lot has happened since then [...]

Now I must stop and hope you get this one and find it partly satisfies the longing within you. We all love you dearly and long and hope every day for your return to us.

Your loving wife

Lucy

Bedford Prison
April 22 1918

Mia Kara Edzino

I have now two letters to reply to. The cause of the delay was the fact that you inserted the letter in the book, which went to the librarian. He happened to be away on holiday and they were not opened until he came back, when I immediately got the letter and read your news.

4. 'THE COUNTRYSIDE IS GLORIOUS'

I must say how pleased I am with the Esperanto. As you see I have commenced my letter in this most elegant language. I am making good progress in it and find it very enjoyable. I wish I had started before. Do you remember when I was learning German, what fun we had, how we ticketed everything with its German name. I expect Dora will want to do the same and you will find it helpful if you can do so. I can't use that method here but my slate is always full and my tongue is in a knot through trying to pronounce some of the words […]

I am <u>pleased</u> to know you have arranged the letting of the house and fixed up your lodgings for the summer. I do not think it selfish of you but am glad to know you can arrange it. Use your time so that <u>you</u> will be stronger for the changes and I am sure you will be nearer to me then because you always have given me inspiration. You will have more time to think and reflect, the new scenery and surroundings will bring fresh thoughts to your mind. Oh I can imagine the great excitement now prevailing at Focabers.[104] What a sorting of clothes, cleaning of boots, brushing and refurbishing etc which must be done before all is ready. The packing and unpacking, the things which won't shut and the straps which are too short and so on, not to mention the toys which must go, Morris's Teddy Bear, Dora's books and Chrissie's paints.

Don't forget to take some <u>cushions</u> for yourself. They do not take up much room and are very light, but make such a difference to comfort. I am glad you <u>could</u> get books for the children. I thought such things had all been long used up […]

I was amused at Miss Pass' prophecy, but the trouble is they keep shifting the date. Thank all my friends for their kindness to me and say how much I appreciate it. Write me fully of your doings for your life is not trivial to me and just enjoy yourself, knowing that I am resigned and waiting patiently for the release that must come at last and that will be when Peace has come.

All my thoughts and Love for you

---

104   This may have been the name of their bungalow.

THE CONSCIENTIOUS OBJECTOR'S WIFE

Your Loving Hubby

Frank

🙞

April 23rd 1918
32 North Avenue Letchworth

My dear Frank

Sorry I cannot put it in Esperanto, it looks nice. Dora seems to be enjoying it and we will study it together when we are away. Was glad to get your letter on Tuesday morning this week. I have a better chance of answering now than I shall have tomorrow. I have the sweep coming in the morning, 8.30, for kitchen and sitting room. If this weather continues my tenants will want good fires (if they can procure the coal. I haven't any just now, been ordered a fortnight) and I do not want chimney fires, then for a clean-up for the last spurt, then a little rest I hope. I saw Miss Amor last week, she is in raptures about Barnstaple and surrounding country; she comes from the next county, Wiltshire,[105] and both her and Mrs Price think I ought to send the children to school, there is sure to be a good council school. Mrs Buckingham's children go to the Catholic school. Dora will enter for the Scholarship next year; she will be better fitted then, as she will go into the 5th Standard on her return.

I am so glad you entirely agree with this step I am taking, it is not nice planning for oneself when you cannot be there, but I will try and write good letters and let you know everything. My days will not be as full I shall be able to let my brain expand and my mental outlook broaden. I feel I have got dreadfully narrow, into a rut and need digging out and feel weighed down with – nothing but <u>myself</u> [...]

This morning I was out at 10 till 20 to 2, had expected to get back by 1 o'clock and wondered how the children had got on: found a note from

---

105   Somerset and Dorset lie between Devon and Wiltshire. Lucy's mistake suggests her (or her informant's) limited knowledge of English geography.

4. 'THE COUNTRYSIDE IS GLORIOUS'

Dora – 'Dear Mother, we have had a bit of dinner so do not worry about us. Dora' They will make up for it at teatime and I started this as soon as I had something to eat and a cup of tea, so I am having a nice rest while writing this and then after it is posted I can go ahead again.

[...] Miss L sends greetings and if you <u>should</u> come home suddenly go to her and she will <u>gladly</u> lend you money for your fare to us, so don't forget. I was to tell you her girls' club is going strong, about 30 members. The girls are affiliated to the Labour Party and they have about 400 members. I have asked to resign the Sec. of Adult School but they won't let me, so have work to come back to and I hope there is one at Barnstaple [...]

The children were waiting for me with a fire and tea ready, they are very good really in spite of cross wilful moments, which all children good and bad indulge in. We have several books ready to take, <u>if</u> we can get them packed. Katie thinks the charm of a holiday is having no possessions. I think she is about right. She has promised to meet us on Sat. morning and very likely Mrs Tickle will see us off at Letchworth. The journey is sure to be interesting and you shall hear all about it next week. Mrs Kearney says we go through beautiful country and she says Barnstaple is a very nice place and Devonshire people are so nice and comfortable, so it all sounds all right.

You will be glad to know that my teeth are finished, quite a number required a little stopping. I asked for the bill yesterday: £2.2.6. I hope I shall never have to wait for money to go to the dentist again when needed. I really have not minded and it is such a comfort not to have toothache any more.

Morris has just come home now so I must stop now. We all send you our love and thoughts. I know we shall be in yours. The books you wanted will come on soon; everyone sends you greetings and kind thoughts.

Lots of love from yours ever

Lucy

THE CONSCIENTIOUS OBJECTOR'S WIFE

28th April 1918
Sunday evening c/o Mrs Buckingham
11 Fort Terrace
Barnstaple
Devon

My dear Frank

Well, we are really here, it seems like a dream. We are all well and going to have a lovely time. The hills and water is simply glorious. I hardly know where to start [a] description. I know you are longing to know all about it and want to see it in your mind's eye. The town is an old market town, not very large and we live about 10 minutes or less from the river which is as wide as the Thames in London at high tide. It is about six miles from the sea proper but of course it is sea breeze all the time.

This morning we walked along by it till we came to a pine wood which had paths winding up a great height overlooking and opposite town and river. The children found quantities of bluebells and ferns and anemones etc, and were in their glory racing up and down. They enjoyed a good dinner and I had a rest and a little sleep this afternoon while Morris wrote a letter to Miss Bracy. He is collecting wild flowers, so he is sending her some we found on the grass by the waterside. The water when the tide is out leaves a small stretch of sand and then a broad piece of grass where pools of water are left. They will be lovely for sailing boats and paddling in and sheep pasture along there too. Plenty of seaweed is washed up when the tide turns.

Tuesday

Had your letter teatime today and I hasten to answer. I knew you would be anxiously waiting for my letter but I am very glad you had my postcard. I thought it would ease your mind to know we had arrived safely.

I had better go back to last week. I got over my spring cleaning very well, finished by Thursday eve when I lit up the copper and we had the big bath and all had our hair washed and then I put the kiddies to bed and washed all the clothes we took off and put them through the wringer. It was luckily a fine morning so I hung them out to dry then did

4. 'THE COUNTRYSIDE IS GLORIOUS'

my shopping, got back to dinner then out again. After tea I packed up and borrowed a push chair and got some of our luggage to Mr Palmer's shop, and called on a few people, paid Chapham's bill and got back at 9.30 awfully tired of course; then I got the children to bed.

Morris was afraid to go to sleep in case I overslept the next morning. I cleared all up tidy, dusted etc. laid everything ready and went to bed about 12.00. Several times I woke and the last time 10 to 6. We had some breakfast and got to the station in time.

I had a busy time I can assure you to get there by 8.30 as everything had to be left in perfect order for the new people. I felt nearly done by the time we got into the train. Katie and Dad met us at Kings X and went by the tube with us to Waterloo. We were there by 10 and found a very long train but only 2 coaches to Ilfracombe which were already full so we had to take another part of the train and change at Exeter. It was no trouble as the luggage was in the van for Barnstaple and did not have to change too. I knew how far you had been. It was very pretty country we went through and the journey was over as you said almost before we knew. I had a cup of tea at Kings Cross and then we had our dinner about half past 12. Bread and butter and eggs. Marmite sandwiches, dates, nuts and orange: we all felt better after that. There were little girls, 6 and 11, with their mother in with us and ours talked to them in the corridor while I read and talked to Morris.

They were very interested in watching the river growing from a tiny stream to the broad River it is here. Of course you know it is the Taw. We find we can go to Ilfracombe for 11d so we plan a long day there during Whitsun.

I was glad to see Mrs Buckingham to meet us and to get here and have tea. She is very nice and we are quite all right. There is a Council school nearly opposite and I shall most likely send the children next week. They are getting used to the place and the change of air. They enjoy it very much. I have got a lot of papers to fill up for the Food Office before I can get Margarine or meat but this morning the Town Crier with a bell (interested the kiddies) called out that all farmers making butter after supplying registered customers could sell surplus to the public. I got ½lb of Devonshire butter and it is lovely too. I also got some lilies of the valley, honeysuckle and forget-me-nots in the market, 1d bunches, and sent to Katie, she would be pleased. Everything is early here, it is almost summer and we have heard the cuckoo and seen strawberries and gooseberries, also new potatoes. Market days are Tuesdays and Fridays, and people come here from miles around to see the stuff.

I have scarcely any work to do and am taking a good rest except when out walking, and the children want to be always out of course. There does not seem to be an Adult School here, but a Theosophical meeting on Tuesdays I might go to sometimes.[106] My box has not got here yet and it was sent off last Thursday. I have brought plenty of sewing to do when I feel like it. Food costs much the same as everywhere, also only rather cheaper I think but we are all more hungry. I daresay that will wear off but everyone thinks ours are fine children. I am very glad when I hear that [...]

Mrs Buckingham thinks I devote myself very much to my children, she thinks they are everything to me. I do hope not _too_ much, but they will always remember the happy times we have had and I do not want them to be saddened early in life, and I try to be a good mother in every way [...]

I hope you will enjoy reading this letter. We all send our best love and wish you were with us.

All my love to you from your loving wife

Lucy

---

[106] Meetings of the Theosophical Society, which was concerned with advancing ideas about a universal brotherhood and the comparative study of religion, subjects that Frank and Lucy were interested in.

4. 'THE COUNTRYSIDE IS GLORIOUS'

Bedford Prison
29.4.1918

Mia Kara Edzino

Your letter received with unusual promptitude and the tone of it real good. I liked your description of a day's work but felt what a pity it is you have not mastered or rather mistressed the bicycle, both your time and your legs would have been saved. You speak of a shortage in coal. I suppose it must have made people very careful and cinder sifters come into general use.

[…] I look forward with great interest to receiving your account of this famous journey so please write fully. I know some of the route but not all. I see no prospect yet of putting Miss Law's kind offer to practical use but the unexpected sometimes happens. I'm glad your teeth are quite alright again. I myself have been troubled with toothache and have had the troublesome member extracted. It was one of my few remaining at the top row. I've only two left so shall have to fall back on false ones soon.

As to the children going to school, I think it will be wise to send them. They will have ample leisure to enjoy their new surroundings and the school hours will but give zest to their pleasure. You will also be ensured a certain amount of time to yourself which is also very necessary. As to the school, I have no objection to them going to a catholic school providing that you can find no other for them. I have not that fear of Catholics which seems still to prevail amongst so many of our so-called educated and protestant friends and am sure a short period spent at a school would be insufficient to make any great impression on a child's mind, especially when the schooling itself is <u>not</u> the main object but just a diversion. I have only mentioned all this because I want you not to feel <u>bound</u> in any way, but quite free to act as you think best.

Prison certainly puts one's ideas concerning others' freedom in good order, for I feel I was not always so keen that <u>all liberty</u> should be enjoyed by <u>all</u> as I am now. I hope you managed to pack your books, and that amongst them are the Adult School handbook and the Esperanto. I want you to study Esperanto as it will be useful for a little trip to the

Continent which I am planning for the future. I have made up my mind to see France, Italy, Spain and Holland so you must be prepared for a good time and Esperanto will help us to be understood. This is not an idle dream, but quite a practical scheme which I feel sure will meet with your approval, when I explain the details to you.

[...] I am glad you were able to get away with everything so nicely arranged [...] I look forward to getting the photograph with pleasure as it will be like having a long visit from you all. Have just had your PC and am pleased to know your journey has been accomplished safely. I hope your lodgings will prove satisfactory.

Eagerly awaiting your letter, I send you my best Love and wishes for a real good time

Your Loving Husband

Frank

❦

Bedford Prison
May 6 1918

Mia Kara Edzino

I am glad you got my letter so promptly, as I am sure you must have looked forward to getting it. Being in a strange place and having none of your usual occupation to take up your time should naturally tend to permit of reflection, and as I feel that I am much in your thoughts my letter should have been especially welcome.

I am glad you had such a comfortable journey, but I feel sure that some exciting events took place although you have not mentioned them. I have been reading *Pickwick Papers* again and I find he could not go on even a short journey without some startling incident taking place, but perhaps they were due to the difference in mode of travelling and not to the natural excitability of human nature. [...]

I am surprised at your description of Barnstaple as I thought it was closer to the sea but perhaps it will be better for you all because you

4. 'THE COUNTRYSIDE IS GLORIOUS'

can get both sea and country. Your description of the surrounding country whets my appetite and I want to know more about it so please make great efforts to describe all you see as accurately as possible for I do not entertain any hopes of seeing you there.

I am glad there is a school to which the children can go for they will perhaps get <u>too</u> wild if they do not have some restraint. I want a full description of your lodgings style of house etc, also of your landlady and family, if any [...]

I have been thinking of your Aunt Kate and her son, have you heard of them lately? I get a shock sometimes as thoughts of long forgotten friends surge through my mind, for it reminds me so forcibly how isolated and shut off from the world I am, and I then wonder can the world outside be real, or is this world inside real. Perhaps you would like to juggle this one out for me.

Weinsteen and Bowery have left here and I suppose are again in the guard room awaiting another sentence. Puts one in mind of cat and mouse tricks, doesn't it.[107] I suppose that this treatment will go on until the war is over and who can tell when that will be. It seems to me to be like a snowball which has been rolled from a hill top, and gathering momentum as it rolls downward, carries everything before it breaks up at last of its own volition [...]

My space is gone and I must close. Forgive my misanthropic mood and put it down to the weather. Kiss the children from Daddy and accept all my love.

Frank

---

107 Frank is referring to the notorious Prisoners (Temporary Discharge for Ill-Health) Act of 1913 which had been passed as a way of getting women suffrage campaigners on hunger strike out of prison until they recovered, and then forcing them back in to serve the remainder of their sentence. This was jeeringly called the Cat and Mouse Act, referencing its cruelty and autocracy. COs could be treated similarly.

THE CONSCIENTIOUS OBJECTOR'S WIFE

May 10th? 1918
11 Fort Terrace, Barnstaple Devon

My dear Frank

I feel so sorry and sad at the sadness of your letter. It is so cruel a thing, this war. The separation of wives and husbands and sons and mothers, but I who am in the world and know how <u>real</u> it is find worse and more lasting sorrow than ours can possibly be, whatever the end may be. Keep up heart, my dear, and know it must end sometime. Be strong. I will help you all I can in every way. I am trying to fit myself and the children for the future we shall live and you are doing the same I am sure. This may all end sooner than any of us think. Keep hope alive. Yes, I know you very well, and all your moods, as you know, by look or word or letter. I ought to after studying you for 20 years. We all get the feeling of dreaming sometimes but 'Life is real, life is earnest' and the conditions we live under, if unnatural or poor health, will give us that dream sensation.

Things are beginning to feel more real with me now. I am just waking up which means I feeling better. I am having a good rest and enjoying the change and freedom from worry. This will renew my youth.

There are a few wounded soldiers here but I have not seen an aeroplane yet and no munitions <u>banging</u> all night like they are at Letchworth.

You ask for a description of this place. I'll try. The town I do not like. It is very old and streets are narrow and the houses small and crowded together. They call them lanes but they are only alleys. They are paved with cobbles and very clean. The town is in a valley close to the river and rises up on the hill behind, so Fort Terrace is higher than the river. We have a nice breeze always here tho' it is not very cold. I was rather afraid we would find Devonshire too enervating but the sea air saves that.

The hills all round are glorious, dozens of them in constant view. Dora says it looks as though we could walk along the tops all round. Wherever we walk away from the river is up on the hills and the view is like pictures constantly changing. It is so beautiful I almost want to weep. I have tried to draw a diagram I hope you understand.

The woods are a favourite place of the children. There are paths like terraces on a steep hill and looking through trees over the river to hills opposite. We went on Monday, took our tea and then walked right through and discovered a lane which we explored and found it led to a road and saw Barnstaple at our feet. It was a good long walk but the children loved it.

This morning we are in the park. I am writing this and Dora is reading *Oliver Twist*. Chrissie and Morris are making paper boats and sails of sticks and loosing them on the river.

On Saturday we went to see Mr Fox at Newbridge, 4 miles each way. Mrs Buckingham — (Auntie Claudia the children say) is his niece. She is only 23 but tall and capable. She married Mr B last Aug, a widower with 6 children. One, the oldest, is away at school, Droitwich. They are Catholics and he is training for a priest. She does not take to the religion but favours Theosophy. We took all 8 children and they walked well. She had a push chair for the youngest, nearly 4, a boy, then one 6 girl, twins next, girls 9, and a boy 11. They are quite nice children, obedient and well behaved. They all go to school. Mr B is 31, went into the army, April '18, stationed in Romford, Artists Rifles. He had leave till Mon the day we came. On going back he strained his leg running and has been in hospital 6 days. He got leave again yesterday till next Monday to get up his strength I suppose. He is rather jealous of his young wife, otherwise they are very happy together. He is one of us at heart but says the solitude would drive him mad and of course he has the children to provide for which makes it difficult. He was Sec. for the Education Board here.

The house is not bad, front sitting room leading off a tiled hall leading through to a conservatory with a grapevine; this also looks into the back sitting room (mine) and the kitchen and scullery 5 steps down to the garden which is small, and a large washhouse at the back of it. There is a little bit in front which was neglected so our children got permission to beautify it, if they could. So now there is a rockery from gate to door and a bed made under the window and under the railings and along the side about 18inches wide leaving a piece of grass in the middle, which Morris calls the lawn, about the size of the table in your reception room. Dora has planted some seeds, nasturtiums along by the railings, (dwarf) columbine and *Linum* under window with night stock between the houses, and Morris bought a root of pansies in the market yesterday. They got some lovely ferns from the lanes for the rockery so they will leave something better than they found it [...]

Mr Buckingham talks of taking us on the river one day so I shall try to row again. I have found out we can go to a place called Instow, lovely sands: early train 6d then across ferry to Bideford and Appledore so we shall go soon. I feel this is better than the sea altogether, I should have felt too lonely in a little village.

I have discovered a Labour Party here so I am going to meetings they may hold. There are a lot of visitors here now. They say a lot come from London in the summer so I may come across a comrade or two.

I am disappointed about the school. They are already too full and cannot take ours but I have heard the attendance officer is looking for me. I think they could go to the Church School or Catholic School or a private one but I don't think I could afford that and they don't want the others but I shall wait now until Whitsun holiday is over [...]

I know what you mean about *Pickwick Papers*. I have always felt that you are getting your senses refined after reading beautiful words like Whittier's.

Lots of love from us all and thoughts going out to you.

Yours

Lucy

4. 'THE COUNTRYSIDE IS GLORIOUS'

Bedford Prison
May 13th 1918

Dearest Lucy

Your letter to hand on Thursday morning and greatly pleased I was to receive it. Your letters are a great source of joy to me, even though they may perhaps reflect at times my own sadness. I am very interested in your account of your lodgings but you have only whetted my appetite for more news about them […]

You mention docks in your most wonderful diagram. I am curious to know what is brought into the town. It will be difficult to judge by what is going on now as I expect that the war has changed the usual conditions but you might get to know, perhaps a guide book from the *Free Library* would 'supply all necessary information' as the advert puts it […]

Give me your impressions of Friend Fox, as I have seen some of his work and feel interested in him. As to the School, do not worry but just set aside a certain time for study with the children and you will be fulfilling the law of this land of the free. For my part, I fail to see the necessity of education if it's to be the end of all lads that they become Cannon Fodder as one of our famous politicians called the men who are forced to lose their lives, and if the girls are to spend their lives in making munitions etc it seems such a waste of time and money. But there everything is illogical in this topsy turvey world […]

I have been reading *Lorna Doone* and it is a tale of Devon and Somerset. The Author gives some fine descriptions and speaks of Bideford and Barnstaple fair […] Needless to say he brought me in close touch with you and I could see in my mind's eye the bells and woods which you speak of in your letter. I could see the delicate celandine and the frail but hardy anemone and I wandered again through the woods at Crowborough with you.

I suppose that Morris will become quite a climber and be wanting to fish and all sorts of things and of course the girls will not be backward in the same pursuits. I hope you will get a good time on the river and be able to put your capacity for rowing into operation but I guess that

THE CONSCIENTIOUS OBJECTOR'S WIFE

Dora will want to try too and that you both will only catch at <u>crabs</u> which cannot be boiled [...]

I have received the photographs and think them fine. It was a real pleasure to get them and on comparing them with the others I have, I can see how the children have grown. The girls are bonny, but you and Morris are excellent. His face is so sweet and innocent and as I gaze I wonder what is before him and would spare them all the rough places of life, but after all it is the struggles with temptation, and the dark days of doubt, which make us strong and real, and fit us for the duties of life even as the rough and rocky county, together with the fields and moors and fogs etc which made the strong men of Devon [...]

I have just thought that perhaps it would interest you to know that your humble servant is in a good state of health and he hopes you all are in a ditto. I have nearly filled my space and of course left out all the things I wanted to say, but as none of them were important and I've got heaps more letters to write it does not matter much [...] I must close now so send lots of love to our darling children and I wish you all a real nice pleasant and instructive holiday.

Yours confined in body but not in Spirit

With Fidela mian Amato

Frank

11 Fort Terrace, Barnstaple, Devon
May 15. 18

My dear Frank

So glad to get your letter at teatime yesterday. I was looking through some of last year's and putting them in order. There was only one for each month last year. What a long time it seemed to wait and now that I have one every week it is long to wait and I have so much to occupy my mind too. I have dreamt of you for about 5 nights and was anxious to know if you were well. Each time you were home and I was so happy.

4. 'THE COUNTRYSIDE IS GLORIOUS'

As Mrs Thomas says (I heard from her on Monday), will it never end? how the time drags on. She hasn't seen George for a year. He is still at Dartmoor and keeps well. Johnny has been ill in the hospital with Mastoid Abcess behind the ear and now he has an ulcer on his eye. She wants to go into the country for a bit so if I was home she would be at Letchworth. Well, I should like to see her but should be awfully tired and knocked up again, so it is as well I am here.

I am feeling more rested but not quite like 20. I often forget we are getting on in years but we need not remember. I feel I am having a holiday, like old times. Of course feeding is a little difficult, shopping is quite an art. I found a little shop on Monday that had potatoes (we had none all last week). I also found they could let me have ½lb cheese, the first since I have been here and they sell Marmite and Fruitarian cakes. It was quite a discovery. Mrs Buckingham was as pleased as myself. She does not find it easy to feed her family of 5 and without potatoes for the midday meal they need more filling up.

I do as little cooking as possible, to save the gas for one thing. I bake only when the oven is going, porridge is off the menu and we use grape nuts.[108] I get a qt of milk a day for 5d sometimes a qt scalded with cream off [for] 2d. Of course I never use my meat and bacon coupons. There seems a very plentiful supply and veg are cheaper and salads are so nice.

Chrissie and Morris are growing so big and fat and so is Dora. As you say she is growing more mature. I have started her at the Private School, a Miss Symmond's. I had an interview and asked her terms, 30/- a term. I explained my position and yours and was sorry that was impossible and she offered to halve it to 1/3 weekly, so she started on Tuesday and likes it.

Chrissie went with these children to the Catholic School to see how she liked it and they put her name down. She told the teacher she did not want to learn the catechism so they let her home as they have that last

---

108   Breakfast cereal made from wheat and barley, marketed as a healthy and vitalising breakfast food.

lesson in the morning and then go into Church which is near. I don't think she will take any harm or much impression, but they will learn early to be broadminded enough to respect other people's religion. These children are slaves to the Church and have to do and say things they cannot understand; their mother brought them up like that. Mrs B is not catholic and will <u>not</u> have the holy water and so on about the house, as she says was here when she came. Morris I am keeping at home till obliged to send him, he does little lessons with me.

We went to a Lantern Lecture on Monday evening, 'The Bible and how we got it'. They were very interested; some of the pictures they recognised, 'Scott's Monument' and 'The soul's awakening', and a few others. It was very good but only about 20 or 30 people present.

Last Sunday I with Chrissie went to the Parish Church in the morning (it is very old and historical). In the evening I took Dora and Mrs B to the Congregational Church. It was a much nicer service and they were having a jumble sale in the week so we went. We could buy nothing but I had a conversation with the Minister. He offered to help me in any way should needs arise, as he said, one never knows, and he spoke rather strongly about the confinement of COs. I took Chrissie and Morris last Sunday and they behaved beautifully. Morris seems to drink in all he hears from anyone. He prefers meetings to Sunday School. I too often wonder what his future will be. Anyway I do not think our children will be a disgrace to you mentally, morally or physically, so our efforts will not be in vain [...] We went a long and lovely walk last Saturday, just our children and a sister of Mr B, over the hills and far away about 8 miles. We had our first taste of cider when we came back, all the shops seem to have it in Casks. We like it much. We saw more Cherry trees than I have ever seen, great trees of them appear to be wild on the side of hills and underneath growing bluebells and primroses and broom, beautiful golden, the bottom of hills running water in a valley another great hill the other side. The glories of nature is here and all round.

I am afraid I have rambled on. Will look through all your letters and answer any questions I <u>may</u> have omitted to answer [...]

4. 'THE COUNTRYSIDE IS GLORIOUS'

Bedford Prison
May 20 1918

Dearest Wife

Your letter duly received [...] I was surprised to read that potatoes are so scarce as they form the staple part of our diet, but I suppose it is just a local shortage. It is nice for you to be able to get Marmite etc and it will not be long now before vegetables will get plentiful. The weather is glorious now but we had a bad storm on Friday with heavy rains which may have damaged some of the crops

Do you remember the Whitsuntide we spent at Jordan's two years ago? I wonder when we shall be at such a gathering again. It was there we saw the great cherry orchards if you remember. I am shocked at you all drinking zider, if you go on like that you will become quite natives of the place and perhaps fall into use of the Devonshire brogue. I wish you all a good time at Instow and I'm sure the weather will be hot enough for you. The latest photographs are better than the first and as to you not being twenty, well I have seen girls at twenty who certainly looked as old as you do. Don't take this for a double barrelled compliment, please.

I have received three books from Mrs Middleton; Thoreau's *Walden*, *Sartor Resartus* and Mazzini's *Duties of Man*. When you write to her give her my thanks and say that the books are a great source of pleasure to us. They not only give us pleasure when we read them but often form the subject of our conversation, as, needless to say, being shut away from everything our talks tend to become philosophic and academic. I think we have discussed every subject under the sun including Women's rights, Expatriation and the colonization of the German colonies.

I am interested in your information about the docks. It seems like history repeating itself, doesn't it. But I think that the cement built boats have a commercial value, and if so I should think it is the starting of a new industry, because shipping will have a big boom for many years to come. It may perhaps mean the growth of Barnstaple from a quiet sleepy country town into a big shipbuilding centre, but that of course depends on local circumstances which you have not mentioned.

It is natural that Morris would like to watch the men at work, and work would be play if the joy of work were the urge, but as I suppose the men just work for wages and have no voice in their own well-being it is just the usual workshop drudgery to which we are all accustomed. It is good for Morris to see all these things as the impressions early received, help to form the character in later years. I am glad you have settled the schooling difficulty and I suppose we shall see Mistress Chrissie crossing herself and calling on the VM for help etc, but it will do her no harm. The only harm is when these things are forced on to one and true freedom denied [...]

Well my Dear I must finish now. I hope you will enjoy this letter and am sorry I have not expressed myself well in it. My health is good, I keep cheerful and have not yet lost hope. I send you all my Love and thoughts for a speedy reunion.

Yours ever

Frank

11 Fort Terrace, Barnstaple, Devon
May 21st [1918]

My dear Frank

I am writing this on the sands at Instow. The children are having a glorious time. There are 9 of them with us, Auntie Claudia & two other aunties. We came on the workman's train from Barnstaple at 8.13. The tide is just coming in, 12 o clock now, it goes out a long [way] and leaves a long stretch of sands just opposite in Appledore & a little higher up is Bideford. I never saw such a lovely place. Dora is hoping to bathe presently with Carl, they will never forget the lovely time they are having in Devonshire. Chrissie has just come up to me so hot & undressed all but comb[ination]s & knickers, of course the other children have had to do the same, what freedom, how shocked our mothers or grandmothers would be.

4. 'THE COUNTRYSIDE IS GLORIOUS'

Now a new excitement has occurred, an airship has passed into view, and after being watched and admired, has gone round the hills and disappeared. Yesterday being Bank Holiday this place was crowded, it is called 'Babyland'. Now I have come over, it will have to be often, the fare is 8d return workman.[109] Mrs Buckingham took tickets first, has asked for 2 and 4 children workman the man said the fare is all the same, we haven't child labour yet, you are looking into the future. Yesterday we picnic'd all day into the woods, it only wants you to make our stay here just perfect. I have sent a card to Katie from here, I am wondering how they are after the terrible raid they had on Sunday night, and I was in safety here enjoying the lovely night and the moon, thinking of you. Mrs Middleton says you feel sad at the distance between us, is this so? I do not feel any further away than I was at Letchworth, in fact my spirit is really nearer and I do hope you feel it so. Of course we both long for your freedom the more that one of us is enjoying such freedom.

The children are now completely undressed except for a pair of knickers each and Morris, Chrissie's thin vest made into a bathing suit, they are having a time of their lives; talk about the water babies, you would just love it. I am sure you will be glad to know about this and to know we are thinking of you every moment. This holiday is going to renew my youth and make me look forward with greater wish to the future holidays we intend to have together, I might be for ever drudging – to what end after all – and I have nearly got over the shock I had such a little while ago. Now all that seems like a dream. Sometimes I live it over again, and endure agonies, but it passes quicker than it did.

Miss Jefferies has written to Mrs Middleton that she 'has a concern to go and see you'.[110] Can you spare a letter from me one week soon! If so, send her the visiting order and tell me you have done so. I will give you her address and write for her to go as soon as she receives it. The

---

109   Cheap tickets for early morning trains had been sold as 'workman's' tickets since the 1840s.

110   A Quaker concern was a deeply-felt discernment for a course of action. Lucy may be being satirical at Miss Jeffries' expense, as prison visiting was a normal Quaker activity, and did not need a particular effort.

Tickles will be coming next, if you like. Mrs Middleton thinks you must miss my visit, I hope you don't – too much. I have got no news only our own movements.

We went to Parish Church on Sunday morning and the Congregational in the evening. I liked the evening one very much. He spoke very straight out, about unity of the churches and not too much sect and so on. The morning Parson is a washout. I could talk better myself but Mrs B likes the singing and the organ which is very fine, about 2,000 reeds. She also likes Mr Lewis the Congregational man, so we go with each other and take our children. Of course hers are not allowed to enter a Protestant church service.

Dora still likes her school very much. Morris is getting rather wilful but he loves me and will do anything for me, you will be surprised how useful he has got. He has got a knapsack to carry the food in for picnics and Dora a satchel so mother is not burdened with a basket of food in the old style [...]

I had a letter from Peter Myles last week, he sent me a little NCF paper. It was suggested in that that your man should use the Concession of extra letters to send one a month to NCF friends, but I don't think I could spare another, as we shall lose one for a visit the next two months. Morris says I am to be sure to tell you he <u>has</u> enjoyed himself and found a lot of cockles. I must finish up now for tonight, keep the thought of our reunion for ever in your mind, I do and we shall have it soon I'm sure [...]

Don't forget we think and talk constantly of you. Your photo is on the sitting room mantelpiece and I look at you often. We all send lots of love now and for ever.

Yours Lucy

4. 'THE COUNTRYSIDE IS GLORIOUS'

27.5.1918
Bedford Prison

Dearest Lucy

Your prompt reply to my letter was received with pleasure. I am delighted with your account of the day spent at Instow. Your numbers remind me of a Sunday School excursion [...]

By the way, who is Carl? The name has a German sound, so you had better be <u>careful</u> or you may be run in for consorting with the enemy. I suppose the girls will not get a chance to learn to swim whilst you are at Barnstaple. I hope the cockles caught by Morris were satisfactory when boiled and eaten and that there were enough to go round. It should be a good place from shrimping. Do you remember the shrimps at St Leonards? I think it is so fine to watch them as they glide along through the water with their long nets trailing and to see the silvery shrimps jumping and sliding about as the nets are emptied. As I write I am again back in the old familiar scenes and am a boy again.

[...] As to the visiting order, I will send it to you on June 10th as I am not entitled to one before then. You can then send it to Miss Jefferies if she still has a concern [...]

As to missing your visits. I shall be candid and say that I have not missed them yet. Visits to me are always a mixed blessing because they seem to contain as much pain as joy, and one can get reconciled to doing without them because time here does not count. I mean that days and weeks are all so much alike that one has to actually make an effort to place events [...]

You will be interested to hear that I am taking a course of massage and physical exercises. No, not to keep me from getting fat, but to keep me in condition, as we do not get as much real exercise as I should like, and I do miss my open-air life so I am keeping really well and my rheumatism is better.

I had intended writing about some of the books I have been reading but seeing I have nearly filled up my space they will do another time. Send along the *History of Barnstaple* by all means but not until you have really mastered it. I look forward with interest to the account you will give of Bideford, Appledore and Westward Ho. I am much more interested in them than Ilfacombe. One thinks of the smuggling days and the exciting incidents connected therewith; also of the brave race of men with childlike hearts who sailed around the world in cockleshells searching for the garden of Eden. There were indeed the days of romance and heroism.

[...] Kiss our bairns from Daddy and say he sends his love and wishes them a happy time by the sea. I trust you will get enjoyment and encouragement from this letter.

You are always in my thoughts

Yours most lovingly

Frank

11 Fort Terrace, Barnstaple, Devon
May 29th 1918

My dear Frank

The contents of your letter has given me much food for thought. I did not realise before that you cannot dwell on thoughts of home and us, and I wonder if my letters which are so full of our doings is really best for you, but you asked that I would tell you. I am always dwelling on the thought of your return, and wondering if there is any possible chance of your release, before the end of the war. That seems so remote, although it seems the ball is now rolling so fast it must stop with a crash somehow or somewhere. Again sometimes it seems to me that the madness or wickedness of people or selfishness that one sees everywhere has so angered God that the world shall no longer be, & the people all exterminated with sword, plague or famine; but I got a grain of hope on Sunday evening, we went to a church about a mile away called Pilton, very old, 1259, and the lesson was taken from Abraham pleading for Ninevah, 'even if ten are found it shall be saved'. I thought of the Friends and the few people who love their neighbours

4. 'THE COUNTRYSIDE IS GLORIOUS'

as a Christian should and the beautiful world as one sees it here, also the sacrifice of the heroes & martyrs of old surely not to end in the entire destruction of <u>all</u>. Then yesterday I had the *Labour Leader* & read the number of killed and wounded 41 … & away goes hope again until something else comes along and renews it, so we go on, up and down.

I am sitting in the park beside the river writing this. It is a glorious morning: the sky is intense blue, going off to a haze over the hills just by the rainbow, the grass & trees a beautiful green. Morris is with me, of course, but the road behind is being tarred & sanded so he is watching the operations and very interested too. On the way we passed Dora's school & music was sounding so I expect she was dancing. She has just learnt the sailor's hornpipe, & tried to teach it to all the other children including 'Carl', who is the biggest boy at home. He is 11 but smaller than Dora, she appears to be big for her age [...]

Would you mind very much if I do not keep it up? I mean all the business. I do not find it easy to get the money sent to me, so cannot send accounts fortnightly & Eastman wrote yesterday, if the agency was not attended to properly, he would have to appoint someone else. He also is worrying me for a new business, I think it most inconsistent of him, & I feel inclined to tell him to do as he likes. I have heard from Mrs Gardner & Mrs Stacey that my tenants are very comfortable and quite alright. Mrs Gardner has been to tea and Mrs Stacey has been doing their washing [...] I had a nice letter from Mrs Harris asking after you. He is still at the fruit farm in Essex.[111] I wish you were. Wiltshire is still on the farm in Suffolk and was home for the weekend at Whitsun. I hear from Mrs Middleton once a fortnight. I do not find it easy to pay my way and have all that we require, everything is so dear and the kiddies hungry. However I don't worry and manage somehow to make enough of what I have and I will not touch what I have put by if I can possibly help it. I shall go home with renewed health & strength to work all the harder later on. I try to think what I should like to do and what would be best, but I stop short with including you in my plans. Oh well, we will both look forward to our heaven and reward for our

---

111 Mr Harris was presumably picking fruit as an alternative to prison service as a CO.

sacrifice. I have got the Esperanto book, and will try to study it with Dora: are you getting on? Do you want any more? I am going with Mrs Buckingham to a meeting tonight for 'Women Citizens' and to one on Sat for the 'Federation of discharged soldiers & sailors'. I like to know what is going on. I am still very much in love with Devon, and am going to read up Westward Ho & go to Appledore & Bridepond as soon as I can, then I will tell you all I can. The real thing is better than books isn't it? [...]

Now adieu lots of love from Dora, Chrissie & Morris & your own loving wife Lucy.

☙

Bedford Prison
June 3rd 1918

Dearest Lucy

Your letter contained both gladness and sadness. [...] I advise you to get Walt Whitman's poems 7d series for, even if you have to stay away from Church to pay for it, he will lead you to the source of Life and settle some of your difficulties for you [...] You must not be blown about by every wind of rumour that floats over the earth but stick fast to the great fundamental things and all will be well.

Now for business. As to Minns, I can't remember what arrangements we made and am not concerned. Settle Eastman by letting him do as he desires. Let it all go and do not vex your soul with the trash [...] It pleases me much to hear that your tenants are so satisfactory.

If you read my last letter again you will notice that I quoted June 10th for visiting order so shall write again next week, but it would be well for you to remember that these letters can be stopped for any slight misdemeanour of mine and not be too much concerned if they did not arrive when expected. Sorry you are finding a difficulty in spreading out the cash, but the new harvest will soon be in and as you say perhaps the snow ball will soon burst.

I find I have done half my sentence so the other half will roll away much more quickly and I'll try then to get a holiday. I am not pessimistic but you must school yourself for a long separation. If liberty of body comes soon well and good, but if it is delayed, still well and good. As to plans for the future, I am always forming plans but they are only castles in the air because we do not know what conditions will prevail, and they to a certain extent will determine our actions. I should like to hear your plans even if I do not fit in them and then I can perhaps help you. I will enlarge on this subject in my next letter.

I am getting along fairly well with Esperanto and have two other chums to assist me, one of whom is quite a Philologist having five other languages at his command. He is a stickler for correct pronunciation but makes a good teacher […]

I send you all my Love and thoughts and will ever be thine own true husband and twin soul

Frank

11 Fort Terrace, Barnstaple, Devon
June 5th 1918

My dear Frank

Your letter has indeed given me the ray of hope I needed. You have always been so much help to me mentally. Your mind works round and sees such different points of view to mine. I know all you think subconsciously but cannot grasp it till I have it from you. I have depended on you for so many years you know, for so much, this is, I believe, the last power I possess, to be able to use separate from you. Your letters are as much help and comfort to me as mine are to you, perhaps more so. You are in peace and quiet and can think, I am in a constant whirl, even when alone with the children in the woods and lanes with nature for our teacher, I cannot express or think my thoughts. I am afraid you cannot understand what I mean.

Last evening, it was cooler after tea, I took the children a beautiful walk, we did not get back till 9.30, it was as light as day then. We followed the river the reverse way from Ilfracombe, and the opposite to the Town, your quotation describes the scene. After we had walked a little way and the children had let off a little wildness of spirit by a game of leaping as we went along, presently came a bend of the river, then the woods and hills rise up on either side of us, in the hollow below lies the river, and all around in peace the children gathered beautiful yellow 'Iris' and 'Ragged Robins', while I got into touch with nature. I only get a few rare moments like this, presently in comes my practical and material mind and I notice perched up in a corner of a field away yonder a group of tiny houses, about 6, each with a tiny yard and chicken coops. In the same field were a few horses and cows grazing. Now why is it people crowd together so when such an expanse of land is in view? I supposed the cottages belonged to a farm and was good enough for the labourers to live in, but you can't think how that annoyed me, for a little while.

The hope I have now since reading your letter is that the future landworkers will not be slighted and I begin to see a lot of things that could not be changed but for a great upheaval and mass pains of nations. I feel more contented now to 'Wait and see how gracious the Lord is'. I think the trouble the we who have humanity in our hearts is, we don't like waiting, and the lesson is hard, just as much for us as you who are inside wanting to be doing [...] I have told Eastman off, and that has relieved me.

I shall have about £9 to come from the amalgamation,[112] so I shall hang on a bit and not worry about the journey home. I shall not mention that to anyone; I would rather you didn't. We shall pull through and I shall be better later on for this change and rest now. I needed it badly. Now about yourself dear.

I certainly hope you will have a holiday and the time will soon pass, now half the time has gone. Freedom of the body after all is not so important as freedom of soul and that you all have. Of course I long

---

112   This was a windfall equivalent to around £400 in 2018.

4. 'THE COUNTRYSIDE IS GLORIOUS'

intensely for your presence and [am] glad you know it. I am always making plans for our future. The children too like doing this. Dora still wants the farm, and likes New Town because she feels they will be nice people and the houses will be large and convenient. Morris and Chrissie have no plans of their own yet [...]

I shall get Walt Whitman's poems today, and read and digest your letter. It will do me more good than lots of books. I am ashamed to own any weaknesses before you, but you will forgive me. I will try now on to be strong and brave whatever the future holds and however long may be our separation. I look forward eagerly for your next letter. I remembered after that you said the 10th the two weeks will seem a long time to wait.

I have got the Esperanto Book, but could not seem to settle to it much, however now I shall be better and go on with it. You are constantly in our thoughts and on our tongues. I should like to send you a book for the 24th: what shall it be? Can it really be 20 years since first we met? I shall soon be the Old Dutch we are going to have some good times together before long, I feel sure.

Lots of love from Dora Chrissie and Morris and your ever loving wife

Lucy

Bedford Prison
June 10th 1918

Dearest Lucy

[...] As to plans for the future, use your imagination and put ourselves down in some country spot with an old homestead, something like Bland's with land attached and the new town near etc. and I think you can draw the picture. Simplicitus is the keynote to be struck. As to books, I shall never be satisfied in this line, not even if our Dometo[113]

---

113   Frank was trying to translate 'simplicity', a key Quaker concept, into Esperanto. 'Dometo' is Esperanto for 'cottage'.

is lined with them, but if you will send a reminder of the 24th, I should like Young's *Travels in France and Italy*, Everyman 720. I also want you to write to Foyles Booksellers, Charing Cross Road and ask for list and price of a *Compendium of Handicafts, Fruit Growing and Market Gardening*. They are second hand booksellers and keep an enormous stock of good class books.

I am glad it was fine on Saturday for your trip to Instow. I was with you in thought and imagination. I am making good progress in Esperanto and can say and read a good many words. Do not be discouraged with it but make a piece of fun out of it by naming all the things around you and getting the children to go in for it too. [...] I hope you will enjoy Whitman and find in him the source of strength and hope which he has been and is to me. I've followed the lessons but have not made any comment because that Carpenter, Whitman and even the straggly and confused ideas I have given of Thoreau, better express the spirit of the age of ourselves than the orthodox language used in the handbook.

Forgive me if you do not find much of myself in this letter but I send you all my love and sympathy, prayers and thoughts. A kiss for all my dear ones and lots of love from Daddy.

Vian Amianto Edgo[114]

11 Fort Terrace Barnstaple Devon
June 11 1918

My dear Frank

I was so glad to have your letter this afternoon, but there was no visiting order enclosed. It had better be sent direct to Miss Jefferies now perhaps. Her address is:- 7 Bigwood Road, Golders Green, N.W.4.

I find there is a Thoreau *Walden* here in this house so I am borrowing it. I could not get Walt Whitman but have ordered it, and expect to have it

---

[114] This may be a misremembered attempt at Esperanto for 'your beloved husband', 'mia amata edzo'.

4. 'THE COUNTRYSIDE IS GLORIOUS'

in a few days. Fancy buying books for myself, such extravagance!

I had already glanced through *Walden* and now I shall enjoy reading it. It sounds so inviting, the extreme simplicity appeals to one, seeing the luxury and trash one sees about.

My plans for the future is really just such a life, for a time at any rate. I do not want to be quite isolated from all humanity, but not crowded, why need we when the world is so large? While I am on this subject I may as well enlarge on my ideas. Of course we really hope to play a part in the New Town, at the same time I really think ours <u>must</u> be a country life, so I should like to have a house, or homestead, not a cottage please, nothing pokey for me any more, 2 or 3 miles at most from a Town, with a good garden and land enough to grow enough for home use and some to spare for market also flowers, which are more profitable than fruit I believe in the long run. I think I should like to specialize in salads. Of course I must keep a few chickens, but no pigs or cows. If we were near a wood we could build our own Arbours and arches and seats and so on. We should not need or wish for much furniture. I agree it is a nuisance, what we do have must be useful and artistic, we must have books and pictures and some china.

I should like the house to be built to our own design if possible. We show how simply we can feed and clothe ourselves, from experience. This must be near a town for School and so on, for the children will need that for many years. I am convinced this is the only sort of life that will prolong our years. We are too old now to go back to Town[115] and the children would not be well.

Your knowledge of tools and machinery must not be used in a factory or workshop of a town, or your health will suffer. We ought to have thought this all out 12 or 13 years ago but perhaps we still have a chance to make good. I do not mean that we are to ruralize and not enter into politics or amusements and so on, but I think you understand and I fancy share my ideas of this plan. Dora does not want to go far from Letchworth, she says no place seems like that to her but she does not like it overrun with Belgians.

115   London.

Down this way would not be bad, but so far away from all our friends. Of course you know that land will be taken up largely by the government for the returned soldiers, so we may not stand much chance. I am wondering whether I ought not to turn my efforts in this direction when I go back, instead of doing a bit at collecting and needlework. I really have some fancy for it and could train the children to help me. I am thinking seriously about it. The thing to remember would be that it would take 2 or 3 years to be really a paying concern and we should want to stay where we land if we could [...]

There is one place I must try to describe, I am going to visit it soon as it belongs to these children's uncle. A low hedge on the roadside about up to one knees, looking deep down into a valley where is built a long sort of bungalow, stables etc. Down the hill to it are rows of potatoes, cabbages etc, quite a large piece of ground, a little to the mill also belongs to him. This mill works a round saw. We saw it work, put on for our benefit. He wanted me to understand they put in very little time in the garden, things grow so easily, or the house which is very simple and is really the mill house and opens in to it. Now for his history. He was a sailor and Irish, he used to like painting and music as a boy but his mother called the first rubbish, till she found a picture he had painted, and the latter she did not understand. He has several pictures in his house and there are 3 here large and small of his own, but he never had a lesson. He can play 3 or 4 instruments and has given lessons in both music and painting. He came to Barnstaple about 4 years ago from Liverpool where he had a business, tailor, I believe (not sure). This place was going and he saw possibilities in it and bought it for £300. He has now paid off the mortgage and just bought the allotments I mentioned before and a quarry on the top road opposite for £90. He is about 56 I should think, a widower with 2 sons in France and 4 daughters at home. One about 30, the others 17, 15, and 13 and a ½. The 3 eldest work with him, he has no other help, they cut trees and strip the bark and make Arches and things as well as he can, they ride the horses and drive the waggon to the station to send the goods away. They can make £3 worth in less than a day.

The 2 youngest come into Barnstaple to the Art School in the evenings,

4. 'THE COUNTRYSIDE IS GLORIOUS'

one for painting, the other for commercial work, shorthand or typewriting; each of them play the violin and piano, and I forgot to add he is a dancer and has had classes in the Town.

The little room we went into had a couch and some chairs, a stove, piano, some books and music. Some odd panels had been put down the walls; painted birds and grasses and the ceiling was calico stretched over, also painted [with a] picture. After some singing and playing (myself on the mandolin), a little girl who was there danced and then Dora did the Hornpipe, then a side door was opened showing a large workshop the other end opening into the mill. That door shut and the floor cleared and swept was the work of a moment.

You can guess what happened next. Lancers, Waltz, Veleta, Hurndilla, Military two steps, and La Rinka was the programme, which we all enjoyed immensely.[116] I had not been very well and it did me a world of good. Previous to the music we sat and talked on several subjects, religion chiefly, and he said he had no creed, but love to his fellows, he said they have a common purse and they all have what they want out of it. They have enough to eat and wear and no expensive tastes. They are almost vegetarian and can grow nearly all they need to eat. They are all very healthy, you may be sure. To really know anyone who lives like this is better than reading about them. I can go and picnic any time I like in the orchard and get hot water for tea at the house but I shall always find them working. I must tell you he has a carriage he bought for £1/5, he says one wheel is worth that. Of course the Mill wheel had worn badly, but they repaired it themselves [...] While we were talking the children were having a fine time on the ponies, bareback and saddle, on the road above.

The hot weather we had has flagged Chrissie a bit but I have got her some malt and she is picking up again. Morris and Dora are well, they were pleased to have your letter, but have not written an answer yet. I

---

116 Lancers is a dance for groups of four couples, the Veleta is a stately dance for couples, the Hurndilla is a round dance for couples with a caller, and La Rinka is also called the Skater's Waltz.

had a letter this morning from Miss Jefferies. She gave a good report of you. Mentions 'New Town' and is looking forward to us working together in the future. She would like to buy a few shares as a gift if I would like. Of course we should, and I shall write and thank her.

I am sorry I cannot get you Young's *Travels in France and Italy* till Tues next. I have ordered it and you shall have it at once, dated for the 24th. I also have not been able to get Walt Whitman but hope for it this week. It has had to be reprinted and I expect will be 1/6. I am getting on with *Walden* and like it much. I like to get alone with Nature and we certainly have too little of it anywhere so I <u>never</u> have it, and as they never go to sleep till I do and are awake the moment I do and Morris is around me all day I do not have the concentration of thought I should very much like. I do not complain though as they will soon be leaving the nest, then we shall be left to silence. I am glad to give myself out to them. They will always remember this time spent with me. It is mine too, to have no set occupation just do as I like and look after myself [...]

I do not think I have much more to tell you and I have had so many interruptions while writing this you must excuse the mistakes I have made. I hope I shall catch this post, else you will be worrying at the delay but I hope not.

You have all our love and good wishes from lots of friends.

Kisses from the children to be given in person soon

Your ever loving wife

Lucy

🌿

June 17th 1918 Bedford Prison

Your last letter was like a cup of milk to a thirsty child or a pail of oatmeal to a parched horse on a summer's day. It was both helpful and invigorating and I even caught a whiff of the sea from its pages. [...]

I am glad you will get an opportunity of reading *Walden* so I will not quote any more of it to you. As to your plan, I heartily agree that the

4. 'THE COUNTRYSIDE IS GLORIOUS'

simple life is what we must have, what other life could suit two such simpletons better and I hereby draw a picture for your delectation. A large rude hut with a few small apertures for windows from which the smoke, after blackening the rafters, finds its egress. It being divided in two parts by a rude rush hurdle, the one half for the domestic animals, pig, chickens, donkey and other livestock, the other in which the family assemble for meals and discourse etc. etc. A stout oaken board runs down part of the latter half and around it are seated a family of nine, Father at the top, Mother at the bottom and children, in order of merit, ranged down either side. Domestic economy in this household has been brought to the most simple of sciences and the fare is Potatoes boiled in a large pot which now stands in the centre of the board upon which an indentation has been made by long use. Each participant has a scooped hollow in the board into which is placed some of the steaming mash. Bread, meat, knives and forks are conspicuous by their absence and the children soon learn to become experts in the use of the wooden spoon which is the one article of cutlery.

I hope you will find this simple enough and there are certain elements which particularly commend themselves to me. For instance, no washing up, no serviettes to keep dropping, no confusion between fish forks and dessert forks etc. No puzzling as to 'what to have for dinner' and above all no need to dress. Continual source of conversation could be found in the dietary. As for instance, is it best to eat the skins, can the potatoes see if the eyes are left in and so on as lib. I feel in a humorous mood so am just letting it out as it were.

Now for news. I had a most pleasant chat with Miss Jefferies on Sat afternoon. If I were of the feminine gender I should describe the plum coloured costume, trimmed with green buttons and set off by gloves and bag to match. The whole surmounted by a steel grey hat trimmed with a plain embroidered band, giving a sweet and neat effect which was further enhanced by the bunch of Letchworth roses worn in the belt. Not being a woman I shall say nothing of these things but proceed at once to the subject of our discourse.

We talked of books, and New Town and of the work women are doing for peace and lots of other things besides. She is staying at Crowley's for the weekend and I have asked her to get him to send me on the books on Fruit growing etc so you need not trouble about them but do try and get the book on Handicraft too if possible. I am feeling starved in the use of tools etc.

I am much cheered by her visit, it was a glimpse of the real world to which I belong and I am assured of the love and sympathy which is felt for us by our friends. 'Do not Hurry, have Faith' is now my motto. [...]

If you see an opportunity where you are and really feel the call do not hesitate but do as you wish. Regarding our friends, they do not depend on locality and of course we shall <u>settle</u> at New Town. I look forward to your account of the furniture maker: ask what the land costs and how to get it, where they market the crops etc, and price of houses or <u>hut</u>s. Is employment obtainable, what religion is needed and can one wear breeches or must one wear trousers and a top hat?

[...]

Eagerly awaiting your reply Dear. I conclude with fondest love my heart's desire. Yours ever

Frank

PS No letter next week x

11 Fort Terrace Barnstaple Devon
June 20 1918

My dear Frank

I was surprised to have your letter this week, of course very pleased and shall not like missing it next.

Have not yet heard from Miss Jefferies yet, so do not know her report of you. I am so glad you enjoyed her visit. I always think her a sweet creature. Mrs Middleton has written to me and said she was in Letchworth for the weekend also Kemp Brown, so he is safely back from America.

4. 'THE COUNTRYSIDE IS GLORIOUS'

Mrs M. also told me that Peter Myles was arrested last Friday and taken to Hereford on Sat. so he will soon be having the experience of you all and his brother first hand.

There will be a lot more soon. I feel more sorry for Mrs M.

I have also heard that Miss Amy Reynolds died last Friday at Letchworth hospital, she sank under a second operation. Her sister is nearly distracted with grief, they were so much attached to each other. Old Mr Lugden also died at the same place last week. Mrs Myles is still going to Derbyshire. I think I should have tried for their house if I had been at home. I do not think I shall settle here. I do not feel called on to do so yet. I certainly want land, but think if I cultivate properly a good-sized garden it will do for a bit. Potatoes on an allotment. I daresay I could manage an acre, so will look out for something nearer to you. I have learned that the climate here is as good as France and possibilities are great for fruit here missed the frost and cold winds that has ruined the fruit crop at Letchworth, so strawberries and gooseberries and cherries are plentiful here, but they are a very high price; it makes me so cross to see everything so dear. Eggs are still 4d each, my chickens are quite satisfactory evidently, as the tenants have paid the £2 I charged for them. They hope they can stay till the end of Aug but I think I shall return the 3rd week to give the children a week before starting school.

[...] I rather miss the many friends and social intercourse and fellowship, but I feel the change has been good for me. The Labour Party Branch I tried to get into touch with has evidently gone to sleep as I have heard nothing of it. We did not go to Church on Sunday as in the evening we paid the promised visit [...] We got there about 6 and did not leave until about 9.30, and had a fine time. I'll try to tell you all about it. Mr C made me very welcome and at once proceeded to walk me round the place meanwhile talking to me, almost the first question was about you. I told him where you were and he sympathized with me and altho he did not altogether agree with you, he did not blame you, but the act that gave the exemption that you have not got.

He showed me the garden, just at the side of the house (the hillside is allotments of which more later) he had some splendid peas and potatoes, strawberries and raspberries, turnips, parsnips etc, on the hillside leading down to the house is his orchard, he had 3 ton of apples last year, the stream that supplies the mill has fish, even salmon in it sometimes. The wood almost adjoining as I told you on the opposite right a 2-storied building and a mill beside it. This is a workshop. Opposite stretches up the hill a wood and one can hear the water running down to a stream below.

This man built these places himself and owns the wood, he gets his living making garden furniture etc. of Devonshire oak. I can tell you more about it when I have paid the visit. I wish I could really convey to you what it looks like.

We gathered armsful of honeysuckle and foxgloves, and we got home about 7. We called at a house for some milk but could only have water, last week I sent Chrissie and Morris to a farmhouse for a drink of water and they got milk, some bread with cream. Cream is not allowed to be sold unless by the Dr orders, and then it is as dear as <u>butter</u> so I should not buy much. Strawberries are very plentiful and cheaper today 10d lb. I expect they will get cheaper still. I hope so. Milk has gone up again to 6d.

[...] Mrs Middleton tells me the cold winds just as I left Letchworth has spoilt the apples, peas and plums, our trees were full of blossom, so we shall not get much this year. Will finish in the morning.

[...] I have a friend in Mrs Middleton and I write to her as one. Wiltshire seems to be well and happy on the farm on Suffolk. Could you do the same? I hope you will have a nice time with Miss Jefferies, I think she must have a special message for you, listen for it, she is rather slow in speaking and a little deep. Give my love to her, I am thankful we have such friends. Now my space is almost gone, hoping you will keep your health and spirits,

all my love for you, your loving wife

Lucy

Katie has written that Uncle Charley has passed on, not long after Mother is he.

4. 'THE COUNTRYSIDE IS GLORIOUS'

1.7.1918

Dear Lucy

[...] I liked your description of Mr Code and am sure such a life would suit us. I hope we shall not have to wait as long as he did, before we find our niche in the world again. Am glad you got a report from Miss Jefferies and am surprised at her generous offer. Send my warmest thanks to her when next you write [...] We had a little excitement in the town on Friday. The king paid it a visit. Our share was the cheering and the volume of sound which emanates from lusty lungs when blown through bugles and when sticks are vigorously plyed to parchment stretched on a vacuum. In other words a bugle band.

I have received the books you sent for which many thanks. I will send along the criticism when I have read them. I have not been reading quite so much lately as Esperanto becomes fascinating and I spend a lot of time at it. Ruskin says it takes a lifetime to learn a language properly and as I am half way through my life I've got a lot of leeway to make up eh. Esperanto will not take so long but I think it will take about a year to really become proficient. How do you like it? do you find the N. get in the wrong place and do you forget the js and so on. I can read it much more easily than I can talk or write.

[...] I saw the moon last night for the first time for months. It was big and full and quite lit up my cell, so that I thought it was the sun until I fully awakened and saw the position of the reflection on the wall. I am like the birds. I go to sleep at dusk and wake at daybreak, but I do not sing. [...]

My Dear I must close now feeling I have not said anything to you. When you write to Tickles get him to bring me a book on fruit growing and gardening. Au Revoir

With all my love

Yours Ever Frank

THE CONSCIENTIOUS OBJECTOR'S WIFE

Fort Terrace Barnstaple Devon
July 2. 1918

My dear Frank

The time seemed long waiting for your letter, but I knew it would come today. The sense of expectancy does not mar any enjoyment that may come, but I must confess I feel a bit restless on Tuesday till the post has called or gone by. I have put the children to bed and sitting with them while writing this they are trying to sleep. I mean Chrissie and Morris. Dora is reading, always her last pleasure.

The weather has been so hot again the last week and is still. I was told there would be a lot of rain in Barnstaple, as it is in a valley, but we have had very little so far, in fact the farmers are complaining of the dryness although everything looks very well and plentiful and I am sure the prices are high enough: 1/6 pk broad beans, 3/6 pk peas,[117] 6d lb onions, 2½ potatoes, 2d small bunch of carrots, 1/- lb cherries and so on, it is a marvel to me how little we can manage to do with and have quite enough. Of course you know how clever I am! (No one else to tell me so.) [...] Mrs Stacey wrote yesterday. They have had rather cold windy weather at Letchworth, and now have an epidemic of Spanish Influenzas. Mrs Stacey says the Dr told her there are 600 cases but Miss Amor says about 1000, so it must be pretty bad [...]

It was Dad›s birthday on 1st so I sent one each of the Photos you had last. They are very pleased with them. Katie says he gets very tired by the end of the week. I am glad they are not being so much troubled by night visitors, though Paris has suffered again. I have written to Tickles asking about the visit, will now write again and ask him about the book for you.

Mr Myles has now gone to Wormwood Scrubs for 6 months, and Mr Gregory has got the paper for Medical Exam. He seems like a grandfather, certainly not a soldier, so I expect he will land with Peter, also Clapham Lander. Have not heard again from Miss Jefferies. I answered her letter. [...]

---

117   A peck equates to about 2 gallons, or 9 litres.

Lots of love from us all to you, the children will write a letter next week.

Au revoir my dear husband

ever your own, Lucy.

8.7.1918

Mian Amata Edzino[118]

I again take up pen to tell you all the news I am well and I'm pleased to hear that you and the children are all the better for your holiday. Reading between the lines I understand that Devonshire does not suit Chrissie so of course we shall not settle there.

[...] Do not imagine for a moment that I have any intention of trying to get a living entirely from landwork, as I know it would not satisfy me even were it possible for me so to supply all our wants or needs by so doing. I want land, but it is to augment my power of getting a living, not to become my master as it has done to so many small holders. Would you like me to be like Bland for instance?

You complain of a sense of farawayness in my last letter for which I am sorry. But I would ask you to make some allowance [if] I am far away: I am in exactly the same position as I was this time last year and shall be this time next year if still in prison. Nothing has changed, even the clouds, as seen from my window, look the same, so what can you expect from me. The affections feed and grow, upon and by, little acts of love to those around us and who are near and dear to us. Such actions are denied to me and I am forced back on the fact not only for consolation but for growth so that the natural result is an unreal perspective which is bound to show itself in my letters.

I am afraid I have not made myself clear, but if you imagine someone whom you know who was a girl with you, and whilst you have grown to womanhood and motherhood etc, has still remained a girl, would you

118 Esperanto for 'My beloved wife'

expect her to be able to fully enter into your life? Such is my position, even the photos of the children are not of the children I left behind and the glimpse I caught of them last August but confirms me in this. I trust you will not be disheartened or hurt by my plain speaking, but it seems to me that no-one can understand what imprisonment means except those who have to undergo the [inhumane] treatment.

I am forced to fill my letters with the thoughts that come through the books I have been reading, as it is the only safe outlet, and if I get digressive and dogmatic or even rhetoric it is but what I should do if my argumentative powers were given full play. You are compelled to read the balderdash when found in a letter but in all probability being buried yourself with some useful occupation.

[...] Well Lucy dear I hope my letter will give you the pleasure and sense of comradeship you would have from me.

Yours Lovingly F

11 Fort Terrace, Barnstaple, Devon
July 9th 1918

My dear Frank,

Your letter as usual this afternoon: yes, you seemed a little nearer to me, forgive me for having criticised the tone of your letters. They are just _you_, and were they any different I should not be pleased. You don't know what an education they are to me, and I am as glad you have such a memory to be able to write so, but just last time I missed the closeness of spirit, perhaps a personal touch, but I will say no more. I quite understand and my spirit is always with you and I hope helps you to bear all that you have to.

I wish I could be there instead of you, you could do so much more good in the world than I am able to. I hope you will find me the same when you come home, but I do not think I shall be content to bring you coffee in the garden and go on _working_ while _you_ are arguing: _now_ I should want to join in, and try to take an intelligent interest in all things. Now

I feel warming up and would like to discuss with you the 2nd question of last weeks' lesson. I believe woman's place in the world, and in the home even, will be different after the war is over.

This will be the great chance for Adult Schools to help in the reconstruction. Of course the change will be among the young women and some of us middle-aged experienced women will find we can be useful and those who have education will find we can be of such help. Don't fear, we shall find our niche alright, this state of things cannot go on for ever, and think how much knowledge you are gaining and will be able to talk to us who have not had that advantage while <u>we</u> work together in the future. I feel as if you are a part of me away, and you can't imagine how difficult it is for me, sometimes especially, to go on, separately. Of course I have the children and they keep my mind fully occupied. Mr Buckingham has been home again and I was telling him yesterday, how different the children will all seem to you, 2 years makes such a wonderful difference in them all, in stature and growth of mind.

[…] I am sorry I did not finish with Mr Code in my last letter. I expect to go and see him tomorrow. He is taking up fire Insurance with me, (if invalids, men or women who could pay well, I need not do work and nursing myself. I could still have land, and you could do something there yourself when you return.

I told him I would think it over, what do you think about it? Of course this could be in or near Letchworth or (New Town) and I could start on my return home. Whatever I do, I cannot neglect the children in any way, they need me and a lot of time spent on them when home from school.

[…] We had a very nice time at Newbridge last Wed. I did not see Mr Fox but I asked Mrs Morgan the housekeeper if we could stay there for a week or two and she was pleased to have us on the same terms as here. I shall have two rooms to myself up and down, separate staircase and door, larger and more airy than here, and the garden and hills and river on the spot, so I have practically arranged to go there for the last month we are here, till Aug 24th: it will be much better, I feel sure. It seems Mr Brunt stayed here once and used to go out there, also both the Miss Reynolds stayed there the year before last. Mr Fox seems very decent, (and clever artist) but none of them with us, but that won't matter, she evidently likes me, although was prepared to do otherwise. The children are very pleased at the idea and were ready to go at once.

I would like Dora to finish the term at school; she likes it very much and makes good progress in some subjects. Last Sat we went out about 3 miles (on the way to Newbridge) to climb a very high hill, Codden. I got about 3 parts [up] and then stopped; the children took off their shoes and up they went to the top. I don't know the height but it is the highest about here and the view, even from where I got, was simply wonderful.

Dartmoor (30 miles) lies one way. Exmoor another and the sea I saw quite plain. I shall never forget it. Barnstaple lay in a little valley and looked nothing, but O the feeling of space and air was almost overpowering. The hill is covered with ferns, heather and Wortleberrys, the same as Thoreau in *Walden* calls Billberrys, they grow on the ground almost and look like blackberries. We gathered some and I made 1lb of jam, it was most delicious, we must get some more.

I took a loaf and some butter and Fruitarian Cake and buns and a qt of milk so we feasted, leaving here about 10 returning at 6. I wanted a cup of tea badly and soon had it too [...]

Now I must leave off,

with all our love to you

Your ever loving wife Lucy.

෴

July 12 1918 Bedford Prison

Dearest Wife

Your letter to hand a little earlier this week. It is nice to know that your long holiday has not become wearisome, either to you, the children or to your hosts. [...]

Talking of books, I should like you to thank Mr Gregory for sending me

4. 'THE COUNTRYSIDE IS GLORIOUS'

the WEA *Yearbook*.[119] I find it most interesting and full of instructive matter. Also give my thanks to Miss Reynolds for the Esperanto books. I have made good progress and find it a most fascinating subject. She will be interested to know that there are four of us learning Esperanto and out of our small number that is not a bad average. I will let you know of any special books I want but of course any books are acceptable [...]

No letter next week but I trust we shall see each other instead. Kiss the children from Daddy. I should like to see them of course but leave all that to you. Best wishes to all friends and all my love to you (I am in good health).

Yours ever Frank

Bedford Prison
July 15 1918

Dearest Lucy

Your letter has been a real treat to me. It brought a message of hope and love and cheered me greatly. I felt your presence as I read it and I enjoyed the picture you gave of the children. I am not worried about Chrissie and my mind is quite at ease about the future. One learns the lesson of not looking ahead here, but just live one day at a time.

I have read the guide and I must say that both description and pictures whet one's appetite for more and create a desire to see these scenes for oneself. I did not think you were so near to the palace in which the coddled conchies dwell.[120] The guide, like that type of book usually does, leaves out all of what I call the most important sights. It makes no mention of industries or workers or the history of all the population but casually mentions a few items and places away from Barnstaple.

---

119 Worker's Educational Association
120 A sarcastic reference to the extremely austere conditions of Dartmoor Prison in the village of Princetown, where many COs were sent.

The town evidently does not lend itself to photography as I see only two plates in all the book. However it is well got up from a printer's point of view.

I like Mr Code's suggestion and feel sure you could make a success of it were you to go for it. You are just the person, strong in purpose, gentle in action and sympathetic by nature all of which qualities would be required. If you are to do it a way will open for you. Do not consider me in the matter for I will agree to anything you may propose. Will even go so far as to buy a bathchair and pony if desired, or wear a livery and clean the knives, windows and stair rods, wait at table, keep the garden in order and fill in the rest of my time by writing adverts or any other odd jobs which may come along.

[...] You say you would like to discuss the question of Women's Emancipation. All I can say about it is this. We must first decide as to what is emancipation. Is it having a vote, being able to work side by side in the manufacture of the devil's toys, or on the land, in the pulpit or the court, school or senate house, or any other field which hitherto has been considered man's prerogative? I think not. All these are right in their proper place and all will undoubtedly help to bring equality of the sexes but, even with it all, emancipation may be wanting. Is man in the mass emancipated? Does not custom sit tight on the chest of many? Is not the fear of my neighbour's irony the stumbling block to many? To be or to do anything out of the ordinary is to be looked upon as a lunatic and how many will face such an ordeal? No, emancipation must be an inward urge and a willing endeavour on the part of the individual to live up to the inward conception and not to allow external habits of thought and custom to rule the life. Such a one is already free and will be conscious of her freedom and though she will see the need for social, economic and political liberty and help to attain them, they will be but aids to her own soul growth.

I agree with you as to the help which can come from experienced elders and that the desire for freedom will be found amongst the young. Many problems will have a new perspective after the war and women certainly will not look forward to sex slavery, ie marriage, as the goal to be desired. I do not know how these things will adjust

4. 'THE COUNTRYSIDE IS GLORIOUS'

themselves but I am sure that sympathy and love, together with the willingness to exercise forbearance will overcome many difficulties in the readjustment. Please do not take me for an oracle or an old Moore.[121] I am but a mere man groping in the dark, fully conscious of my own failings yet proud to know I belong to the great human family which is slowly but surely working its way upwards to the light of perfect love [...]

I have sent Tickles the order so shall expect them sometime this week. No letter next week so let me have a new address. I suppose I must not forget to say I am well or perhaps you may think otherwise. My best thoughts I send you with sweet desires and fondest love.

Yours always Frank

---

11 Fort Terrace Barnstaple Devon
After Sat next: Newbridge Cottage, Bishop's Tawton, Nr Barnstaple, Devon
July 18th 1918

My dear Frank

Very sorry for the delay in answering your letter, but as you are not having one next week I hope you will forgive me, and not be over-anxious about reasons for such treatment of you.

Well, yesterday I went to see Mrs Morgan about staying there and found everything quite alright and we can go on Sat. see above address. It has been rather wet and stormy all the week and Morris had a little cold so I left him and Chrissie here while Dora and I went by ourselves. How we enjoyed our walk! We did it easily in an hour and the road is all up and down hills. The sky was stormy and bright by spells and the glorious smell of earth and damp hay. It did us so much good and then when we got there the doors and windows stood open (always)

---

121 *Old Moore's Almanac* had been staple source for enquiries for generations, and also contained predictions for the future.

straight on to the garden, and hills beyond it was just like home, even when presently it poured with rain, it only brought out the scent of flowers etc., jasmine over the door; never can we live in towns.

I am glad to say Chrissie is much better, she is gaining ½lb a week. I told the Dr this morning I was taking her out to Newbridge on Sat to stay, he said 'Good'. They give me a very generous supply of malt they call it Robeline and it is more like Virol.[122] I am giving some of it to Morris but he is growing very fast. I can get plenty of milk out there from a farm, 4d qt here it is 6d and skim at 1d. We are going to have a good time for our last 3 weeks.

I am going to stay in London for the weekend when we go home, it will break the journey and it would be so late by the time we got to Letchworth and then have to make up beds and so on. So we are chancing any raids. They are ever so pleased. Katie did not go down last week as she was so queer had the 'flue'. It has got here and one of the schools closed on Wed, where Chrissie went, 60% away ill. Mrs Middleton tells me it is dying out in Letchworth, she is pleased I am going out of the town.

I have not got Mr Code's fire insurance yet, hope to go up this evening. Mrs Morgan is also going to insure for fire with me, see how I try to work up your agency for you. Of course you would see the funny side of my 'Home for Invalids'. I cannot see you playing such a meek and mild character as you say, you would do better or rather more in your element as boss to the boy who could do all you say. No don't you worry, I shall find something far more profitable for you to turn your hand to. I often smile to myself when I remember how I got my way of a cottage in the country, when the idea was considered mad. I don't think I mind what my neighbour says, so I consider myself emancipated, though I agree that men in general are not and I warn you that when women start and see what they can accomplish, things will get a move on, and they will become far more emancipated in 50 years than men have. You say I am strong of purpose, I always imagined I was not, I should never have called myself so, but we do not see ourselves as others

---

122 Robeline and Virol were malt extract supplements given to children.

see us. Anyway I feel sure that whatever step I take when I return, will be what I am led to, and a way will open and I certainly must include you somewhere. How could I do otherwise? Even coming away like this seemed as if I was pushed here, I don't know why yet, but we have all got our brains stored with the most lovely pictures. I am sure the children will never forget. I should have like to have taken them about a little more, but it is money all the time, however we have done very well and when they are grown up they will be able to come again and see what we have missed. I myself am quite satisfied and know I am ever so much better in every way, and I have saved myself a breakdown in health. I feel I can go on now, till your return fighting against all odds and one day soon I hope it will be all even and plain sailing.

I have wondered the same thing as you say about the rationing: will people go back to so much flesh eating and beer drinking after the restriction has become unnecessary? I am afraid so, you see people are not doing it willingly, not because they see it is best or because there health will be better, but that will come later on. People like it less now; while they are earning such large wages they could afford what they have never been able to have, but the increased prices of everything else helps them to get rid of any surplus they may have, and also makes it harder for a soldier's wife and family who does not trouble about the meat and beer.

I am exchanging the children's meat coupons for extra fat ration. I am keeping my own for the sake of Katie and Dad when they come to see me. There is no cheese about, I have had ½ and ¼ since I have been here.

You may have heard we have new Ration books for Butter and Margarine, Lard, Tea and Sugar and Meat, all in one book, much better than all the separate cards we had before. This all makes a great deal of work for shopkeepers, they are all nearly off their heads this week. You see the books start from this week and some people have not had them yet. I had mine on Friday last. Came with Mrs Buckingham and they are being sent out Alphabetically, nothing can be purchased till each one has been signed 5 times by the holder and stamped or signed 5 times by the shopkeeper then the signed counterfoil cut out, and a coupon cut out for each article purchased: is all this clear to you, I wonder? When I leave here I have to take all my counterfoils to the food office and do the lot all over again at Letchworth, think of this being done this week all over England. Of course I must admit we have fared much better since we were rationed, everybody has had some of what was going. We shall probably have coal rationed soon. It will be a strange world when you come back into it.

I was telling Dora yesterday on our walk, how many strange things would be seen by anyone who could come to life again after 200 years. I do wish you were here often to answer the many questions I get from her, she said yesterday that Daddy always was able to tell her what she asked, sometimes by a long word that she could ask what that meant too. If she put a few to you to write, I am afraid I should get no letter myself so please don›t suggest it, as I know you would like […]

I must stop now, hope I have told you what you like to know, lots of love and happy thoughts from the children and all the love of your loving wife

Lucy.

🙞

Bedford Prison
29 July 1918

Dearest Lucy

I was pleased with your last letter. Its tone was so cheerful and bracing. I forgive you readily for your tardiness in sending it as you are usually so prompt to reply. I am delighted to know you are settled in such a lovely spot for the finale of your holiday and that you do not have all the fuss of getting ready to go out, which is such a nuisance when in a town. I suppose that Dora will be getting the remainder of the time free of school which will be nice for her.

Mr and Mrs Tickle paid me a visit on Wednesday. It was the best day of the week as the weather is very unsettled, heavy showers constantly falling with but very little warning. I have no news as per usual but of course I am well. I have been thinking about your stay in London and should like to suggest that you go on the Friday and leave Saturday clear so that you can take the children to see something of London; St Paul's, Westminster Abbey, Houses of Parliament, Thames and lots of other places I can think of. Make a regular tour for a country cousin as it were, because it may be years before they get a chance to see London again. I may be wrong but if so I expect that they would enjoy it all the same. I am told that New Town may be somewhere between Bristol and Birmingham so if we are to go there London will be further away. If you think well of my suggestion let me know and I will try and draw up a plan of campaign for you so that you can see as much as possible in as short a time as possible for I flatter myself I know London fairly well for a cockney [...]

I am still pegging away at the Esperanto but it is unfair to say it is easy to learn or else I am a dullard.

[...] I hope you have not found the last fortnight very long but really for all there is in my letters it would not matter much if they were not written. Space filled up at last. I send you all my love.

      Yours ever Frank

      Newbridge Cottage, Bishop's Tawton. Devon
      July 31st 1918

My dear Frank

So glad you find my letters cheerful. What a blessing it is that one can keep good spirits in trying times like the present [...]

Mrs Morgan has interested herself in the Adult School movement and thinks of starting one here in the village. She thinks the lessons in the handbook are fine and do not at all offend her patriotic spirit. As I told you she is not at all in sympathy with you, only with me, of course I am trying to show her things as they are [...] She has a son of 15 in the

Navy, Fred, also one 16, Robert, who is in a butchers shop and they are almost vegetarian, have been for years [...]

I am writing this letter very haphazard but I daresay you will not mind. The children are very much improved in health already for the stay here it is so free and open for them. Our kitchen sitting room opens on to the garden and just at the side is the orchard, where we sometimes have our tea and dinner and sometimes on the lawn in front of the house overlooking the road fields and river. The house itself is built in a very nice spot at the corner of crossroads, one going downhill to Exeter, the other up the hill towards another village about 2 miles away with a few houses between, so the front of the house looks over a veg garden below the lawn, slopes down to the road, then faces south and the side of the house by the crossroads is west, so last and north is sheltered by the hill road going up. There are 14 rooms and the end I have is an addition and has a separate staircase so we are all to ourselves when we like. I only wish we could have spent all our time here but then Dora would have had no schooling and we could not have gone to Instow and so on so it is as well as it has been.

Yes, Dora left her school. Miss Symonds told me she was sorry to lose her, not as a scholar only but as a friend. She gave Dora a pretty little handkerchief and hope we might meet again. She found Dora very persevering and taking an interest in her work. I do not think time and money was wasted there. Chrissie got no good at her school, only a little experience. She is ever so much better, I am glad to tell you and I think has got over another crisis in her life. She is growing fast and so is Dora. [...]

I had a little adventure and experience coming out here, not very pleasant perhaps. I had a bag or two and a parcel (carrying to save cab fare 5/-) when I missed my brown bag containing money and various treasures including your last 2 letters and ration books. I went back to where I had it last only 5 or 10 min but it was gone. There happened to be a shop near with a telephone and a gentleman who I asked for advice gave me 2d which the shopkeeper would not take from me. I got onto the Police Station gave description etc, asked for the crier to go out for me (charge 1/-) offered a reward of 5/-. I had left the children

4. 'THE COUNTRYSIDE IS GLORIOUS'

sitting on a seat at the roadside and when I joined them, having done all I could Dora said Don't you worry a bit Mother. Have faith and you will get it again. So I had her advice and luckily having enough food to last a few days you see, we are taking that up with us. [I] just dismissed it from my mind till Monday morning when I found it had been taken to Mrs Buckingham, having my address in it. I called to thank the finder and pay the reward, which was <u>not</u> accepted. So I was only 1/- worse off and had learnt two lessons, more faith and not to struggle too much to try to save. Hence I am going to have a cab to the station when we go home.

About your suggestion, I do not think we can go on Friday for several reasons, then we could not go about London for nothing and I feel this will have cost quite enough by the time we finally get home, nearly £4 you know for fares if there is no further rise, as Mrs Middleton says Mrs Harding told her is to be in Aug. I hope not. We might go somewhere on the Sunday. Mr Parker might like to take us all, anyway I feel we must leave this for another time.[123] I do so want us all to go with you and children will enjoy it better. There will be an opportunity again I feel sure perhaps sooner than we think.

Katie and Dad are so looking forward to our little stay with them, it would be unkind to suggest being out all day just as we got there. I might have stayed a little longer, if it was quite safe from aircraft but our house will be empty on the 12th and Mrs Palmer goes away on that date so he will want to come to us right away.

Dad is working all the Bank Holiday to get a weekend in Letchworth soon. He did that last year and then we all got Scarlet Fever and he could not come. They are having such a little fruit in London and so dear. Plums 2/-lb and small green apples 10d, did you ever hear. I hope we shall have a few in the garden when we go home but Mrs Middleton tells me and Noel Palmer too that it has been a very bad fruit season.

So the site is fixed now for 'New Town'. I had not heard anything about it. I have written to Charles Fritton but have had no reply yet. [...]

---

123   Mr Parker and Katie would marry after the war.

Now I must stop, hoping you will enjoy this letter and forgive me what I have omitted you may have wanted.

Lots of love from Dora, Chrissie and Morris and your loving wife

Lucy

August 5th 1918 Bedford Prison

Your letter to hand yesterday which much revived my drooping spirits. The letter days are the bright ones, you may be sure, and realization is always better than anticipation in this case. [...]

I am glad you recovered your purse, it is another example of the goodness of humanity, so rare nowadays when everyone is preached the doctrine of self first and, if anything [is] left, supply self again. I liked your picture of the children bathing: I am sure the salt water must be splendid for their growing limbs. The liberty which they enjoy would quite shock our parents could they see them.

I apologise for sending suggestions to your conduct in London but I find I am not yet cured of a great fault of mine, namely impulsiveness, and must say that I did not think of the attitude which some persons may have taken towards it. As to the expense I rule that out as a plea, because as all the museums etc are shut, it but meant a shilling or two for tram and bus fares.

Do not delude yourself into thinking of an early reunion as it may mean a disappointment for you if it does not come off. [...]

Well Lucy Dear I have filled another letter and I hope you will have an easy journey home and find everything in good order, returning refreshed and strengthened to again take up the work of life before you. Eagerly looking forward to your loving reply.

Yours ever, Frank

4. 'THE COUNTRYSIDE IS GLORIOUS'

Newbridge Cottage, Bishops Tawton, Devon
August 8th 1918

My dear Frank

This is the last time I shall write to you from this address, next week we shall be at home again. How quickly the time has gone since we have been here. The people here are as sorry to let us go as we are to leave. The children too hope to come again one day which proves they are not tired of it, only two days have they missed the bathe in the river. They are all very well and myself too […]

Mr Palmer seems to be looking forward to his stay with us and has a mind (has promised) to give Dora lessons on his typewriter, I shall have a go too.[124] He is bringing a goat which might so amuse Chrissie and Morris. He has sent the tenant's money to settle up so I shall have plenty to get home with and no worry. We may see a bit of London after all. I hope you did not think me making excuses because I do not want to take the children. You know I do not like to spend a penny more than I feel I can afford and even a couple of shillings are of value these days.

I had a very nice letter from Mr Fritton. He was pleased I had written; he had forgotten our address or would have wrote to me before. He is very pleased to know about you and will be proud to shake your hand. His health must have suffered very much altho' he says very little about it. He is busy gardening again and hopes to go to Letchworth before the winter when he will call and see me.

My dear, do not tell me not to hope for a speedy reunion. I hope for it every minute of time and that is why I can keep cheerful. I know the darkness will clear soon there must be dawn and the time we are passing through is like a night(mare). Do not think I could be really happy away from you even in this lovely country, but like you I dare not think of it. I can only hope and believe we shall have a bright future together again soon. I would like to know if your caravan scheme

---

[124] Their friend Noel Palmer from whom they sublet the cottage was to become their lodger.

includes me (sometimes perhaps) [...] I could get knowledge here on all subjects, there are books and books and Mrs Morgan is well read and Mr Fox too. Yes you are right in thinking her strong minded, but very pleasant too with a quiet voice like Miss Guys at Clifton and I like her and I think she does me. One thing she told me tonight, she has never had such good well behaved children stay here before, they do not bother round me but make their own amusement. I was very pleased as I consider that shows how natural they are. I always seem to have some praise of them for you, but I know how you love to know the good points, you have had your share of training them and I do not think you will find them spoiled.

[...] Send me the visiting order when due as I want to come to see you. I shall come alone unless you wish to see any of the children. Mr Fox went in to town this morning and took all the children with him for a bathe. They came home very hungry for dinner.

Mrs Middleton has heard from Mrs Sidney Palmer. His exemption expired in June. As he is so indispensable he has not been discharged but his salary reduced so much that he is on a level with a temporary employee instead of a member of the permanent staff. She (Mrs M.) is very indignant, she is fond of the Palmers and she is very faithful to her friends. She says she will be pleased to see me again and tells me of Mrs William's visit to her husband and says I must go too soon before the [tan] wears off. She seems to think I am brown. You would love to see the difference between Morris's body and his face and neck and hands and arms and legs and feet, he never wears shoes and socks, neither does Dora. Their feet are hardened to such things as thistles and stony roads. Chrissie likes her shoes on. There are a good many little streams about here, runs down the hills and Morris is often dabbling his feet. There is a running brook just at the bottom of the orchard, he is fond of running to. Sometimes he takes a scout pole with him where there are some fallen apples. They have a good supply of these, they each had 3 before breakfast this morning as he got his knapsack full yesterday afternoon. It is quite allowed but they are 1/- lb in the market so I could not buy for them. They had a qt of skim milk 2d for supper last night so they ought to be well and get fat. I am so pleased about Chrissie, the improvement is remarkable.

My letters to you are always so simple, just small talk it seems, but I enjoy yours when you touch on big things, I am so glad you are able to get books. Let me know what you want when I come to see you. I am sending a shorter letter this time, I hope you get it sooner than you did the last one. I am going to town so will post it myself so you might have it by Friday morning. I did not get yours this week till Wed. Dora, Chrissie and Morris send sweet thoughts to you. Have you tried to use the power Stead had of writing a message from me? I have tried it but it has not worked yet. Now I must stop.

Lots of love from your ever loving wife.

Always in my thoughts

Lucy

32 North Avenue, Letchworth
August 14th 1918

Dear Frank

Well here we are, home once more everything quite alright, no damages. They seem to have been nice people so I was lucky. Mr Palmer has settled down with us and the goat too. It is nice to have someone in the house and will help me to be a little more independent. I wish I could quite. I hope you will be able to read this letter written in pencil but I had no ink and could not buy any at the Post Office. I wonder what you think of the typing. Dora will soon master it.

Now you are anxious to know how we got home. We got to the station at Barnstaple in good time, ½ an hour to spare. We rode in a trap and I allowed for breakdowns which we did not have. The train was crowded, coming from Ilfracombe. We got in expecting to stand all the way but after a little while we went into a first class and so we travelled comfortable. It was a good train, only stopping at Salisbury after Exeter till Waterloo where we arrived at 4.20. Dad and Katie met us as I had to bring all my luggage with me. Dad and I took it to Kings X in a taxi (as it could not be sent through). Katie took the children up on a bus and we landed at 39 exactly together. I left all except your brown bag in the cloak room till Monday.

[...] After church we went round some of the old haunts, showed Morris and Chrissie where they were born and went into Gospel Oak fields but the lower part is allotments and they look well too. The top of Parliament Hill is fenced in, they have a searchlight there [...]

After dinner we went to Regent's Park to see the zoo animals, Katie and Jack with us and in the evening we went to the Spaniards Road and home over the viaduct and Lily Pond. On Monday morning we took [the] bus to Westminster, went into the Abbey, then bus again to Liverpool St and so through the City and past St Paul's. Then we came back the same way [...], had a picnic lunch in the Green Park and walked past Buckingham Palace to see the Victoria Monument and home to Chalk Farm by tube at 3 o'clock, left at 4 and came here by the 5 train first stop Hitchin, so we had a good day, the children did not seem at all tired.

Mr Palmer brought some of the luggage up on his bike and the rest came on Tuesday morning, costing me no more than if I had sent it on and I was sure of getting it and had it safely. As you say it was very nice to feel the Letchworth breeze, but how strange a place looks after a long absence. We found the house quite clean and tidy, but the garden rather wild except where I have some potatoes and cabbages growing. I am glad to say I have a few nice apples, Mr P. says quite a good number considering the fewness about. They are 1/- lb now and no plums at all round here. My fowls look quite well and I think I shall just leave them as they are. I have had no eggs yet but as they are moulting early they will lay again presently and eggs are 5d each. Mr P is marmalade-making and sells as quickly as can make it. There is nothing else to be had, no jam or syrup or fruit.

I have had a letter from Miss Jefferies telling me to expect papers of shares taken up in your name for New Town for £5. She seems to think we were tired of our holiday but we were not. It still seems as if I have had a pleasant dream.

I shall come to see you next week but cannot say what day and I don't think I shall bring any of the children. I could not bring them all and I could not choose.

Mrs Middleton has been to see me and seemed glad I was home and very glad I was so much better and I feel I am too, all the tiredness and weariness gone. I can work with a will. The children are happy all day in the garden. Chrissie spent the morning at Mr P.'s shop weighing up etc. I am not writing a long letter this time. I want to see you and talk. [...]

We all send you our very best love and hoping to see you soon.

Your loving wife Lucy

5. 'These last days are the most trying', August 1918 to April 1919

August 26th 1918

Dear Lucy

Once again, with the permission of a beneficent govt whom it is presumed over rules all our deeds for our mutual improvement and benefit I am writing to you, though what to write is as big a puzzle to me as what to get for dinner is to the much tried and worried housekeeper.

I do not feel in the humour to discourse upon some abstract philosophy, such as should dogs curl their tails out or let them hang limp, should COs be allowed to complain when their eggs are boiled hard or given extra allowance of salt. Is it unlucky to walk under a ladder with a top hat on, or get out of bed the right foot first? All these and many other subjects may be crying out aloud for discussion and solution but I pass them by with a cool indifference, feeling that none but the exalted and lofty minds of Smith, Brown etc can deal adequately with such weighty matters.

I am tired of saying the commonplace things so intend to leave them out altogether, although I know that it is the common things which make up the sum total of life. As I am <u>not living</u> it does not refer to me so I can look down from my exalted altitude, or up from the depths, whichever way you like best and smiling, say, why all this thusness, why worry so, why bustle, why scramble for what you can get? Come this side of the wall and you will have all you need. A regular supply of food, diet varied, a sufficient amount of labour to keep you from ennui and leisure enough to cultivate the habit of contemplating. A vast array of servants to wait on you, both for temporal and spiritual needs. Healthy books for the mind and occasional music, both military and sacred. All these things are to be had by the slight sacrifice of all that man most desires and loves.

Our talk the other day was the epitome of brevity. You managed to tell me all about your four months' holiday in one sentence of fine words. [...]

Lucy Dear, my space is gone and I feel that the letter is very unsatisfactory but I trust you will feel my love is <u>yours</u> X

---

32 North Avenue, Letchworth
August 27th 1918

My dear Frank

How can I answer your letter as I wish. We both feel the bitterness of this struggle very keenly just now, you particularly because of the monotony of your existence. Now is the time we must not let our courage falter. I felt very bad about it all on my way home last week. Our interview was not very satisfactory I admit. While I was waiting at Bedford station I opened your books as I had an hour to wait for the train. I chose Browning to read and found a little help in 'Evelyn Hope'. We shall love and be united in other lives after this and I often feel it would be easier to die than live as we are doing. I am so sorry I could not say what I wanted, but I felt rather full up. What could I tell you fresh about our holiday when I gave you almost a diary of our doings. Although I could not talk as I wanted it was something even to see you.

We shall be together again some day. I know just how you feel and know this mood well, but dearest, it will pass. You must not deny me asking your advice on plans. You are still living and present with me in spirit. Doors and keys cannot part us. I think of you every moment of time and feel myself incapable of helping you even mentally. I know how difficult you must find it to write to me and I think it wonderful you have managed so well. Your letters have been so much help to me.

[...] I had your letter this morning and also a depressed one from Mrs Thomas. She is not looking on the bright side just now, really no one is, but there must be a silver lining dear and we shall see it soon.

THE CONSCIENTIOUS OBJECTOR'S WIFE

Do not give up hope. You say I have the hardest part but I have not, only to keep cheerful and try to keep others so. I had to cheer up Mrs Williams this morning. Sometimes this is very hard especially when I get depressing letters.

I have been thinking over what I can do. I went to see Miss Walkden, but she was out. [Taking] the little cottage and let[ting] this house again is not possible, as I could not get one near here and I do not feel inclined to go right away for the winter, so the only thing is to keep on as I am going till Mr Palmer leaves me again and then let his room again and do any needlework that comes along. This is about all I can do to give the children proper attention. I shall manage all right as if I get short of money I can sell the piano or anything else valuable. I suppose your idea of selling up is that we shall want all different stuff when we go to New Town but do you think that cannot be for a long time? I suppose shareholders will have first chance and I should like to be in the making of it.

We are indeed fortunate to have progressed in thought as we have, to make it possible for us to be in the beginning of something fresh which will be so much for the good of the future generation. It cannot be said of you that your life was in vain. We shall accomplish something yet and I hope we shall be allowed to work together. Life to me without you is nothing and not really living but I have to make it appear so for the children. I do not wish their happy young lives saddened by our sorrows. They will have, there's no doubt, in years to come, and they do not understand now what we are going through. I feel you are storing your mind with knowledge which will be useful for them later on. You have a good memory and I only have constant and faithful love and would never fail for whatever you set out to do.

All this is writing just as I think and perhaps does not help you one bit, but I do not seem to be able to write trivial events. Our doings are so commonplace and I think are of no interest to you just now.

[...] Mr Cree and Miss Wilding came up last night and we played a game of Whist, such a long time since I handled cards.

5. 'THESE LAST DAYS ARE THE MOST TRYING'

Katie has come today for a week, she is rather worn out so I have to look after her and cheer <u>her</u> up now. Dad is coming on Friday till Wednesday. How lucky for them I am here. Of course they bring their Rations.

This is a funny world to live in now. Mrs Middleton tells me that it is almost impossible for people to get leather and nails except through a boot mender, who does <u>not</u> sell. The boot menders are afraid they will lose their jobs after the war [...]

Now my space is almost gone. I shall be anxiously looking for you letter next Tues and do hope you will be feeling better. We have accepted our position willingly. We had the choice and can do nothing but take the consequences, however hard we find it. We felt this the right road for us and it will widen out to the fields presently. Just now it is very stoney and dark.

Cheer up my dear husband. I am sorry I am unable to help you.

Ever yours lovingly

Lucy

September 2nd 1918

Mien Amato Edzinon[125]

You can tell by the heading of my letter that I am in a sweeter frame of mind than when I last wrote. It is always funny to me the way you watch my varying moods and generally you diagnose them correctly, but permit me to clear away some notions, which it seems you possess which I think are erroneous. Firstly, as the parson says, I <u>have not</u> lost hope. I am as certain now of winning through as ever I was. My words referred to the rumour of an early release which seems to be prevalent amongst both ourselves and our friends and I both spoke and wrote strongly about it because I feel that to place any reliance on such things is <u>weakening</u> [...]

---

125   Misspelling of 'Mia amato edzino', 'my beloved wife'

Seeing you gave me permission to speak and even desire that I should do so, I will mention what I have in my mind. As to your nursing institute I think that would require too much capital and take too long to get a real return. Lodgers of the ordinary type do not pay and are generally a nuisance, so don't think of them as being able to render what you require. Your idea as to needlework is good and it will be the wisest plan at first but what I have been thinking of is this. Why not try and start a post trade. Lots and lots of women are now in industry etc who have hitherto made their own underclothes, or their children's etc, who must now find little or no time now to do so, are compelled to buy at shops and you know what shop goods are. You must think out what stock things are most needed and work out prices etc, then get someone to write a good advert and insert it in the most suitable papers and books and when you orders come you can execute them on the spot, your cash will always be to hand and I should think it possible such a trade has the field for a large output.

See what Miss Walkden says about it. Buying your own materials and not dealing with the middleman should give good profits. Get all the ideas you can and put the best to your own purpose. Such a trade would be independent of locality although in a large way Letchworth would be a set-off against sweating etc. The capital required would not be great.

I do not want you to leave Letchworth for you must have the sympathy of friends and the pleasure of pleasant company. I shall always have pleasant memories of the garden city as I have spent many pleasant hours amongst the sturdy champions of the ideals for which we stand.

[...] It is nice to know you have a house full this weekend, the weather is grand and the clouds are really beautiful. Such rapid changes in them. First huge leviathans passing by, then triumphal cars drawn by glorious animals and filled with laughing nymphs or some majestic personage, and these pass rapidly away and in the blue are seen filmy dappled clouds like the sands on the sea shore or the mudflats of a wide river reach. Here and there an island will arise around which can be seen sea horses sporting in the incoming tide, but there I shall fill my letter with these babblings if I don't stop.

Sorry to hear that Mrs Thomas is so downhearted but her husband will be home soon, as he has nearly done twelve months on the scheme and can claim work where he would like to be. I feel that if all had taken our position the whole question would have been settled long ago. However every man to his taste as the old lady said when she kissed the pig.

[...] You expressed a desire for knowledge when you were here, well now that is just how I feel. I should like to start afresh and take up Drawing, Mechanics, Elocution, Music and languages together with lots of other subjects. As I am half way through this life and still got to live under the curse I'm afraid it will all have to be left for the next few incarnations. I've just read *The Valley of the Moon* again and must say I got more real incentive to live and greater knowledge of human life than one would get through reading Ruskin for a thousand years. Adieu.

Sept 3rd 1918

My dear Frank

I was very relieved at the brighter tone of your letter this morning. This reply will be in instalments; I now have a few spare moments so am commencing. I was out collecting all the morning, got home at one and then had to get a move on to get some dinner by ¼ to 2, have cleared away and tidied up and just going to get tea ready. Katie has taken Morris to the post and Grandpa is dozing in the front garden, under the laurel which now makes a good screen from the road. The girls are playing in the back garden. Miss Wilding is coming up this evening for a game of cards. Yesterday at 6 Katie Dad and I with Morris went to the 'Pictures'. I had not been for a year. It was not bad but I never was keen on them. I was glad they were not war pictures. Morris was highly delighted and very interested. Mr Palmer has taken Chrissie and Dora once, and Dora is going again on Thursday for remember he has tickets. The house was packed for the 8 o'clock show. People want amusement.

This is a lovely day, the best Katie has had; she looks very worn (didn't you think I looked well?). I expect she feels the anxiety of housekeeping. I am afraid that does not worry me very much. I feel rather ashamed of myself sometimes, for worrying so little considering all things, and looking cheerful. My father is very well. He and Katie seem to get on very well together. Their tastes are somewhat alike so they agree; he also likes 'Jack' so there is no friction there. Mr Palmer has a large trade in marmalade just now, and made 3 gallons in the copper last week and more going for tomorrow.

Katie has just come in with a bad wasp's sting on her neck so I must leave off to apply the blue bag etc.[126]

<u>9 o'clock</u>. A little more while the four are playing cards. Supper over, children gone to bed, my application effected almost instant cure. Dad seems to be enjoying the game and Katie says he has not played for a very long time. Do you know, somehow they appear to me to live only on the surface, as it were. They do not go deep into things and I believe that is the general way with people, they just take things as they are and are contented with everything as it comes. I often think of *The Valley of the Moon* and the Harvester and cannot but find how enjoyable such a life must be.

Going into two houses this morning where women were washing and cooking and children were playing [and] crying, I felt how silly to crowd together like that and thought so much better my cooperating scheme of living would be, but not one in ten women I mention it to agree to it. They seem to think a number of people could not live in harmony.

[...] About your idea for my work, it is good, I do want to rescue my economic independence, but it will be a hard struggle to attend to home and children properly as well, but I shall do my best and they will have to be useful too, but I do so want them to have a real good time and plenty of liberty as they have now.

---

126 The 'blue bag' was a 'blueing' bag used in laundry to keep the whites white, containing bicarbonate. However, this is only good for bee stings: wasp stings need vinegar.

5. 'THESE LAST DAYS ARE THE MOST TRYING'

I have been asked to take two new lodgers who would pay me very well, but I have decided not to take them. As you say, ordinary lodgers do not pay and it means giving all one's time. I also want to feel free. How strange this desire for knowledge should be so strong within us now, when our lives are half run out. If we satisfy this desire will it benefit the future race any […]

<u>Wed evening</u>. I have not had one moment since 7 this morning when I got up. Dad and Katie have just gone, and Mr Palmer and the girls with them, so I am left with Morris. Their coming and going still seems strange without Mother and it makes a little pain, tho' I think we all feel most sorry for her, missing so much in life, we none of us can talk about her. I encourage the children to keep her garden tidy and pretty at Norton. Next Tuesday I shall be all alone with the children.

This afternoon Dora has been to Miss Bartholomew to tea with some of the Esperanto Class. She had a good time, I think, and the class commences again next Wednesday. I am so glad you have got on with it so well. I am afraid I have too much to think of to concentrate on it but I intend to have a good try. I have got to see about the Adult School again soon and Miss Reynolds has sent for me to go and see her so I look like having a pretty full time.

If my letters are a little disjointed I hope you will forgive me, and know that although the time is long since you were in our family circle in the flesh you are with us so much in our thoughts and conversation, it would not seem at all strange for you to share our next meal. Now I must get this off to post.

With best love, hoping for a good letter next week.

Your loving wife Lucy

The children's letters are postponed till next week.

THE CONSCIENTIOUS OBJECTOR'S WIFE

32 North Avenue, Letchworth
September 11th 1918

My dear Frank

I must apologise first for being late getting this letter off, but Mrs Bland came yesterday morning and as she stayed till this evening I could not get the time to myself for writing [...]

Our picnic for last Sunday was off, the weather was much too wet. Dora particularly was disappointed, because she had got the loan of Mrs Palmer's bicycle and had invited Lily Wheeler to come too and bring hers. However she went to Howard Hall Adult School with Mr Palmer as he was giving a paper on 'Hardy Country in his books' and she had a few little runs during the day. She likes it very much and will soon ride very well. I am sending mine to Munts to be done up.

Mr Cree is coming up tomorrow to fix up a place for the new chickens. O yes, Morris will help; rather, he likes to be in everything and he is happy working (like his father). He and Dora have been digging potatoes for me this evening. I have not got a very good crop but shall be glad of the small ones for the chicks. Sorry you think them dear but Mr Tickle and I think them very cheap. Pure bred birds are selling at 25/- and he is trying these cross-bred on the strength of my good luck with our 'Mongrels' so [I] hope they are a success. The greatest difficulty will be food and that will be rationed.

Now I am on my own again and have a little more time I must see about the Adult School. I am going to call on all the members and see what can be done to start again in the hope of making it go [...]

I went to the ILP Branch meeting at the Skittles on Sun evening last [...] There were quite a number present, including Mr Pease who looked much better. Miss Lawes as chairman did her duty well. We are commencing the Sunday evening meetings from Sunday next week and of course I hope to attend all I can. Mrs Osborne is doing most of Moss's work while he is away from the office (National Labour Press). She and her husband have had a little holiday together and he has recovered from the slight illness he had.

5. 'THESE LAST DAYS ARE THE MOST TRYING'

I saw in the press that the Government had decided to send you all to Wakefield. I hope I shall be able to get all the children to see you first. Mr Hall Jones would like to come next time, he said, but I think it had better be Dora and Morris as I said and you are expecting. It will have to be on the Sat. as I cannot keep them home from school just as they have restarted.

I am afraid nothing can be done for poor Katie. She would be a great deal worse if it were not for Jack. She may be better in a few years, her health is not good and the conditions of living are not the best she could have and housekeeping is not easy for her just now or for anyone.

[...] I think I must stop now. Mrs Middleton has given me two books for you but I am reading them myself first, I hope you don't mind.

Lots of love from the children and myself. Kind thoughts and greetings from a number of friends and comrades.

Your wife

Lucy

September 23rd 1918

Dearest Wifey

I must say how greatly I enjoyed your visit. You looked so well and happy that it was like walking into a garden of beautiful flowers to behold you. Morris and Dora too seemed to me to have dropped from some celestial city, so sweet and clean and full of love were they. I cannot express all that I feel but must say that I know the real joy of a father's heart and were I a poet I could perhaps then express it in words. After all it is not what one so badly expresses by words or deeds but what one really feels that matters. I want you make it up to Chrissie dear for not being able to come. Give her a special hug and cuddle and lots of kisses from Daddy and tell her Daddy knows she loves him dearly.

I trust you had no unfortunate adventures on the homeward journey. The weather seems to have been especially favourable to Jack for

Sunday has been awfully dull and cold. We did not say much to each other but to be together is enough when Love and Sympathy flow so freely. I am shocked at the skin disease you spoke of. Perhaps it is a new species of bacteria from the front. I hope you will be able to steer clear of it ... Does it recur?

I am pleased with the books and you must thank Mrs Middleton and Mr Cobbold for them. The New Testament is just the thing because I can read a portion every day and being familiar with the content I shall be better able to transpose the Esperanto. Do you remember me asking for a Handicraft book some time ago? Well if you want to set Katie and Jack on the book stunt just ask them to go to Foyle's Charing Cross Road and look one up for me. It will open a new avenue of interest to them and perhaps result in me getting what I desire. The book I want should give a fair knowledge of nearly all the handicrafts and trades. As Foyles' have about 10 miles of books on all and every subject under the sun, moon and stars and are ready to assist buyers by all means in their power this journey should not be in vain. The last paragraph reads like an advertisement but it isn't really.

[...] I still have a hankering for that Cabinet[-maker's] shop and when we get to New Town I shall see that I get it. If you can get any information relating to NT I should like to hear it. Ask Clapham Lander or Dr Crowley if you see them.

I am glad you are taking up the school work again as I feel it is most important and I wish you all success. I understand that one of the privileges at Wakefield is unlimited correspondence, so you had better practice on P's typewriter so that you can get your replies off a little more quickly; also they will not be supervised. In many ways it will be better but I feel it is being shunted into a siding. Whilst we are in prison we are a thorn in the flesh to the Govt, when we get there they can say look how well we are treating them and the real issue will be lost. [...]

Lots and lots of love to all of you

from Daddy to Mother Dora Chrissie and Morris

5. 'THESE LAST DAYS ARE THE MOST TRYING'

32 North Avenue Letchworth
September 24th 1918

My dear Frank

Your letter received as expected, yours are always to time, sorry you cannot say the same of mine. Yes, we did have a nice visit on Sat. How could I help looking happy when it is such a pleasure to see you and to know you can keep well and cheerful. As you say we did not say much to each other but have spent many silent ½ hours together since first we met and I hope we shall again and before 10 years too.

I have not much news for you now. Miss Bartholomew has sent some Esperanto books, which I am sending on to you. [...] I went to Miss Blackburn [to do her] sewing, yesterday afternoon and this morning. What a fine room Miss Gay has, large and beamed, 2 fireplaces one at each end, windows each side and door into the garden and one into hall. Miss Blackburn is one of the many I suppose who want someone to sew for them. Her wardrobe is in a sad state of neglect. The children do so dislike coming home and finding me out. It makes them cross and this evening Morris and Dora had a few words while out, up by the post office and Dora left him. It began to get dark and I felt anxious so went off to look for him. I met Sheila Matthews and asked if she had seen him and presently she came running after me with him. She had found him in the hedge in the lane to the Manor House [...]

About that skin disease: I suppose one is likely to get it at any time while the germ or parasite is about. I have unfortunately got one on the ball of my right thumb, can scarcely hold the pen. It was very painful all night and all the morning but is getting better. I was afraid I should have to go to the Dr again [...]

Adult school meeting on Thursday afternoon but no lesson. I found Mrs Myles out today so have to call tomorrow. She goes to see Peter again on Monday. He is keeping well, but she is very downhearted so I must try to cheer her up. They feel the separation like us. Now I suppose I must stop and I have only written chatter.

Love from the children and myself.

Your loving wife

Lucy

A letter from Fritton on Sat. He sends kind regards to you and I am to tell you they are doing all they can for you all. He says, what a Meeting there will be some day! [...]

September 30th 1918

Mia Amata Adzino

Your letter was prompt and gladly received. So your new chicks are satisfactory, that is well. I trust they will take a copy from their near neighbours and prove very fruitful in the egg laying department. Don't forget that there is big can of tar in the garden and it might be useful if Mr Cree and Cobbold want a job. Glad that Marshall is giving you a clean-up for the winter. He is <u>most generous</u> and deserves great merit as a landlord.

As to the books, you need not trouble as they are now in Letchworth even if you have not already got them. The Esperanto books will be welcome and you must tell Miss Bartholomew how much enjoyment I am getting from this study. I'm sorry to say my memory plays all sorts of tricks with me and refuses to act as I would like but I have never yet forgotten mealtime.

So you have got another job. Well it will probably pay better than needlework and certainly will not be as tedious. Have heard nothing of Kays lately. Are you still their representative? I saw a good tip the other day and pass it on to you. Get a Continental Commercial directory and write to the various firms asking if they need a representative and to forward samples [and] particulars. You may light on something which would pay you well and be easy to handle through the post etc.

You always were fortunate in having men friends I believe, both young and old, and I hope you always will be for after all men can be useful at

5. 'THESE LAST DAYS ARE THE MOST TRYING'

times and though women now are trying to do all the men's jobs I think it will not last or if it does the human race will suffer [...]

ஓ

Oct. 1st 1918
32 North Avenue Letchworth

My dear Frank

Glad you got my last letter more promptly. I know it must seem too bad of me, when you have to wait, but I know I am forgiven for the many times it has happened. I will try to get this finished tonight then posted in the morning. I feel very tired though. I was walking round from 10.0 to 1.0 this morning and then sewing all the rest of the day except getting meals ready and putting children to bed. It is now 9.30.

Mr Palmer has been to the Branch meeting of ILP, just came in. I felt too tired to go and it was a dreadful night wind and rain. I never was out in a worse. It was worth going to, the speaker was a Miss Stevens from Bermondsey, Trade Union organiser. She gets through a vast amount of work, holding meetings, 24 in a week, running clubs and classes of all sorts and socials but the women are joining up at the rate of 2,000 a week in London. (Miss Lawes said I was to tell you they have a 1000 members in Hitchin and Arlesey). The subject of her talk was the demobilisation of women, she was very enthusiastic and knew what she talked about she had been in jam factories and domestic service.

This is an important question: what will happen about women workers after the war? Miss Stevens was staying the night at Crowley's so I saw Mrs Crowley. She wishes to be remembered to you and I was to tell you the New Town scheme was going on, the next book is ready for you and you shall have one at once. The site will be the next thing to decide, two are being considered, but she did not say where [...]

I have filled in a paper now for coal, coke and gas ration. I daresay I shall be allowed far more than I need or can afford. I am going to have Pugh for my coal merchant. He brought me 5cwt coal today. 10-5 for each so you can see what an increase since you used to pay Perry. Mrs Middleton can have 6 tons if she wants. Of course if Mr and Mrs Palmer are here they will help pay for it and it will keep the house warmer [...]

⁂

October 7th 1918

Dearest Lucy

Your cheery letter to hand. Glad to know all are well and shall be more pleased to hear that the spots have all disappeared [...]

Now I am stowed away out of danger and deprived of activity BUT there is a time coming and let it be soon when I shall be back in the ranks of those who are fighting poverty and greed, ignorance and evil. Undoubtedly the woman worker will be a problem after the war but I think the man fighters will be the biggest problem. How to get him back to work, along the lines of old and existing ideas, I mean, of course. Will he be content to go back to the weary unexciting and monotonous labour of the prewar workshop? Again, will the housewife be content to struggle on with the small wage of old after having had the opportunity of endless lodgers at high prices, high war wages and regular allowances?

I know high prices for goods and food are the order of the day and that many people are feeling it very much, but the very searching makes money cheap, as it were, for its outlet is so restricted. At any rate mine is for I have not spent anything for over twelve months.

Glad to know that New Town is coming into being, for I can go on building my day dreams about it and I find it pleasant occupation to visualise in my mind's eye the rising town, filled with an energetic, virile people working and playing with equal pleasure and eagerness. The children a joy to behold, free and happy with full opportunity to learn the lessons which nature would teach, together with the wisdom man has acquired through the ages at hand for them to draw upon.

What has Perry done that you discard him? Has he been called up? I know he was a patriotic stay-at-home who liked to get his fighting done

5. 'THESE LAST DAYS ARE THE MOST TRYING'

by proxy but he was a decent sort in spite of that […]

I amused myself last night by reading some of your letters of <u>last year</u>. In one you say 'I don't think this awful war can last much longer'. A year has rolled by since then and still it continues and we are no nearer <u>Peace</u> than then […]

All my love to you all from Daddy

❧

Oct 9th 1918
32 North Avenue Letchworth

My dear Frank

Glad as usual to have your letter. I suppose you are well although you omit to say. We are all quite well, all spots gone but one on my arm which is nearly well. I don't think we shall have more trouble with them.

I got through a good bit of needlework last week but it was a great trouble to me with sore hands it feels so nice now they are better and I shall be able to get through a good lot this week. As you know I am always busy and so keep well and happy as possible.

I went to the Adult School last Sunday evening. Palmer gave a paper on the country of 'Hardy the Novelist'. There were quite a large number present. All the young men land workers seem to belong, the only 2 of the oldest men were Jones and Brayshaw, oh I forgot Francis of Sollershot End. Brayshaw has to go before the tribunal on Friday next. He has been left alone till now but he is 50. He may get off, you know he is at the Estate Office.

I also went to the ILP meeting at the Skittles on Sunday evening. It was very Political, a subject I am not keen on but I was interested. It is well to know all I can. The speaker was a Mr Humphries and his subject was Proportionate Representation. I expect you know all about the scheme. It seems to be working well in several places and I should think it decidedly better than the present system. There are quite a number of people turn out to these meetings […]

Mr Perry has really done nothing. He left me very short of coal all last winter though he will be very glad to be discarded he has more custom than he can supply and the other man is near at hand. I am more likely to be served. Coal is short and so are men for carting and we cannot very well carry it home.

[...] Dora has read a lot of Tolstoy and likes them very much. As to the other by Gould, I only read here and there, but I rather liked it, however, as you say Campbell's *New Theology* is more concise.

In some curious way all those sorts of books seem to feed as I read, I digest them and they pass away and I am sustained for the time, then want fresh food. They certainly help me very considerably to live my life, I suppose in the same way as people must go to Church or Chapel. I do not mean to say I have not my own thoughts but I can only live by them and not easily express them. I think you understand me.

The problem of the women workers is involved in that of the new fighter to a great extent. In the first place he will not go back to work along the old ideas and the existing ones will not be [enough] when the war is over for the housewife. I fancy there will be trouble. She will not be willing to give up going out to work where she has been doing so, or having lodgers where she has been having them and the returning husband will probably object. But there are thousands of wives who will have to work to keep themselves and children to help out and it will be allowed by a grateful country. There are many now who are having a struggle now to manage on the allowances with a young family they cannot leave to go out to work for. Then there are the girls earning £2 or £3 a week: will they be willing to go into service for 5/- or Laundry or anything else for under 10/-?

Mrs Middleton and I were talking about this yesterday and she predicted plenty of crime and misery for some time, so you may well get ready to fight against ignorance, evil and so on. I hope I have a privilege of doing a share somewhere. I have a feeling I should like 'Welfare' work in Mothers' 'Welcomes' rather than Trade Unions or Clubs. Anywhere I shall be willing to help in anything that will be any benefit to brothers or sisters. Surely that would be better than making fripperies even if by so doing I could make plenty of money.

How quickly this month has gone. I will hope to bring Chrissie and Mrs Middleton (if she can come) one day next week, perhaps Thursday.

Now I must stop, thinking of the Labour Song 'Goodnight, Goodnight'.

Lots of love from us all.

Your ever loving wife

Lucy

&

October 21st 1918
Bedford Prison

My Dearest Wifey

If your visit gave to you as much delight as I myself derived therefrom, then it must be counted an unqualified success but of course there is always a fly in the ointment as they say, ours was the brevity of the time of bliss. I think Chrissie has grown a great deal and looked very well. Just get them all to look after their teeth and clean them every day. In these days of decadency it is so necessary and nothing adds to beauty more than teeth like pearls. I am not afraid of you making them vain by saying this.

On reviewing the visit you seemed to me like a study in black and yellow. The effect was excellent and if you are having a dance this year I suggest black and yellow for you, but perhaps you would prefer to wait until I get home again before you indulge in such frivolities.

I am afraid we did not say what we wanted to say to each other and that I felt rather tongue-tied, but it is impossible for one to describe the feeling which comes over one when he suddenly meets with two such sweet but rational creatures as yourself and Mrs M. You bring a glimpse of a different world and I have been here long enough now for these conditions to have gotten very commonplace. It is strange how man so readily adapts himself to [his] environment. In outward things at any rate, for instance one never thinks of such things as collars and never has to hunt for a collar stud or run to catch a train etc. These things, if thought of, seem to belong to a dim and distant past and yet we know that, given the opportunity, we could take up the old and real life just as if no break had occurred. Let the time be soon I say and I'm sure you will most readily endorse it [...]

Frank

✣

32 North Avenue Letchworth Herts
Oct 23rd 1918

My dear Frank

I am sorry I could not possibly get your letter written yesterday. I hope I am forgiven. Yes I got a great deal of enjoyment from our visit last Thursday. Chrissie too and Mrs Middleton. It is the first time she has visited a prison, she enjoyed the chat immensely, but as you say the time is all too brief. Glad you liked my colour scheme but why only at a dance? I should always like to look my best, not vanity you know. I gave the children your message about tooth cleaning. I am always at them but they are always so busy enjoying themselves. Glad you thought Chrissie looked well, she still increases in weight so must be better. I have had a dreadful cold at the weekend but it has nearly gone. I was afraid I was in for 'flue; it is very bad in different parts of the county again.

We had a very pleasant time in Bedford last Thursday, had a nice little lunch in a café and walked through the arcade. On Hitchin station we saw Miss Lees on her way home with about 70 girls. She told me this news, that the Skittles had been commandeered. We find this is correct, also the Howard Hall and the Reading Room [on] Gernon Road, also the boys' club, so now we have nowhere to hold meetings. There is a Labour meeting at the Skittles tomorrow, but we might not be able to get in. [...] Isn't it shocking? [No-one] knows why but the general impression is 2000 munition workers coming and they are to be billeted there, I have heard 2000 Serbians. We shall soon know.

5. 'THESE LAST DAYS ARE THE MOST TRYING'

Miss Armstrong is working hard to get members for the Women's section of the Labour Party. I am giving her names of likely people and the latest to join is Mrs Barker [of] Cromwell Green, they will be glad to attend the meetings Mr Cubbon is going to talk to. I believe they are to be a Study Circle for Hobson's book on Finance. I have been asked to take a meeting, finance boiled down to everyday affairs. I don't think I feel equal to it, but I can talk in discussion.

My next piece of news – I have a Belgian girl lodger (temporary). This is the tale: on Saturday evening Mr Palmer was rather later than usual coming home and I felt so queer I told Dora she could stay up for him and I would go to bed, 8 o'clock, when in he came with this girl. Would I shelter her for the night and could she have his bed and he would sleep on the couch? It seems she came from Birmingham to work, never dreaming Letchworth was so crowded. She was sent to Mrs Rix and she got him to try and get her somewhere; they did try and found it impossible, so he could do no other than bring her here (are you thinking of another Belgian girl he took home?) They went to about 40 houses Sunday and Monday and she is still here.

He went to London yesterday, home, till tomorrow, then he will try again to get her put in somewhere. Of course she has started work and has to be there [by] 7 o'clock so I have to be up early and it makes more to do all day somehow. And only on Friday I told someone that I did not like Belgians and would not have one in my house nor take munition money but what could I do, not turn her into the street.

This just proves the need for a hostel for girls we are agitating for, you would be surprised at the overcrowding here. I know of one house with 11 new lodgers and father, mother and daughter, 3 bedrooms only. It seems a dreadful state of affairs but there everything is of a piece these days. My great hope of a speedy peace seems to be fading away. I have felt very disappointed today, and sad with intense longing unsatisfied. I suppose it must come some day this year or next, but I somehow feel afraid of what may happen first. I daresay you know that Ostend and Lille have been evacuated and Antwerp next, then the Belgians will begin to get busy building up. They have already commenced in Ostend […]

Love from everyone the children and all the love

from your wife

Lucy

October 28th 1918

Dearest Lucy

Your letter is full of surprises [...]

Miss Lee's news is very cheering, also your last remark re women. Surely now we shall soon see some of the stalwarts marching in honour to Westminster, and I'm sure they will make things lively if only in the tea room. As to the Belgian girl, does it not strike you that whenever we make foolish boasts we are often confounded. Have you analysed your dislike? You have now a chance to put internationalism into practice. It may be nasty but the result will be good.

As to munition money you are quite right not to seek it or lay yourself out to cater for those out to get them. [...]

As to the taking of the halls in Letchworth, perhaps your surmises are all wrong. Where are the munitions works in which the workers are to be employed? Why should Serbians be sent to Letchworth? Have you thought what will happen should peace be declared soon. The army will <u>not</u> be disbanded at once and housing them will be a problem. Perhaps the Skittles may be wanted for the boys to come back to for the winter.

Glad Dora is settling down to Esperanto, she will find it very useful when she gets to other languages at school. Send me along some more Esperanto books and also the French as suggested. Don't bother about the other books whilst you are so busy [...]

Did you see the airship when you were here?? I got a good view of it on Sat. It is a lovely thing and sails through the air so gracefully and seems to be easily managed. Man has accomplished wonders in the material world and when he has made so much progress in the moral world which of course will happen, then indeed he will have cause for self-congratulation, but until then progress is like putting the cart before the horse [...]

32 North Avenue, Letchworth, Herts
Oct 28th 1918

My dear Frank

I hope you note that I am writing this letter, or beginning it, on Monday eve, before receiving yours. We are all well and I still have the girl here so I am kept pretty busy with 2 lodgers. We have been unsuccessful so far in getting her a home. The children and I have just been to a missionary Pageant at the Mission. They liked it immensely, especially Dora who is very keen on plays and acting. If we do go to London at Christmas time and there are any Pantomimes I shall let Katie take her.

We had a meeting at the Skittles last Thursday, first to protest against the probable near loss of the place for meetings. Aneurin Williams[127] has been written to and several others and it might be left to Letchworth. Secondly, to hear Mrs Hunter report on the first Women's Conference at Caxton Hall of the Women's Labour Party.[128] It was splendid and shows what ideas and ideals we have and what good must result if allowed to put them into practice. No doubt we are on the move and must keep moving on and forward. Ethel Bentham, Mrs

---

127 Liberal Member of Parliament, and Director of the first Garden City Ltd, which was responsible for planning and building Letchworth.

128 Mrs Hunter was Harriette Butler, wife of Edmund Hunter, founder of the St Edmundsbury Weavers, based in Letchworth.
http://www.meg-andrews.com/articles/st-edmundsbury-weavers/10/1 accessed 10 April 2018.

Snowden, Maria Philips, Mary Macarthur, etc were on the Platform.[129] […] Sorry about the neuralgia, lots of people are suffering from wrong nerves now. I went into a Chemist shop today and all along the counter were bottles of neuralgia mixture but they are more busy with people buying quinine for this 'flue. It is very bad about indeed, almost like a plague. Leonie, my Belgian girl, tells me they are expecting to close down again, so many have fallen ill today. I hope we all steer clear of it and you too. Chrissie says 'don't think about it or talk about it then we shall not get it'. Drs and Nurses have it as bad as anyone. It is the same as trench fever so you can guess how it comes, brought of course by the soldiers.

[…] I cannot analyse my dislike, it is only a silly prejudice against [the Belgians] as a race and perhaps because I do not know or understand them. Of course I get on well with this girl, and it is one more experience for me, only I am not pleased at getting up at 6. However the next fortnight it need not be till 7 as she will be working at night and leaves at 7. You might amuse yourself by thinking how I can sleep 7 people and a child in 2 double and 2 single beds. Mr P. sleeps by himself and at present lays a mattress on the floor in the sitting room. I have given my cradle away at last. A woman with her ninth child was very thankful to have it […]

We had a splendid evening at the Skittles on Sunday eve. last. Mrs Vali— spoke on a certain Regulation that the women are up against.[130] This Reg is to get rid of an evil very prevalent and at the same time makes it appear that vice is necessary. I was glad to see so many young men and soldiers (quite a lot) to hear the women's opinion of it and they were quite keen and joined in discussion and questions. I think we are certainly getting on when men and women can meet and talk together

---

129 Ethel Bentham was a politician and doctor, and in 1918 had been elected to the Labour Party's National Executive Committee. Mrs Snowden was a prominent suffragist, married to the Labour MP Philip Snowden. Mary Macarthur was a Scottish trades unionist and suffragist.

130 This could have been to control and penalise prostitutes but not their customers.

5. 'THESE LAST DAYS ARE THE MOST TRYING'

on delicate and hitherto banned subjects. I will explain more fully if you like. The Howard Hall are trying for the Vasanta Hall Sunday morning meetings.

I have still not heard for sure if they are Serbs coming, but there is a new factory to be opened and I heard today it is for shell filling, so they mean to carry on a while yet. But I also hear that the Belgian factory have a form for Belgian men to sign if they wish to stay on to build bridges when peace comes. None have so far, as they all want to go back to Belgium, so perhaps the Serbs will too, then it will leave the Halls clear for the boys. [W H] Smith's factory will be clear too of the air boys. Did I tell you Hendon Airdrome is [to be used] for a postal service?

Yes we saw the air ship when in Bedford and remarked how steady it sailed along. It will soon be a common way of traveling. [...] We think things, or rather the peace offensive, steadily moves forward.

[...] Mr Palmer has gone to Guildford today to a sale of a fruit farm and nurseries, he only to be a small partner of 3. I told him it was only another spasm of his, he wants a change he says [...]

Best love from Dora, Chrissie and Morris

and your loving wife, Lucy

November 4th 1918

Dearest Lucy,

Your letter was like a gentle shower of rain falling on a thirsty field. It is so full of human interest that I can live through the scenes quite easily as I read its pages. Am glad to know you are all well during these days of epidemics. So am I and the neuralgia has been better also. I trust your fit of depression has passed away. For myself I feel very hopeful that the end is near and that we shall once again be able to talk and work for Christ without incurring the wrath and venom of Government and their satellites.

[...] It is very strange that the Belgians do not wish to remain in this 'Land of the Free' but prefer to go back to be neighbours to the family of Beelzebub after all we have done for them too. Where is their gratitude?

[...] The book you sent on Town planning is interesting and it was good to read the words of our compatriots Brunt and Kidd. I think that Garden Cities will come into being providing Govt make it possible to get both lands and money cheaply, to be used through local authorities or Public Companies. Private efforts cannot cope with these things as it is too spasmodic and too greedy. I eagerly look forward to hearing more of [the] New Town.

If you feel so inclined you may sell the <u>newest</u> additions to my wardrobe whilst prices are high. Am not sending the visiting order next week unless you especially wish it.

[...]

Lots of love to you all and regards to the lodgers.

Yours lovingly Husband Father

✍

32 North Avenue Letchworth Herts
Nov 3[131] 1918

My dear Frank

Sorry again this will be late reaching you but you cannot imagine what little time I have. You need not send the order next week, we will have the letter this time instead of a visit. Perhaps I shall not have to come to see you again. I should soon solve the puzzle if you did walk in, only too pleased if it should happen.

I had a nice time in London on Monday. Leaving here 7.55 I was up at

---

[131] Lucy seems to have mistaken the date for this letter, which Frank replies to on 11 November.

the Priory by 9.20. Katie and I spent the time from 12 till 4 in Oxford St in Selfridges. I had never been in before and really enjoyed seeing so many people and so many goods. I also bought 4 towels which cost 10/-. We could have gone to a theatre but did not care to venture risking the 'flue'. It rained little and was an awful night. Dad, Jack and Katie saw me in the train at King's X and Mr Palmer met me at Letchworth 11 o'clock, so I had a good long day. Everything was alright at home too. The change has done me good. I have so much to do, the same things it seems over and over again and catering is none too easy just now. In spite of what you say I think I cheered the folks up too. […]

Our Belgian girl is supposed to be on night work this week but she hurt her arm on Thursday and the factory was closed on Friday and Sat for 'flue' cleaning and the Dr will not let her start yet. She had to go and see him on Friday. He asked who had bandaged her arm she told him the missus where I live. He said is she a nurse it is done so well I couldn't do it better myself. I tell you this to show I have not forgotten your first aid practices and I felt rather proud of myself. Isn't it just my luck though, always to have to look after people.

[…] I have got some news for you about [Noel Palmer]. He has bought a fruit farm at Guildford with Milton. 41 acres freehold, 14 tomato houses, Grape House etc, possession at Xmas. He has sold the business here and the house next door and he thinks 'Redcroft' is sold. He saw Milton last Sunday and they are thinking of applying[132] for your help, sort of general repairs and useful help. There is a staff of 8 or 9 now, also a motor lorry. Should you like it? Providing of course we could get a cottage near; be sure and let me know next week.

I am writing this letter with the children playing schools with Nellie Briant. Norton School was closed on Monday for a fortnight on account of flue. The epidemic seems to be abating, glad to say. I hope you keep free, of course. I have heard Bowry and Williams have it and hope they are better. I felt anxious about you till I had your letter.

132 Lucy suggests that Noel Palmer was offering Frank a form of non-combatant agricultural labour, to get him out of prison and protect him from being called up again.

THE CONSCIENTIOUS OBJECTOR'S WIFE

I think now we shall have 'peace' very quickly; if only the fighting ceases it will be something. Tonight's news is Germany must accept terms of armistice <u>at once</u> and yes or no, no discussion, so it looks like only a matter of hours. I tell Leonie she will be back home in the new year. She could hardly believe it, she does not read the papers although she <u>can</u> read English and speak it well. She is quite the ordinary type, short and fat with a lot of black hair. Of course [she] makes a great favourite of Chrissie, and [is] generous with them all, she is fond of children and is 21. I took her to the Skittles meeting on Sunday evening and as we went in the Internationale was being sung in Belgian.[133] The [...] subject was the Internationale.[134] I think she understood and enjoyed the meeting. The large room was full and half the small one, but we got a seat up near the front and I was glad to see Miss Lawes and Miss Lees there [...]

Dora and Morris went into the Common this morning and got 1lb of blackberries which I have made into jam. We shall only get 4oz ration now and 24 oz don't go far, just about enough for Mr Palmer and Dora. We are getting used to Marg, we have our one once for Sunday tea. Cheese is much more plentiful. The extra ration of fat in place of meat will now be nut butter which we can get in the Co-op.

Sorry I did not give you the subjects discussed at the ILP Conference: they were many. We were chiefly interested in housing, or at least I was. It is very important for the women to have every convenience and comfort to carry on the work of housekeeping properly; it should be catered for [??] as a business and not for women, or rather mothers, to have to put up with any old thing (such as stoves and baths).

I shall have to stop now. The children are very interested in the story.[135] The Skittles is still available for meetings next Sunday; Mr Butler is taking Esperanto the International Language. Dora seems interested

---

133   Flemish, or possibly French: there is no Belgian language.

134   The *Internationale* was the anthem of left-wing political groups, originally in French.

135   Frank wrote a continuing story to the children as part of his letters (not included in this edition).

5. 'THESE LAST DAYS ARE THE MOST TRYING'

in it and enjoys the lessons. We are having our school each Thursday afternoon now till the general meeting at the end of the month. I have quite a job to keep up interest and get the women to come. Our study circle on Finance has not commenced yet but the women's section [of the Labour Party] are having a meeting tonight.

Now I must stop. Lot of love from all the children

and your loving wife Lucy

November 11th 1918

Dearest Lucy

Your letter breathes of London rush. As I did not expect it until Friday I was not disappointed. Am glad to know that all are well and to be able to say ditto with regard to myself [...]

How the munition workers will like being stopped of pay for all time? When they get back to civil employment after receiving pay, whether at work or not, is one of the questions I am going to keep an eye upon. They are certainly being taught some lessons. Everyone seems to think that the sorry business will soon be over, but I am not so sanguine about release as some of our chaps are, so do not be too optimistic. Of course you cheered the old fogies up. Your very presence would do that. A ray of sunshine will make even the darkest dungeon bright [...]

Now as to your momentous news. What am I to say. First I congratulate Noel on his good fortune in getting so lovely a spot to settle down in. The surrounding scenery is just delightful. All hills and dales, woods and dells, with little brooks and rivers flowing through them. Then the people of Guildford are quite proper, even classy I am given to understand, whilst the educational facilities are equally excellent I think the ILP and NCF are strong there too and even errants are tolerated. After reading all this tosh you will wonder what on earth I am driving at. It is just to show you how you have put a proposal to me which may alter the tone of the whole of our lives. Something like the way you sprang the other job on me, eh?

I appreciate the offer of course and am quite willing to give it my fullest consideration but what about terms etc, of which you say nothing. Is it just a generous impulse to get me out of prison, or army services considered of real value to them? It is just such a job as I would like and think I am fitted for, but will it give me the freedom I desire? What about its effect on my ideal and the New Town of the future, the better environment for the children and their education? I do not want to develop into nothing better than a money grubber. Now I have put some of my thoughts about it before you to show you that I have considered it a little and what I suggest is this. Let Noel make whatever arrangements for my release on these grounds which he thinks fit, and after I am released we will undoubtedly come to an arrangement satisfactory to all parties. I think that he will <u>not</u> be successful in obtaining my release on these conditions. As for myself, I have done two years and can now see the end in sight, so shall not make any effort to get free by accepting conditions. If they give me my liberty to assist Noel, well and good, but if they say I must abide by any rules laid down by them I'm not taking it. You need not tell Noel this unless you like as I feel sure he does not understand our attitude towards Work of National Importance.

Do you only want a <u>cottage</u>? Four walls, tiny rooms, water outside, no bathroom, no private garden, and probably a troop of disorderly animals always around. How does it fit in with you remarks re housing in a later paragraph? I know what I want and it isn't a cottage unless you stretch the meaning a good bit. I shall await your reply to this with impatience so don't keep me waiting any longer than you can help. I hope I made myself clear as I do not want you to have the impression I am not enthusiastic about it. My thoughts are full of it and I have built many air castles but the cold light of reason dispels them and leaves me doubting. This environment is conducive to doubt as everything is so unreal and nothing happens.

[...] Oh as to Insurance. Get rid of it as I do NOT want to have any more to do with it. I might become an Eastman. I am sure I have a dual nature, one of which is grasping, selfish and practical in the worldly sense and with which I could become a cynical 'buyer in the cheapest and sell in the dearest' sort of chap. The other is idealist, gentle and loving full of sympathy for humanity which could if followed lead me to do something for the race. These are always in conflict and whilst I have been here I have seen myself, as it were outside myself, and what I have seen makes me fear for the gentler elements. Perhaps this morbidness is largely due to the prison influence which will be counteracted when I get back to natural life again [...]

Lots of love to all of you from Daddy and Hubby

❦

Nov 14 1918
32 North Avenue Letchworth Herts

My Dear Frank

I expect you are very thankful to know that at last hostilities have ceased, I cannot rejoice knowing that so many precious lives have been sacrificed – Hitchin has gone mad, and London I believe – and expecting industrial trouble. The Belgians have demonstrated here and the Belgian Socialists have paraded with the red flag. Yes it is fine to know how Labour in other countries have rallied round the Red Flag. I thought Germany would fall in line when they threw off the Military Power.

Of course lots of people are asking when you are coming home. I had a letter from Lizzie yesterday asking. Your mother is still with her for a few days longer, she keeps fairly well.

I have told Mr Palmer what you think of his scheme and he wrote a letter last night (in Milton's name) to the Sec of Home Affairs. I shall be looking for a reply every post and you will eagerly look forward to my next letter, I know. Mr and Mrs P have gone to 'Normandy' the farm today and they will probably look around Guildford and round about for a house. I told him what we thought about a 'Cottage' [...] of course it will be the standard rate of pay, which now would not be more than 38/ or 40/ but I am sure you may leave it, they will be quite fair and just. No doubt Pass would be glad of you at once but somehow I don't want that for you. New Town will not be ready yet and we have got to get a living till then and it may as well be in good surroundings and happily.

[...] I have got my Belgian lady into Mrs Barker's house, she went on Sunday (unwillingly). I have had a very bad cold this weekend and felt collapsed and crumpled up on Monday, but had a little rest and feel better again. I have been overdoing it again, I do a good lot, you know, single handed and always feel anxious about you and want you home. I felt your presence on Monday. I have got some work allotted to me for the Election because I haven't enough to do.

The Labour Party are having a dance on Sat evening at the Howard Hall. I expect I shall go, having promised to help with the coffee. Hope we shall have a large number present. It is for the election fund. Do you know that Lovell is to be the candidate? Of course we do not know when the election is to be but it is expected soon.

You will be sorry to hear that my cousin Marie passed away last week after a few days' illness, Flu and Pneumonia. It will be sad for Jack to come back, a stranger to his children, and she has worked pluckily to keep things going for him.

[...] One cannot help feeling morbid at times in any environment, but it must be shaken off. Everyone looks happy now and flags fly from nearly every window, all kinds. The street lamps are lighted and many curtains are left undrawn including mine.

[...] I have heard no more news of New Town but shall probably write to Miss Jefferies in a few days, the papers have not come she spoke about. They will be able to go ahead now, it is lovely to think work will now be construction instead of destruction. All the works here [were] closed until today. Now my space is gone and my news has run out. We all send our best love, still hoping to see you soon,

Your ever loving wife Lucy

Am airing all from wardrobe. You have nothing to <u>sell</u>, I ought to <u>buy</u> for you.

5. 'THESE LAST DAYS ARE THE MOST TRYING'

November 18th 1918

Dearest Lucy

Your letter is full of all the emotion to which human frailty is heir. I detect the quiet joy which runs deep and needs no outlet in noisy demonstration. Also sorrow for the lost friends in which I join you. I received quite a shock at the news. So Jack is one of the fortunate ones who have come through the whole campaign without a scratch and then to get this blow [...] As to the reply to Noel I am not greatly concerned because I feel it is all a frost. The more I think of the proposal the less it glitters and time alone will tell how it will turn out.

Glad to hear you helping in the election; having now the vote brings with it additional responsibilities with which you can help to mould the future, and if the future is to bring forth better results than the past woman must play a large part, as from her alone can come the impetus toward a saner, sweeter world for she inherits the race urge for conservation, whilst man, who has always been the fighter, inherits the force urge which is the desire for present satisfaction. I hope you will understand the gist of these few words as they are pregnant with meaning for the future generation and around them will the battle of Life be played.

I should much like to be out to help in the coming contest but [Lloyd George] is too astute to let us go until after that is over. Remember me to Casey when he comes and tell him I often think of his sweet music.

Your news re the Belgians is cheering as it omens well for the future. They will not live at enmity with the Germans but you will see them fraternizing with the German comrades. The collapse of the war is not a satisfactory thing from the allies' point of view in a political sense, because to treat with a socialist govt is quite a different matter from treating with a capitalist govt. The game of diplomacy has no place in socialist politics because openness and publicity coupled with justice and fair play completely rout the orthodox diplomat who wants always to make economic or territorial bargains the foundations of his treaties and above all will not allow the light of day to shine upon his works.

The terms of the Armistice are stiff, but, in spite of that, if a spirit of reasonableness does but prevail at the peace conference the whole business may be conducted in such a manner as will ensure an opportunity being given to all to recover sanity and a real peace become the aim of democracy. It is up to the common people to settle once and for all what is to rule in the earth, force with its wars in all phases of life or goodwill and cooperation, based upon the belief in the oneness of humanity no matter what colour, race or nationality.

[...] No need for you to air my wardrobe yet as I do not expect to get home for another three months if then [...] I send you all my love and lots of sweet nothings which mean so much to those who understand.

Yours ever Husband and comrade

32 North Avenue Letchworth
Nov 20. 1918

My Dear Frank

Your letters give me as much pleasure as mine do you and for the same reasons, we look for and find the personal touch and shows how much we long and look forward to the society of each other. It will not be long now I feel sure. We have now had 2 years of separation, and still wish for the company of each other. Enough of this, forgive me please.

We have no news yet about Guildford and you. Moss is applying for Ray Cree in the same way. I hope it comes off as Marshall wants this house and I only want to have one move. You see I am in a peculiar position. Mr [Noel] Palmer is [the] tenant and sublet to me. I could be turned out. Now he is leaving they want me to go too. Of course there are no houses to be had here at present. The Belgians are going very soon, some at least and Mr P is asking Ladd if there is a chance of one this end of town and I can ask Miss Bartholomew. Mr and Mrs [Noel] Palmer only went for the day to see their new home. Milton went too, also his mother and brother Maurice, M is very keen on having you, and a house (or cottage) is coming vacant in the village and he is speaking for it in case you can go. I have been wondering if I should go straight there and wait for you, or whether you would rather come back here. I should have to go and see it first and find out about school. I had hoped not to have to move till I had you to help, but what is to be will be and whatever comes to be done I can tackle. I should like your thoughts and advice on this matter. Of course I am not very keen on a fresh place till you come too, but I wondered if it would be best. New Town will not be ready yet, and you would be getting more fit perhaps in a beautiful place and congenial work. Of course I shall make them promise to take you on as soon as you may and try to get a wage settled. Just think this over well please, I don't suppose you would have any trouble to get work if you cared to stay here till you go to New Town and no doubt you could start work there as one of the earliest settlers; that is what I should like in any case [...]

I am glad to say my cold is much better but I cannot quite shake it off. About the needed rest: we could very well change places for a bit. Mr Palmer is more help than anyone I have had here and he always gets up first and lights the fire so they are not so bad. The children are very well and <u>all</u> go to Gym now on Monday evenings, that is 6d. 2d each and I had to buy them new rubber [shoes] but it will be worth it all, I want them to grow fine men and women. I had a serious talk with Dora on Sunday evening about herself and the race and her future and the advantage of getting all the education she can. She takes it all in with great intelligence and is not too young for it, she is developing very rapidly and is going to be a big girl. Her mind will also be large and opinions broad. You will be able to go teaching her where I leave off. Chrissie and Morris are growing very fast too. I often think they are quite different to what they were two years ago. I feel I have lived nearly a lifetime since you went away and have had so much experience. Will it be of any use to me? I am afraid I shall not be of much use in the coming election though workers are badly wanted for the Labour Party. You seem to get all (after) War news, and your remarks are generally about right. There is much to discuss and great problems to settle. I don't know how the late Munition workers like the great decrease of wages, it is such a big drop to 25/-, and 30/- girls up to 18 12/- with the cost of living as high as ever: it is not sufficient to live on or to be kept in lodgings. Of course people will gradually go back to their own homes and their late employment where possible. We heard yesterday that Germany was going to mobilise again and make another stand. It would be very dreadful, wouldn't it, to start [the] slaughter again. Last Sunday was thanksgiving services everywhere and I went to Howard Hall. Mr Sadler spoke on Humiliation and spoke with great courage of matters not mentioned by War parties.

I went to the dance on Sat and enjoyed myself very much, dancing with 4 different men. There was only a very small number present, 34, but we had a very good time, they are to be continued every other week. I am taking Dora next time. I shall have to stop now. We send you all our love and kind remembrances and regards from all enquiring friends.

We still hope to meet soon,

best loves from your ever loving wife

Lucy

32 North Avenue Letchworth Herts
Nov 24th 1918

My dear Frank

Your letter helped me very much. It gave me the suggestions I was wanting. Do not worry about me, I am not at all overwhelmed with my difficulties, though of course it troubles me a little to have to make a new home for you to come back to. This will make the third time you will have come into a house you have never seen. One thing I know, you trust me to do the best possible for you, but I must say it seems as if I am arranging your life for you at any rate for the immediate future. I do hope the move to Guildford is the right thing to do. It seems the best for your sake and you say the place is lovely. P says so too. I also will regret for several reasons leaving Letchworth, but we are doomed to have many changes it seems and it all means new friends and new opportunities for good if we use them.

5. 'THESE LAST DAYS ARE THE MOST TRYING'

The village is called Normandy and is 5 miles from Guildford and 3 from Aldershot. A station called Wanborough is about 10 minutes [away] and a good train service. Mr Palmer is going next Tuesday, coming back on the 14th to vote, and hopes to be able to move his furniture on the Mon. Mine could not go with his, but could go at the same time and if he has not found me a cottage he will store it for me. His house is not large, only 2 bedrooms, 2 sitting rooms and kitchen scullery. There are two houses together but the other one is for a market gardener. They have a staff of about 10 men which will be increased as soon as possible. There are 14 tomato houses, stables and outbuildings and you are wanted for repairing and keeping in order those barrows etc, general carpenter or wood-worker or everything else as far as I can make out. It seems to me what you will like to do. Is it? There are 41 acres and Jones has 6 so you can guess the size of the place.

I must see Mrs Middleton before I finally decide. She will have to see if I can still have help because we must live and I cannot possibly keep us all. How glad I shall be when you are allowed to work for us again. I shall of course sell the piano and perhaps the couch and the big double bed and get one of Palmer's small ones instead and also have his rush pull-out chair. I will take those long planks and posts of mahogany [...] and all that is in the coal cellar. It may be useful for you.

I have asked again about the amalgamation fee due to me, and Eastman says I shall have it direct from Birmingham soon. I have not got my agreement but believe I have to give the Cooperative Society the option of buying the business, but I <u>may</u> go to see Pounds. I have asked for this agreement several times [...] I should like to get settled for Christmas in case you come home, but I am not hoping too much. Of course, I know it will not be before the election. Am sorry I had this cold so bad, I could not go out with bills last week. We are disappointed that Lovel has withdrawn and a new man will be standing as Labour candidate, such a pity I think.

I went to Spirella Hall with Mr Palmer last Sat eve to hear Lord Robert Cecil, my first visit there. I expect he will be returned again but, as you say, this is not an important election, just a scrap one to try and clean up the mess and straighten out a bit. There are so many important matters to arrange and Lord Robert C said there [are] troublous times ahead, or words to that effect, I am afraid so too. I should like to come again to see you if possible before I leave here, if I go and you stay. How uncertain everything is, we can only arrange from day to day it seems […]

I must now stop, keep well and cheerful, we shall meet soon.

Lots of love from us all

Your loving wife Lucy

Harvey Smith has bought the goat.

Dora will write to you next week

November 25th 1918

Dear Lucy

Your letter is so full of problems that I do not know which one to tackle first […]

Now as to future arrangements I can only suggest, of course, but you must act as you think fit. Firstly about the bungalow. They cannot turn you out, and if necessary you could get any magistrate to give you a restrainment order, so make your mind easy on that score. Ask Brunt as to this if you feel inclined. For my part I say get out as quickly as you can. I know you feel like that too. I suppose Noel is moving down to Guildford at once and that the house he is going to is fairly large. If so why not all go together and then you could be ready to take the cottage when it falls empty. At any rate the furniture could go with his even if he cannot put you all up for the time being. He could surely store it in a room for you whilst you could get a lodging in Letchworth for a time, or stay with Katie for a time, or perhaps Mrs Thomas would be pleased to welcome all our little family. Mrs Williams could accommodate you perhaps.

I quite agree about taking the cottage and will accept the job tentatively, as the scheme I there worked out for myself could just as easily be

5. 'THESE LAST DAYS ARE THE MOST TRYING'

carried into effect at Guildford as elsewhere. The scheme would only be put into operation if the job is not a success, so I need not elaborate it to you as it will afford you food for thought to try and guess what it is and needless to say you will not talk of it.

[...] Even if you succeed in getting a cottage I suggest you end all but absolute necessities with Noel's move and do as the Belgians did, be content with a bed, fire and cup and saucer etc. and visit your friends when you feel the need for looking at pictures etc. It is a great pity you are to have all this trouble, but I can see no other way out of it. Is the Adult School let? If not, try that, as it would just suit for the time and I dare say they would let you have it. I have no more suggestions unless you buy a caravan and live in that which I am sure would suit the children but you would find somewhat cramping during the winter time.

You are mistaken when you classify Ray Cree with myself as the position is quite different. He is one of the HO scheme chaps and entitled to his freedom at the end of twelve months' compulsory employment, whilst I am a prisoner who has refused to make a bargain with the government. I have not the least reason to think that they will grant Noel's request so don't count on it at all. The absence of reply is just what I expected. Put not thy faith in autocrats.

[...] As to Germany remobilising you must be wrong, as it is quite impossible for her to do that. She is no longer dominated by one central force and [...] all the little states which comprise the German Empire are busy with their own internal affairs although linked up loosely by the socialist movement amongst them.

I hope my suggestions will be useful to you and that you will soon see a way through all your difficulties. You said that when Noel came to stay with you again it would lead to something, and by jingo it has. It seems to mean leaving Letchworth and all old friends and starting afresh. I shall regret this for many reasons but as you know I have always felt that Letchworth was only to be a sojourn by the way and as much as most of our friends are scattering too and the island is small after all, we shall meet them again from time to time. Put all the work you can into the election and give my word of cheer to the comrades who are working hard for the cause of the people [...]

I trust your next letter will contain some suggestion of the brighter days which I feel sure are ahead for us. Take courage and struggle on my brave comrade and all will come right. Accept my love and heartfelt desire for our speedy reunion

Your loving Hubby FTS

December 2nd 1918

Dearest Wifey

[...] Of course I know that the dream is the reality and will come true again, whilst prison is only the transient thing but the present is very much with me just now. Perhaps it is the weather which certainly is not good and dull days do react upon us. But enough of this, to borrow a phrase from you, am glad my suggestions appear useful to you and as to instructions I would not dare issue such things. Are you not a modern woman and would you not feel it an indignity to be ordered to do anything by your husband?

Your description of the village has given me food for thought. I do hope you will land at a decent cottage. As to coming to a house I have not seen, as you say it is not a new experience and there is a spice of novelty about it. Some people go through life placidly and smoothly, seeming to get no startling incidents to disturb them, whilst our lives seem to be all incidents and no placidity. I hope the future does contain a peaceful time in which we can look back on the past and feel that our time has not been ill spent. I think that the prospects you hold out to me, regarding the new employment, are A1, as there seems to be infinite variety and variety is the salt of life, just as constancy in love is the chain anchor upon which all happiness depends.

I cannot say how eagerly I look forward to coming amongst you all again. Undoubtedly I shall find you all changed to a certain degree as the events of the past five years have wrought a change in everybody, whether they are aware of it or no. I expect to find the children grown both in body and in mind and though I naturally should have preferred to have watched the growth on the spot, as it were, I am sure that I shall better understand them through my absence, because the change takes place so gradually that it is almost imperceptible to those who are constantly with them […]

Have you written to Mother yet? If not try and do so as soon as you can. I often think of her.

I shall have to spend a day or two in London so as to buy tools and things for those I possess will not be sufficient to meet all requirements.

[…] The New Town book is a long time coming but I do not despair for the Quakers move slowly when they are on a big thing. Don't trouble about Lovel. He was not the right sort of chap for the job and has been useful as a peg to start operations with. The women should have run a candidate but of course as Lady Lytton is related to Lord HE such a thing would be bad form. You cannot realise how much our political machine is a family affair. I had meant to keep politics out of this but King Charlie's head must appear.

As I have exhausted all my suggestions for your future in my last letter I will not add any more, beyond saying could you sell the swing but keep the rope belonging to it and so I'll make them another if it is needed when I get home again. Isn't it rather running our heads into it to move so near to Aldershot seeing that it is such a large military centre? Did not Noel stay there for some time years ago?

I will send you the order form to visit me next week but if you find you must come before then you can come without it. I would prefer to see you next week and will put my books ready for you to take back as they do mount up so, and I do not want to hire a cart when I leave here to take them away […]

Kiss all the youngsters from Daddy and accept the blank space as being filled with all the sweet things you would have me say. Kind remembrances to all the friends and all power be given you to carry you over your arduous task of house hunting and removal. I expect Morris will enjoy it. I trust they are all well and the Flue will not come near to any of you. I eagerly look forward to you reply. I send you my Love and Desire

Yours ever Frank

32 North Avenue Letchworth Herts
Dec 3rd 1918

My Dear Frank

I did not receive your letter till this afternoon and as they come so regularly in the morning of course I wondered all sorts of things [...] Lately I think we have had more difficulty to keep contact by writing, at least I know you have, myself I can always feel I am talking to you while writing.

Yes, my life is very real and I believe I <u>live</u> every moment of it. But I must admit that the dull days of last week made me feel very 'off', or was it your spirit heavy with me? You know how much we rely on one another for strength. I shall be glad when you get home or the acc may be overdrawn on one or the other, eh. As you say these last days (we hope) are the most trying for the uncertainty as the 'duration of separation'.

Anyway we <u>will</u> be strong now, won't we, you in your small corner and I in mine (large one). I feel a great responsibility rests on me to decide what to do for the best. Mr Palmer went off this morning and will look out a cottage and let me know [...] I have got some boxes and tubs from Palmer but I am still undecided about waiting for you. The Belgians are leaving here on the 10th Dec to the 13th so there will be houses, but they will want doing up, I should think, so in any case I expect to spend Christmas here.

Katie wants to have the girls for a week in the New Year to take them out. I have written a card suggesting the probable move but have had no answer yet. <u>They</u> will not argue, I know, to a change again! I shall most likely take the opportunity of leaving them, and staying for a week or so at Mrs Thomas's or elsewhere. I wish you could be in London at the same time. My fowls, the four new ones, will go straight to Mr Palmer's till I can house them, the others I intend to sell for Christmas. Mrs Clarke has bought the goat.[136]

[…] As you know the Polling day is the 14th but we shall not know the count till the 28th. I am doing my little best. I think after all this is an important election tho' the next one will be more so. I am afraid our new candidate does not stand such a good chance as Lowey but they seem to think the village are sound and he is an agricultural Union Man. I do not think we were ready to run a woman, but I hope some of those who are running will get in. Have you heard about the Albert Hall meetings and the electricians cutting the fuse because the hall was refused or rather cancelled? Of course it was granted in a few hours so Labour got a victory.

[…] The site for New Town is chosen and they want £75,000 to buy it. I don't know where. Mrs Crowley promised me the book as soon as it was out. Mrs Middleton says once the place secured it will soon go ahead, so 'Normandy' will be only by the way. Then I hope our days of peace will come. One thing, we have not stagnated you know, and although your body is confined your thought is free as air and your mind is busy all the time in the land of make believe if you like. I must stop now. Dora is writing you a little letter. We all send our best love to our dear daddy and husband.

Your loving wife Lucy

December 16th 1918

Dearest Lucy

Once again I sit to pen you some thoughts. I feel you must be a trifle anxious as to my health so I will say at once that my pain has left me and I am now as usual. I trust both you and the children are in good

---

136   Harvey Smith must have changed his mind about the goat (see 24 November 1918).

health and will remain so. The election has come and gone and I hope the results will prove satisfactory as the most ardent enthusiast could wish. As for myself I feel that the true issues at stake have been obscured and that the workers will once again find that they have been cheated. But enough of this subject.

You tell me that although my body is incarcerated my mind is free to roam where it will. That is true but liberty always becomes licence unless there are natural boundaries to keep it in order. Social customs hatch law and order from these boundaries in ordinary life and thus keep one in check. With thought too, the everyday contact with life, the family circle, papers, books and events give balance and tone to one's thought but if released from all such restraints and forced in upon itself the human mind must either stagnate, revolve upon itself and thus see all things out of proportion or else indulge in the license of invention.

[...] I have been reading *Dombey and Son* again. It is surprising how fresh these old stories are. I think it a good habit to read books over again. You get them fixed in the memory and points which are overlooked in the excitement of first reading come out clearly and a better estimate of the author's purpose is obtained. Of course there are some books which will not bear re-reading and their name is legion in these days when everyone endeavours to get into print.

I am adding to my very small stock of knowledge by reading how to doctor animals. It is very interesting but if anyone wishes to keep horses or sheep, pigs, cows etc it would be well not to take a course of training first as the impression one gathers is that the animals are always ill and but rarely recover from most attacks. However some time will elapse before I shall be buying stock so the fearfulness will have passed away by then. Perhaps this is the result of too large a dose, eh [...]

5. 'THESE LAST DAYS ARE THE MOST TRYING'

Dec 19.18
32 North Avenue Letchworth Herts

My Dear Frank

I certainly have been feeling rather anxious about you and I am very glad you are a little better. I hope you won't get the pain again. I am really very sorry I do not answer your questions in your letters, I thought I did when I could. The words 'you notice I forgot' sounds like Eastman and not as if I read your letters through a dozen times and carry each one about with me even to bed till I get the next.

[...] I can quite understand how you must feel about so much time and liberty for thought, I myself have often wished I could or need only think of <u>one</u> thing at once, so many different occupations and so many people and so much knowledge of outside affairs makes one's brain inclined to whirl. I am glad to tell you I am having a rest and more peace and room in the house.

Mr Palmer took Mrs P and baby back with him on Monday morning, they will come back some time in Jan to move when their house is cleared of people. He had not been able to find me a house, so I told him we should have to wait, in the meantime what about staying here, he said go somewhere else if I could get, so I am applying for the one next door to Mrs Williams. I think that Marshall cannot turn me out while Mr Palmer pays him my rent, it must be Mr P that gives possession. Marshall is nothing to do with me, all the same I do not want to be awkward and shall get out if possible, but not to leave Letchworth just yet. I shall do as I think best and when you come home will do just as <u>you</u> wish.

You do not mention my visit to you. I always am glad to see you and to feel and know you really are still in the flesh, it helps me so much to go on and renews hope of you being home with us all again some day, although the time is so brief it seems like a dream. It makes quite a day out for me; I do not get home till nearly 3.30. I have found a Cafe where I can get a cup of coffee and bread and <u>butter</u> for 5d and a large pleasant room, only I always wish you were with me [...]

Yes the Election is over (this one) and we all wonder what will be the result, seems a long while to have to wait a fortnight to know. I went to 'Greens' meeting on Friday night, and was not home till after 11. It was in the Picture Palace and was full up [...] We had enthusiasm from speakers and audience and the women seemed to turn up well for voting, Wittimore was full of it when he came here, you know I suppose he is an ILPer and to think how he went on in 1914, do you remember? G Thomas is still at Dartmoor, altho' his year was up in Sept and Mrs Thomas has not seen him since she was here when you was home. Jack is also there. Ray Cree too. Also Wiltshire, he expected to be home last week but was kept back for another month. Frances is still at Shillington and White is working at his own trade in Hitchin, Clarke is still free not at home.

[...] I am writing to your mother again this week. I should like her to see the children, I do not think she is happy with Alf's wife. She told Katie she always got on so well with me, I hope she is at Carrie's when our girls go up to London. You will be glad to know my new chickens have laid 2 eggs today, they are fixed at 5½ each, so I must keep count and pay myself back the 2.10.0. 3 of my old ones look like laying too, so perhaps they won't die yet.

I find I am on my fifth page, hope it will not matter. We are all well and try to keep smiling in spite of our troubles which seem all manmade but we forgive all our enemies and love everyone. The children all send lots of love and plenty of kind loving thoughts from everyone you know or who knows you. You know how my heart goes out to you and all my love with it. I hope and pray we shall soon be together again. May you have peace and health,

Your loving wife, Lucy.

5. 'THESE LAST DAYS ARE THE MOST TRYING'

32 North Avenue, Letchworth
Sunday evening, Dec 22nd 1918

My dear Frank

I am feeling a bit sad and lonely so thought I would start my letter to you. I have just answered your mother's letter, she sends her love to you and hopes you will be home soon, everyone says that now and seem to expect it.

It has been very wet and rough all day and we have not been out. The Esperanto class gave a little concert last night. Dora only had a sentence or two, but she sang with the others (5 of them) of course all in Esperanto. Mr Cubbon was there, also Mr Brunt. I asked him about that book and he knows where it is and it is quite all right.

The children are quite happy and full of Christmas, went to the Common yesterday for ivy and decorated the rooms. Dora made a lovely laurel wreath for your photo. Of course they often talk of you and wish you were here – we should do this or you would say that or sing something that we remember, they all sing like birds.

[...] My space has run out as the girls have taken a page. I have not written all my thoughts to you. Remember I am <u>always</u> thinking of you and sending my love across space to you.

Your wife, Lucy

December 23rd 1918

Dear Lucy

Your letter was just what I needed to put me right again. After my bad turn I had become very down, as the old ladies say, and could only look on the black side of things, due I suppose to loss of vitality through not getting my usual outdoor exercise, but am feeling quite myself again.

Isn't [it] wonderful how the time flies away, here we are at another Xmas. I have just enjoyed reading your letter of last year in which you described how the children enjoyed themselves and how even you managed to find the time passed pleasantly even though I were not with you. My sincerest wish is that you may this year have a happy day too and it is certain that the horizon is much clearer now as it can only be a question of weeks to our reunion. The war is over and peace will come speedily because delay is so dangerous to the financial and commercial interest of this country. There is bound to be a rush for the markets of the world and the longer England keeps her war strength the slower she will be in recovering her previous peace condition of industry.

I don't suppose for a moment that things will ever be the same but somehow or other the authorities in these matters do not learn their lessons very quickly and they will try to go on in their old ruts until compelled by the forces to alter their course. The arising of Labour will mean a new outlook and a new moral tone, if only Labour can be established as the first charge of industry, and thus a sound subsistence level established. Then, in spite of the greedy competitiveness with which society is permeated, we shall see the coming into being of a nobler and better race. A race whose ideals will be large enough to embrace all mankind in a fellowship of love and service.

[…] I should like you to get Chrissie a tambourine and Morris a triangle as I am sure they would appreciate them. These things will help them in their plays and dances and if Morris has any musical talent in him he will find an outlet through this channel.

[…] Lucy, dear, please send me some Esperanto books. Get some of the periodicals if possible as the subject matter is good.

My letter does not convey what I should like to say but you must fill in the gaps believing that my thoughts are always with you and my love constant.

Your loving husband Frank

5. 'THESE LAST DAYS ARE THE MOST TRYING'

December 30th 1918 Bedford Prison

Dear Lucy

I got your letter on Xmas Day. Sorry to hear that you were lonely and sad. Perhaps your liver is out of order, you had better try a course of regular diet for a while, that, together with a strict routine of exercises, may work wonders. Perhaps you are pining for the 'flesh pots of Egypt' or are feeling the loss of your genial lodger who has been so indulgent to you. All things are fleeting in this life so make the best of it and cheer up.

The weather seems to be making the best of it for I am sure the rise of the sun from his bed of down, ie the clouds has been glorious on several occasions lately. If I stop in prison much longer I shall become a sun worshipper his beauty is so real and his significance is unbounded.

There are one or two things in your letter that call for answer so I will attend to them before I forget. Glad to hear news of Mother and to know that she is well. Also that the chickens are doing their duty in that sphere of life in which it has pleased the Lord to place them as the prayer book has it [...]

Do try and send me the Esperanto book I asked for as I am making headway with the language and wish to keep up my interest. As you know I am a bit of a butterfly. 'No not in looks' but in jumping from one interest to another sticking at nought [...] If by any chance you should see a copy of Shelley's poems or could borrow one I should like to have it. I have had my interest aroused in Mythology and his poems are a good exposition of the Greek myths. I'm afraid that from a commercial point of view all my reading will be useless but I will endeavour to make amends when I again get my liberty [...]

On reading the letter through I notice I have omitted to mention my state of health. I therefore rectify the omission (I am well). Trusting that both you and the children are in the enjoyment of good health and that you have recovered you usual cheerfulness of spirit, I send you all my love. F

PS Wish Chrissie Many Happy returns of her birthday from Daddy.

THE CONSCIENTIOUS OBJECTOR'S WIFE

32 North Avenue, Letchworth
January 1st 1919

My dear Frank.

Once more it is New Year's day. I hope this will be better than the last two for us all. Glad to know you are <u>Well</u>. I am <u>better</u>, the children are best, at least Morris is. The girls are not home yet. I expect them tomorrow, on the one train they can come on without changing. This will be their first experience of travelling alone; how they are growing up. An invitation came for them to go to [the] Browns [on] Wilbury Road to a tea party today. This is the first time they have been taken notice of since Wilfred was here 2½ years ago. I meet Mr and Mrs Brown sometimes. It would have been a dreadfully rough night to come home from. We are very lonely, just we two, but [Morris] likes to have me to himself. We read and play draughts, which he likes very much and we go out. I treated him to the pictures last night, 6 o'clock show with Miss Wilding. She is leaving her old ladies in March and going to [the] Palmers in June.

I hear that Wiltshire is home and I saw Francis on Mon. He has been home, very ill, but is now recovering. He sends you greetings. We are all disappointed about the election results, all those who are at all pacifist are turned out, Snowden, Henderson, Macdonald etc.[137] I expect you know there was a big Coalition Majority. I hope the country won't be sorry for what they have done. Only one woman in and she

---

137 The 'Coupon election' or 'Khaki election' of 1918 was the first in which women could vote, and returned a large victory for the incumbent coalition government of David Lloyd George. Labour politician Philip Snowden lost his seat but was re-elected in 1922. Arthur Henderson, who would become leader of the Labour Party three times, lost his seat but would be re-elected in 1919 in a by-election. Ramsay MacDonald, founder of the Labour Party with Henderson and Keir Hardie, lost his seat but would be re-elected for a Welsh constituency in 1922. Constance Markievicz was the first woman to be elected, for a Dublin constituency, and like others of her party, Sinn Féin, did not take her seat, since they refused to take or affirm the oath of allegiance to the Crown, which all British Members of Parliament must do.

a Sinn Fein. So many people did <u>not</u> vote at all. Katie said Dad wanted to vote Labour (coming on) and then said he wouldn't go at all but she persuaded him to vote for Dickenson but he is not in.

Well, we had quite a nice time in London: children happy and good as gold, so made things very cheerful, although Katie had muscular rheumatism and could not stand upright. I had to Dr her. They still feast but Dad could not get any drink (what a blessing to many). I took the children to see Carrie on Christmas morning; of course she wept [...] I will see Miss Bartholomew for the Esperanto books you want and will send you a Shelley [...] Mr Fox has come to Letchworth as the people are leaving his house. I have not seen him.

I have not got a house yet, so no answer from 'Morris', Mrs Williams' landlord. It is rather expensive but the convenience is worth it and only 3/- more than this and easily let too.

[...] Of course you know a lot of Belgians have left here and more going. There will be 120 houses vacant and 150 applicants, without me.

[...] I note what you say about a tambourine and triangle. Morris wants a flute! Will see what can be done. He also wants socks and boots. It is quite nice to go out at night now, all the lamps are alight. How did we endure all the time of darkness? Our dawn is coming too, soon I hope. Now I must stop, roll on time with my next letter. Have done as you asked with the two you sent me this week.

Love from Morris and

Your loving wife Lucy

℘

32 North Avenue Letchworth
January 2nd 1919

My dear Frank

I do hope you will forgive the delay in answering your welcome letter, but last evening when I settled to write I had an attack of my old enemy neuralgia, and all this morning I was out and this afternoon the girls went to a party at Nellie Briant's house, and I had to make an extra fuss of Morris and read to him till he went to bed, and then the girls came home and have just settled them to bed and having my supper while writing this, 9 o'clock now. My time is very fully occupied. I am sorry to say the children have all got bad colds and coughs. I am afraid they have been indoors too much. I also had a bad turn of Sciatica, [it] took me on Sunday and I could not move. It was better on Sunday afternoon, though it stopped me going to the social and I have not heard if it went off well. The weather has been very damp and that may have caused it. I believe a great feature of the Socials now is the performance of the Labour Choir, under the direction of Mr Gomersal and it is very good too. We went to Mrs Gregory's last Friday and Chrissie had her birthday party on Sat; only 4 little girls and I could get no margarine, only ¼ of butter to last the week, and I had had none since before Christmas but as long as I can get nutter I can manage. The children enjoyed themselves and I provided a grand feast out of nothing as usual.

We went to a Christmas at Bedford House. Miss Wales next door [to] Miss W was there too with her eight, making 15 children.[138] They had rare fun. It is wonderful to watch children enjoying life and its pleasures and they ought to have plenty of it I think. The seriousness of it comes soon enough.

[...] I don't know whether it is really more cold than usual or whether it is the quality of our food does nourish sufficiently. Miss Lawes holds this view, she told me yesterday; she had never felt the cold so much. She misses so much dried fruits: currants, dates, prunes etc. which are not impossible to get, are quite beyond people only receiving a small income. They are very sad just now and Miss L very rebellious. The sailor brother has been drowned. He leaves a young wife and a little boy of 3 in Canada. This sort of thing one is always hearing and makes one wonder what do we live for [...]

Chrissie has got a new game, Snakes and Ladders, and Morris dominoes so they have now plenty of amusement but they will be glad to go back to school. The girls go next Tuesday and Morris a week later.

138   Probably refugees and/or evacuees.

5. 'THESE LAST DAYS ARE THE MOST TRYING'

I certainly have less time when they are at home and seem more tired. Of course there is always more to do in the winter time and the days are very short just now. I sometimes wish we slept all the winter; it would suit me fine, only it would be wasting one's life.

I do not think I have anything more to say this time, only to ask if you would like the Adult School handbook or lesson sheet with daily readings. Will you let me know if I may send them to you?

Now I must stop. Sorry the letter is not so long as usual, but perhaps more news next week. The children all send love to Daddy and mine as usual to my dear hubby.

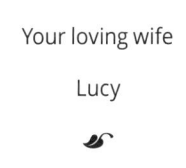

Your loving wife

Lucy

January 6th 1919
Bedford Prison

Dear Lucy

Your first letter this year to hand. It is not nearly as newsy as the letter of last year nor does it cover so large a field of social welfare. I am afraid you [are] unwell or at least as little faint by the way. You must cheer me up and make an effort as Dickens says.

I know the time of separation has been long but surely you have had some compensation for my absence. Friends have rallied round you and I feel sure you have had opportunities of getting closer to the children than perhaps would otherwise have been possible. Just compare yourself and the children with Carrie and her family. I think much unhappiness can and does come to homes in which the father is placed too much to the fore.

Your picture of Morris and self playing draughts gave me great pleasure and I trust the companionship between you may never be broken [...]

As to myself I can say that in spite, possibly because, of my imprisonment I have not altogether wasted my time. I have made progress in Esperanto which may be useful if I ever get the chance to travel on the continent and will certainly be a great help to the getting in touch with progressive movements in other countries. I have had the opportunity to think over and thrash out many of the problems which have perplexed me and have done a considerable amount of reading, some of which has been useful. After all our lives are not given us just to get enjoyment from but that we may play our part in the great programme of progress laid down by the Master Mind. I am well aware that we differ as to what constitutes progress but in spite of that there is a guiding star for us all and it comes to each separately. I mean the knowledge of right or the voice of conscience, this must determine our action and if we follow whither it leads all will be well.

You are downhearted over the election. It is disappointing from one point of view, I admit, but when one remembers how persistently the glamour of victory [was promoted] by the British, and no mention of the other Allies and the part they have played or the uprising on the part of the enemy, coupled with almost fanatical hero-worship of [Lloyd George], one has cause to be proud that there are as many workers who are not led away but are determined to work out their own destiny. Promises by politicians of the LG type which are not carried out are like fowls, they come home to roost and the future contains some very grave and serious problems which will require careful handling. Clap trap does not cure social ills any more than Beecham's pills cure poverty.[139]

[...]

---

139 Beecham's Pills had been marketed for decades as a cure-all remedy for a wide range of complaints, both physical and psychological.

5. 'THESE LAST DAYS ARE THE MOST TRYING'

32 North Avenue Letchworth
January 7th 1919

My dear Frank

It seems my letters to you lately do not give you the satisfaction or pleasure they used. I am sorry but I do not intend to convey the impression that anything is wrong with me, altho' when I wrote to you last week I had rheumatism badly in neck and shoulders and knees and felt the miss of the girls. I am quite better again now.

I am afraid I cannot agree as to the compensation for your absence. I have perhaps kept closer to the children so that they should not miss you very much but of course I cannot be you as well as myself. As for comparing us with Carrie and her children, or any of them, we don't come on the same page. The girls heard Katie and Carrie say I was wonderful and they cannot understand how we can be cheerful. I hope too that my son and I will always be pals, I think so.

I did not feel equal to New Resolutions. I don't think I have ever omitted to before but they so often come to nought. We can only go on from day to day, so many changes happen in a year nowadays. This time last year I never expected such a long holiday in lovely Devonshire.

I saw Mr Fox on Sat. He finds it colder here but he will have to stay awhile […]

I cannot say that last year was altogether a failure although it contained some, and some disappointments too. For one thing the Adult School has been. The last 3 weeks I was the only one present. We are having the Annual Meeting tomorrow when I give up office and Mrs Myles too. The last year certainly contained experiences, one of which I cannot ever forget and seems always with me, but [a] change of house and you home to talk to and be with, especially at night, will soon wear it off. I am glad you feel you have not altogether wasted your time and perhaps you will be able to help me when problems perplex. No, our lives are not given for enjoyment, but for the progress of ourselves as well as the race. I feel sure it must be so, else why these trials and experiences? This short span for each one cannot be all, but that I am content to leave, the next life is of little interest as no-one really knows or remembers (for sure) a previous existence [...]

Katie seemed very poorly and the girls said she was really ill one day while they were there. She is much happier than she used to be and Jack is still around; that is the reason. He lives in the house and is very good to her, makes her take care of herself and does it for her. Dad just accepts it and takes no notice. Of course they did not talk about you, only asked how you were and when coming home. We avoided subjects we do not agree on. We have made our stand and they know it.

On looking further into the Election results, the position is not so bad and not so hopeless as at first appeared and as the [*Labour Leader*] has it 'our propaganda must be unceasing and our organisation strengthened. We shall soon be in the flowing tide' [...] Another correspondent says 'the five ILP spokesmen in the last parliament have as the *Times* truly says "paid the price" of loyalty to their principles, but I fancy the organs of reaction are rejoicing too soon at the "annihilation" of the ILP. Mr MacDonald and Mr Snowden and their colleagues are as powerful out of Parliament as in and the ILP is not robbed of its spirit by a parliamentary defeat.'

I have not got a house yet. I called on Mr Morris on Sat but he would not give me an answer then. Miss Whale next door is leaving for London and would like me to have stored her furniture, so that would have been one room let till June and I should have had no increased rent, and then another room to spare. That would have suited me nicely but as she was to know tomorrow morning and move on Friday and I have heard nothing yet, I may consider that is off and not to be.

[...] Mr Eastman wrote on Monday telling me to send him my book to save rewriting as I could no longer continue to collect! Cheek. I answered by return that I wanted to be quite clear about purchase of business before I finally gave up. I am still awaiting a reply.

I had a letter last Friday from CO Information Bureau, Adam St, Adelphi asking your previous employment, if it was still open, I said doubtful, and if there was any other sympathetic employer willing to give you

5. 'THESE LAST DAYS ARE THE MOST TRYING'

work. I gave Bradley Pass and Milton … Guildford as he has applied to War Office for you. A reply was asked for immediately, of course I did, by return. I never heard of them before, nor has Mrs Middleton. Perhaps it is some idea about release on the expiration of your sentence as you have done over two years. That was one of the promises that was not fulfilled, and with men who had done one year on the scheme, some seem to get out alright. Mr Thomas said last year there were 1,200 odd at Dartmoor and now there is only between 300–400. Of course some can't stand the work and exposure. Jack is very unhappy about accepting the scheme, but they have not got the Friends in London so you can understand why he did it.

Rowntree Gillet is coming here soon to speak at Howgills. I might get to see him. I have heard nothing of Newtown, but have you heard of a Commonwealth Community to be opened near Ross? I was told [the] Wiltshires were joining them eventually. He is home and started work at Kidds (temporary), soon find something better. The pay is small and work impossible some days. Yesterday I received interest 1/5 (2/- less income tax) for the London City and Midland on Stock, to be signed by you. (I think it can wait.) I believe it is what Miss Jefferies spoke about, but I have received no papers in your name, as she said I should, so now I must write to her.

I have not said before how nice it is to go out at night and have the street lamps and electric lights to guide us from the ditches […]

I hope I have not exceeded the limit in this letter but the sheets are smaller than usual. Paper still keeps very dear, but some things have come down a bit and we shall soon do without coupons.

I hope you are well. Love from us all.

Your loving wife Lucy

THE CONSCIENTIOUS OBJECTOR'S WIFE

January 13th 1919
Bedford Prison

Dearest Lucy

Your last letter was an evidence of the fact that you were in a better frame of mind, for which I am thankful. I like to think of you as always cheerful and bright, surmounting all the obstacles, as they rise in your path, with a courage born of faith. Sorry to hear of the Rheumatism. It must be catching for I myself have been suffering a little with it. The weather keeps mild and the sunrises and sunsets are very beautiful but do not last very long. I hope we do not get so severe a winter as last year, but time is rolling on nicely.

I do not know whether you find time drags or not but for myself the weeks fly by which is a great consolation as each week brings us nearer to freedom and to reunion with those we love. Do not dwell too much on a <u>speedy</u> reunion but just wait patiently. It will come all right. Am sorry to hear about the Adult School but perhaps it will revive. How is the Men's school? Have you paid them a visit recently? I have heard nothing concerning the Ross Community but should you get the details please send on the information as communes are in the air just now.

Now for a startler. Are you willing to go to the South Sea Islands and settle there? After getting your breath and giving the matter a little consideration perhaps you can reply. I have just read the life of Henry Drummond who was a great man in the Presbyterian Church and he paid a visit to those islands some thirty years ago and describes them as containing all that man can desire. To be sure the natives were cannibals, but such trifles as those should not deter COs.

The scenery is magnificent and the temperature is subtropical. One can get three crops a year and grow everything one wants from maize to melons. As to clothes, well the natives wear but little and they work less. Drummond says they are better off than Scottish crofters. Conscription and such like troubles would vanish and general elections would be things to read of but not take part in, whilst the women's question would solve itself. Capital is necessary of course, so perhaps it is as well that you have got such a goldmine in your chickens from which you may perhaps draw that which will be required. We could buy a fairly large estate for a small sum and native wages are low compared with European. Do not mention this scheme to anyone but think well on it.

I have received Shelley and it is like having an old friend from home to see the familiar binding. A world without books to a man who can read would be a solitary world indeed. I am at present reading a most interesting book by A Upward, *The Divine Mystery,* in which he describes the origin and growth of religion. It is most interesting and I am afraid if widely read will cause a great stir amongst some of the orthodox folks. For instance he connects the taking of the sacrament with the ancient rite of human sacrifice, when it was supposed the virtue of the victim passed to him who should partake of the remains. I will tell you more of this when once again we sit together round the fireside.

Esperanto books not yet to hand but I await them patiently [...]

I hope you manage to hear Rowntree Gillett as he is sure to have a cheerful message. Sorry New Town does not seem to be making headway but we must have patience. Evidently the parent company is not formed yet [...]

32 North Avenue Letchworth
January 15th 1919

My dear Frank

Glad to say I feel much better. Had a very busy time since I wrote you last week, helping [the] Palmers move. Mrs P did not come because the baby would need all her attention, so he came last Thurs eve, and we were Friday and Sat packing etc. The house and furniture was in a dirty broken condition. He went back on Sat eve leaving Miss Wilder, Mr Cree and I to see things in the van. Leeke packed goods in [the] Railway van. Such a day too was Mon and Tuesday; the horse broke down so could not finish till Tues. They like Normandy very much and still want you. I told him you would go for a holiday, perhaps later on, and see how you liked it.

I shall probably be going to the first house opposite here, Mrs Hardy's; her husband was discharged last Sat and has work in London. My application will come before the Directors last Tuesday and I shall hear by post. Mr Pearsal is giving the preference to Soldiers' wives, but Mr Ladd the Sec. said he would do what could for me. The house and garden will be small but convenient and the move easy and cheap, so I hope it comes off.

You certainly gave me a startler by what you proposed. You mentioned it before but I did not think you were serious. It would require great consideration of course. Would the climate suit Chrissie? I'm afraid not, and what about New Town? Aren't we getting too old to make a fresh start in a new country? I should like very much to travel for a year or two. Of course we can only think of such plans. We may all have to leave England. There are rumours of you all being sent to France for four years on reconstruction so it is well to prepare ourselves for anything in the way of surprises or shocks, more separation or anything.

I have no details about the Ross Community and have heard no more.[140] I saw Mrs Wiltshire at the Social on Sunday evening which was a great success, such a social feeling of fellowship, everyone seemed cheerful, I quite enjoyed it, only it is not nice to come home alone and all the children asleep. They are very good about me going out. We have started our Adult school on Tuesday evening again, now there is no fear of raids. We had only a few [people] last Tues but it was such a night yesterday, and today the weather is lovely, quite a feeling of spring in the air. I am sitting with the kitchen window open and washing blowing in the sunshine outside. We shall miss the openness but never mind; perhaps every disadvantage has a compensation.

[...]. The women's Labour Party are now holding meetings once a week at Common View, with the idea of the coming election to do with the changing of Rural to Urban, and local matters [that] should be of interest to women, if parliamentary [ones] do not. I heard of such a lot who did not vote at the Election because they did not understand and

---

140 This may have been a village community scheme like that of Jordans.

5. 'THESE LAST DAYS ARE THE MOST TRYING'

did not know their husband's views and would not go against them. I believe even the majority of men do not understand politics.

I have two Esperanto books for you; hope you will find them of interest. Tickle tells me he has sent you some *Punch*;[141] hope they will help to pass the time. I do not find the time drags at all heavily. I am too busy and even the time you have been away does not seem so long, unless I look back and think what a lot has happened and how we have all grown.

[...] Love from us all hoping you keep well and strong in spirit.

Yours ever Lucy

20.1.1919
Bedford Prison

Mia Amata Edzinon

You last letter cheered me muchly. It was newsy. So the Palmers have gone at last, lock stock and barrel. I thought somehow you would be requisitioned for the job. I hope your own will soon be over

I am pleased with your arrangements and hope that Mr Pearsall will give a favourable reply.

Now as to the South Sea Bubble, it is only a bubble as far as I am concerned but I thought I would send you a shock and had a quiet laugh over it to myself. My work lies here in England if there is anything more for me to do. There are troublous times ahead and it seems cowardly to me to run away and find a place to take it easy in.

As to the rumour you sent, I suppose you did not trace it to its source. I do not believe it because it is absurd. Do you suppose that men who have spent nearly three years in prison for refusal to be coerced against their will for one thing will accept coercion for another thing

141 *Punch* was a celebrated weekly magazine, full of cartoons and jokes of a very high quality, reflecting the politics, culture and society of the day.

equally bad? The idea underlying the rumour is not 'Can the CO's do useful work?' but make them do something and so smash them. I do not think the Govt want any more trouble: this they can avoid even if it means keeping us in prison longer.

I am glad you are strong enough to look a further separation in the face calmly as it shows you still have a reserve of faith. Glad the ILP Social was such a success and that fellowship was its principal feature. Wish they could pass some of it on to us, as we so often feel shut from the world which we know so well and it is not good to be forced in upon oneself for so long. Thank Tickle for the three vols of *Punch* he has sent and say they are very welcome. Talking of books, Wiltshire has my *Ingoldsby Legends*. Perhaps Dora would like to read it [...]

I wish you all success in your school efforts and I am sure it will go on again and become a force for good amongst the women of Letchworth. Women are awaking everywhere and although the war has temporarily diverted their attention from this thing and drawn them into its many ramifications it cannot hold them always and this thing will look for fresh channels for their energy. Schoolwork offers just such an opportunity for coming together to gain strength and courage and knowledge.

[...] I send you all my love and my spirit longs for thee. Be of good cheer. After the clouds have broken the sun will shine for us.

Yours ever, Frank.

32 North Avenue, Letchworth
January 21st 1919

My dear Frank,

Glad to get yours this morning and glad to see no depression. I must tell you first that I cannot have the house opposite, so goodness knows where and when I shall be moving. Mr Cree and Mr Cobbold were going to help me this week. I believe Mr Cree goes to Normandy next week, but I don't think he will stay there long somehow. Of course

5. 'THESE LAST DAYS ARE THE MOST TRYING'

they want him when their goods arrive to help put straight. He would have been so much use to me helping with chicken houses and sheds. However I have not got a house yet and doesn't seem very likely to get one, although 800 Belgians are going next Monday. I am not worrying and will get better weather, perhaps, by the time I do go. I quite think Marshall cannot turn me out, it will have to be Palmer.

Anyway as it happens I am very glad I am not moving this week, as I have got both the girls ill, with very bad feverish colds. Dora has been in bed since Friday night and Chrissie since Sat night. They were not improving at all so thought it best to send for the Dr yesterday. Wilson came (a great improvement on Mac). He said they must stay in bed and I had to go down for some medicine which has reduced the temperature. The weather is so bad and the house damp and cold in spite of fires; I shall have to be careful of further chills. They are both together in the back bedroom and happy enough with dolls and books. They cough and get so hot at night. It came on rather sudden. I thought it was flue as it has come about again. Of course it makes more to do for me, they want reading to and feeding with little tit-bits, you know. Morris is my handy man. I kept him in bed last Thursday with a cold but he has nearly recovered. It ties me to the house as they do not like to be left. I could not go to school tonight and Mr Hal Jones was going to speak for us.

I am sending you the handbook and I will get you the Fellowship Hymn Book as soon as I can. Have you the Esperanto book and the *Mayor of Casterbridge*? Miss Bixley wants it taken care of. She is Sec pro tem of the ILP. I quite agree that our work lies in England. It was too bad of you to try to give me a shock but I am nearly used to you and to your startlers, and warn you that I shall tell you exactly what I think of any future proposals. The rumour I spoke of came from Thomas for one. I agree with your view altho' I had not thought of it like that. No doubt some would go willingly but it does not seem fair to make a man help to reconstruct what he refused to help destroy [...]

Some day you will be able to tell the children all about Politics and I shall understand better than I used. They will soon be old enough; just now it is fairy stories and Chrissie is beginning to like reading for herself but they all enjoy being read to. If you was here to do it I should be able to sew or knit. We are going to have some happy hours I really believe.

I am afraid I have no news for you this week but I want to tell you the lilac trees are still alive though not grown very much. You asked me this a little while ago. I have also been asked how to remove blisters from veneer. It is on the top of a burr walnut table and I thought you would know.

I am glad to know the spring is coming and it cannot be such a severe winter as last year. We may have a cold spring but not so much frost and snow. I hope not, as coal is not at all plentiful and lots of people are without any now. I get a little and have to eke it out with coke and wood.

[...] Mrs Bartholomew is going to ask Mr Pearce the CO for me as he has some cottages and people are beginning to move about, beside Belgians. I also have my name down for one in Westholm Green. Next door to Tickles is likely to become vacant soon.

I must stop now. Morris is waiting to go to the post with it and he does not like to be kept waiting. His chief amusement is modelling with plasticine. He had a box for Christmas and makes some very clever things, such attention to details which I consider a good thing.

We all send lots of love and long for your return, but I am waiting patiently till the powers that be decide to give you freedom and your help and companionship to your family

and loving wife Lucy

January 27th 1919

Dearest Lucy

It was with very mixed feelings that I read your letter. The news of the illness of the girls brought back the memory of my first months here. I am glad we can communicate so much more frequently as suspense is the worst punishment because it leaves the mind free to all the ills of imagination and morbidness. I trust the girls are themselves again by this time and that you are none the worse for your enforced confinement to the house and additional strain in nursing them. I should much like to be home with you and be able to read the book both they and you and I could enjoy. I like your picture of future happiness [...] Sorry to hear about the housing problem but quite agree that you should not worry; something will turn up, if it is only the bailiffs to take possession of the property. If you wait long enough the weather will get warmer and you might even carry out the caravan idea or camp on the common. It would be well perhaps to have your good trunk packed and keep your bonnet on so that you are prepared to meet any eventuality.

Now for serious matters. You ask how to remove blisters etc from [a] table top. The easiest way is to sell the table or burn it and buy a new one. If this advice cannot be followed and an attempt to procure a remedy is determined on you must procure a Man, failing a man try a woman. Next get some hot water and swab, dip swab in hot water and place over blisters. This will cause the glue to become soft and allow of a sharp pointed knife to be run underneath the surrounding parts. When a sufficient part of the surrounding surface (which must be determined by the blisters and their nearness to each other) has been raised it will be necessary to run some hot glue, which must not be too thick nor used too liberally, underneath the veneer and a hot piece of zinc or wood must be cramped down on the surface. This will, if done properly, cause the veneer which has stretched through the action of the heat and the water to dry and again lay flat. If the blister is too far from the edge of the table to allow of cramps being used the process is a slower one because the hot water must not be used so freely and the glue must be squeezed out with the point of a flat nosed hammer and the work cannot be left until it is quite certain that all glue is squeezed out and is nearly dry. After all is set hard, scrape and clean up for polishing in the ordinary way. If the blisters are not too bad and the person who is going to do the job has had no experience either in veneering or polishing, my advice is let it alone or the result may be worse than the blister. Grease the zinc or wood to prevent it sticking. This sort of thing makes my fingers itch and I long for my workshop but I must wait patiently [...]

32 North Avenue, Letchworth Herts
Jan 28 1919

My dear Frank

Your letter arrived this morning in the snow, and such a heavy fall too quite a foot. One thing, it is a little warmer today, but the sky looks very much like more.

I know how anxious you are to know how the children are and I am glad to tell you they are improving. Dora is up again on Sunday for the first time, but she must not go out of the room. Chrissie has been very ill, but is on the mend and with care I think will soon be herself again. I have had a very anxious week and often felt very much alone, but have been helped and strengthened and have faith enough to know I shall not want for anything.

Morris has not been ill, just a little cold and he could not seem to understand the girls could not stand his high spirits and noise, and unfortunately he had to be in the room as I could only keep one fire going. I am right out of coal now, so went to Mrs Middleton and got a pailful this morning. She carried up some logs too for me, so I can go on for a few days. I should not mind only for the children; they must be kept warm, in fact that is more important than medicine. Many houses are without fuel just now, and now the snow has come that will make a further delay. My chickens have struck, too. Perhaps they are not getting sufficient attention. I was very much amused at the idea of waiting for something to turn up, quite Micawber like.[142] We seem to have been all our life waiting always for something to turn up, a turn of fortune. I wonder will it ever come. I do not wish for wealth but comfort and not struggling. The people who have sufficient to live on comfortably or who earn good wages do not seem to be short of coals nor are they troubled about houses, having their own or renting good ones. I look forward to our own in New Town and a comfortable old age, but we have a lot of work to accomplish before then. The

---

[142] Mr Micawber was a character in Charles' Dickens' novel *David Copperfield*, whose defining characteristic was his eternal hope that something would 'turn up', to keep him and his family from debt.

children are all my work just now; it is not only the nursing, day and night, but cooking, cleaning, washing and shopping all by myself and all spare time reading to and amusing in many ways. I have been reading *Dombey & Son* to myself while sitting up at nights. I shall try another Dickens; they are so very interesting and life-like, it makes the time pass more quickly. One gets tired of the long evenings and nights with only candlelight too. I am wondering if you find them long and if you feel the cold; you will almost certainly forget what a fire looks like. In our house we will have one grate at least for burning logs. Palmers have only one for coal, that is in the kitchen. They have got their goods all safe and sound (thanks to our packing) and are getting straight. I should think Mrs P will be glad to have her own home again, living in other people's houses since August, with a baby too, they seem to like the place.

Arthur Fiennes is not getting better very quickly and is going away for a bit to the Home Dr Salter has opened for the COs.[143] I met him last week and they sent greetings to you. Quite a number of discharged soldiers are coming back now. I have seen Parsons of Glebe Rd working in gardens, still in Khaki. I did not know he had been called up. Lindsey's son is not home yet; he is at an airdrome at Grantham and they all went on strike because they were not being demobilized as fast as promised

[…]

Mr Brunt says I cannot be turned out till six months after the war is over (when peace is signed) so I need not worry, and if you are home soon one move will do. Of course I cannot possibly think of it while the bad weather lasts.

The story is highly appreciated and the next instalment eagerly looked for. Your letters must still wait for another week when I hope they will all be well.

143 Alfred Salter was a doctor with a practice in Bermondsey, south London, where he and his wife Ada worked to improve conditions for this very poor area. They were pacifists and socialists, and both were elected to public office after the war, Alfred as the Labour MP for Bermondsey West, and Ada as London's first woman mayor.

Wed. Sorry to say Morris is now down with the same thing as the girls, same symptoms; he came on in the night, so I expect another week with him but I am thankful that some coals have just come. How glad I shall be when the winter is over; the snow lays so thick up to my gaiter tops going up to the chickens. I always think how much you would <u>enjoy</u> all the trials of weather and so on, had you the freedom to do so. I have no news, only grumbles it seems: forgive me. I am really keeping quite cheerful and smiling. Arthur Francis has just been in. He feels unable to write to you or anyone, cannot concentrate his thoughts. He hopes you keep well and cheerful. He says things are not looking very [good] for COs but the government won't have it all its own way. There are 2 proposals dealing with the question of demobilisation which will affect you all. The first is release [of] all men (from military) who joined up previous to Jan? 1916; the second to release all men over 35. The first of course will mean no COs. This is not decided yet, anyway I myself do not think you will be kept much longer. I feel we shall soon see the dawn of day for us. We have had a long night but surely day must come soon. I am thinking of writing to Fritton next week, also your mother; have you any message for them? I know you will understand this letter being shorter than I have written lately. Do not be over anxious about us, everything will be quite alright. Lots of love from our children and myself.

Your ever loving wife Lucy

32 North Avenue, Letchworth
February 3rd 1919

My dear Frank

The children are nearly well again, so no further cause for anxiety. So sorry you did not get my letter till Sunday. No one came in and I could not leave Morris to go out and post it. I watched for Nelly Briant coming home from school on Thursday afternoon and asked her to take it for me so you should have got it sooner. Morris came into the sitting room today and the girls have gone into the front bedroom to sleep so now

5. 'THESE LAST DAYS ARE THE MOST TRYING'

we are altogether more comfortable and better. I shall keep them indoors while the snow lasts, but I hope they will be able to return to school on Monday [...]

We are all very concerned at the state of affairs, strikes etc, but of course we expected it all. I only hope the worst of the winter will be gone before the trouble reaches the climax, although it is bad enough in Glasgow, soldiers, machine guns and tanks ready for the word to quell the mobs.[144] The trouble is no doubt spreading and this will give you an idea of the state of the world at the present time. There is also trouble with the soldiers at Calais and in Belgium.[145] The Belgians who were to have gone back last Wed have not gone yet, but their luggage was collected and still lays at the station, while the people are living in almost empty houses, no beds, or blankets or extra clothing, cannot get coals or firing. Some have been supplied with straw mattresses and some are sleeping in the Howard Hall. It is a serious matter altogether [...]

I understand the mood of your letter perfectly and feel you are right, but I really do not know how is best to write to you. I <u>must</u> talk about the children and home matters. I never feel that you are outside <u>our</u> lives and every day I expect you <u>may</u> return. Our part in this fight is quite equally divided and each of us as we can bear it best, you mentally and I physically. Sometimes I feel I am tried to the uttermost, as you do, but we are still able to go on. I feel the promise very true, 'As our day so our strength shall be'. It does not matter about you having the power to <u>ask</u> for help, does a child have to ask its father or mother for its daily food?

---

144   Workers had been striking in Glasgow since 27 January 1919 over proposed changes to the hours of the working week, and rioting began on 31 January. The government had agreed that only non-Glaswegian, Scottish troops would be put on standby in case of violence, and over 10,000 were deployed. Tanks had arrived by 3 February. By 18 February the strikers had returned to work.

145   The Calais Mutiny ended on 31 January 1919, upheld by soldiers relatively new to military discipline and service, and had been caused by grievances over food, punishments and slowness in demobilisation.

Our faith is kept strong that we have a Father, or power above us [...]

I hope you will get this soon this week. I am posting it at once.

We all send lots of love to you.

Your loving wife, Lucy

February 3rd 1919

My Dearest Wife

I received your letter on Sunday and I must say that I have been anxious about you all. Since being here I have learned something of the anxious spirit which we have seen expressed in some folk we know well, and at whom we have often expressed dissatisfaction because their fears were usually groundless. This fear is bred from inaction and impotence and is a real thing, bringing with it to any one possessed of the power of imagination, great horrors and vivid pictures of the improbable if not the impossible.

You know my characteristics very well and know that inactivity in any form was almost an impossibility. This experience has compelled me to relegate to the nethermost part of my brain all active thought about you and the children and home and I have to feel as if you are all apart from my life, as it were. It may sound harsh and cruel to you as you read it but nevertheless it is only by so doing that I have been able to preserve my health and sanity [...]

All this must seem strange to you but remember I have been away from you and the children for over two years and have been compelled to preserve my outlook on life and contact with you all by the use of mental pictures only. The result is that I have become like a well-fed and groomed horse or ass, sound in wind and limb to do the task allotted and to enjoy the food supplied, also to sleep well, but were I when sitting at my tea to think of you and the children other than in a happy state, my enjoyment would be gone, impotent need for action and thwarted desire would burst out and the result would be chaos.

5. 'THESE LAST DAYS ARE THE MOST TRYING'

You mentioned some little while ago that the contact seemed difficult. I think you will see why that should be so. Your letter tells me plainly how hard a time you are having and I can and do realise it all and I write to you like this. What is the use of me saying how sorry I am and that I hope the children will soon be well? My whole body and soul is just asking to be with you and to help you as you know I would, and words are useless to convey real true love and sympathy. I think this expression must be similar to the experience of the dead, if after death they can still retain the love and sympathy towards those they leave behind unless there is a means of communication of which we at present know nothing [...]

&

February 10th 1919

Dearest Lucy

Your letter came to hand quite promptly and the news it contained has relieved my anxiety and given me much joy. I am glad you are all in the improvement stage and trust you will none of you have a relapse. The weather is quite wintry now and the winds are treacherous so you must be careful, as undoubtedly the pleasure of sliding and tobogganing are great temptations for the youngsters. We here have all the disadvantages of winter without any of its corresponding pleasures. No fireside chats or merry dances and laughing exploits on the ice, such as Dickens loved to write of, but our consolation is that it will pass away like all other things and the summer will come even though her journey seems somewhat tardy.

Sorry to hear that the friends are so downhearted, but you must tell them that we do not expect them to get our liberation and are content if they just extend their sympathy to those we love and then make their part easier to bear. The future belongs to us so we can afford to wait patiently and we do try to be so.

Your news about Glasgow is startling but quite what can be expected from the government. They are powerless to deal with live issues and know no other method but force. It is a fine object lesson to the working man conscripted into the army to be ordered to shoot down his fellow countrymen because he dares to demand a better share of the country's wealth which he himself creates. Every act of the government makes our attitude stand out in greater clearness, and of course they see in us a menace to them and I do not think they will let us go before they are forced to do so. The strikes represent more to my mind than a mere demand for better conditions of labour. It is the commencement of the end and nothing but full freedom will satisfy the workers. This will mean a long and bitter struggle carried on only in the industrial and political planes but I think that a new moral spirit is coming into being and this will temper the efforts of the workers and make them feel that their struggle is not against men as such but against old ideas and ideals which are holding men in thralldom as surely as the wage earner is held by wage slavery. The time is not far distant when a man will be considered as immoral and base who dares to make a fortune by exploiting his fellow men and when such ideals are generally held the better time will have arrived. The worker can afford to laugh at tanks etc, if they will only be wise enough to make no demonstration and give the military the chance to use their horrible weapons. All they need do is to sit quietly at home and let the owners do their own work. What a change it would be. Fancy your next door neighbours having to go down a coal mine to get their own coal. I think such a state of affairs would soon put a different complexion on the matter [...]

Accept my love and fond caresses,

Yours *Ever*

Frank

5. 'THESE LAST DAYS ARE THE MOST TRYING'

32 North Avenue, Letchworth
February 11th 1919

My dear Frank

Your letter received this morning as expected. What a blessing the post is (sometimes).

Glad to say we all continue well and the children have gone to school quite happy. Dora went to Mrs Gregory's on Sat evening and Chrissie to the Gym display last night and neither seems any worse. I took Christine and found Leslie Barker's mother takes a great part with the children, marking register etc. She came and spoke to Chrissie and myself, mentioned you, of course, and said the latest date of release is Mar 31st; what tales we hear! I shall let Dora and Morris go again, the experience is worth the 6d, 2d each. I only wish we had such things when we were young, but we must not deny our children these things that make for progress and improvement of the race. I was told last week of a girl who had been well educated at the sacrifice of her parents and at 18 had married an Australian soldier and would have to go back with him presently, so she would probably be lost to her parents. The fact was bemoaned but I pointed out she would undoubtedly be a better wife and mother for knowledge, and would not allow her children to know less than herself so we must sink ourselves in the lives of our children.

Dora had a good time on Sat. I went to fetch her home and was made very welcome and we had cocoa and biscuits before we returned. It was very cold and slippery. How the snow and frost is lasting! It is rather trying, but today in such a lovely sunshine all the snow sparkles and the children are having a lovely time sliding and sledging. Glebe Road slopes and on to the Common and Wilbury Hill are very much alive, and really it is warmer out than indoors.

Coal is still very short. Katie tells me there are queues at coal shops with bags and sacks for a little to go on with; much good the Rationing was. Of course those wicked strikers are to be blamed for all shortages now. Katie thinks it is too bad of them. They are like a lot of spoilt children who cry for the moon. There is some sense when there is a real grievance. She does not understand of course. She says now the Tube has started again the lift attendants are so cheeky, have that air about them that they are indispensable! Of course they are, all the workers are, and as fast as the wages go up cost of living goes out [...]

I have many bad hours thinking of you and your experiences, especially this severe weather. I expect some day we shall look back on this part of our lives as a bad dream. One thing, although the children will remember it they have not suffered either physically nor by any bad feeling at school among their little friends or teachers. This week in a special CO No. of the *Labour Leader* and even the *Christian World* is taking up the question of your continued imprisonment, so I still feel we shall soon be together again.

Mrs Williams on Sunday mentioned the South Sea Islands and the children were very interested as I had not told them when you wrote to me about it. Dora wants to go. She has a spirit of adventure in her I believe which will out some day. Mrs Williams was telling me what she learnt from Mr Ogilvie by the way. Mrs Hunter tells me the boys are still in the guardroom not court martialled yet, but Francis has again got calling-up papers and now he is in bed with Bronchitis.[146]

There is quite a lot of excitement here as 1,800 Belgians are leaving tomorrow, Wed morning. They go in special trains straight to Tilbury. There are 40 trucks of luggage as the shops are full of the people buying up to carry with them, food and clothing. Some of them will not reach home before Sat and such cold weather for them to travel, but they are happy enough. One thing they have done very well here and have plenty of money and many of them have their homes to go back to just as they left them, taken care of by neighbours [...]

There is a new large dock to be built in London and a lot of houses, slums, to be demolished to make room, but 207 new houses to be put in the place of them on Garden City lines. We shall have a new London in time no doubt, as the people wake up. I was interested in an article

---

146   The upper age for conscription was raised to 51 in late 1918, and continued until 1920.

in the *Manchester Guardian* on Labour unrest, a working woman's point of view and she says many women voted for Coalition at the Election because they thought they would nationalise the land and railways etc […]

This article was written by a dressmaker who 'wants England to be great in the wealth of a happy, wise, generous and brave people, healthy and free'. I am going to cut it out and send it to Katie. Mrs Middleton gave me the paper to read what they say about the continued imprisonment of COs.

Sorry to say only Mrs Vandyke and myself at [Adult] school tonight. I really think I must give it up. It seems hard work to keep alive just a tiny spark and is it worthwhile. The Church Hall have taken our women on something on every afternoon or eve; they leave ours.

Now I must stop. Lots of love from us all, always hoping to see you home soon.

Lucy

Should you like a visit?

February 17th 1919

Mia Mata Edzinon

Your sweet letter came along quite quickly and was full of interesting matter. It was with great satisfaction that I read the news concerning the children and I sincerely hope you will not suffer any ill effects from the strain of nursing and the cold weather. As you say it has been wintry but there are signs now of it disappearing. The snow has nearly all gone and drizzly rain fell yesterday. Everything looks very cheerless indeed. If we get a little sunshine we shall see the trees begin to burst their buds, and even now the bulb plants are well out of the ground and I expect you will soon see the snowdrop flower. Our old chestnut trees here are always beautiful in their leafless state; they show the delicate slender branch formation which when in full leaf is hidden, and two mornings last week during the heavy rime frost they were covered with a silvery white garment which gave them a most beautiful effect.

I quite agree with you that it is easier to keep warm out of doors than in, but am glad to be able to say I can sleep warmly at night. Am rejoiced to know that the children were able to enjoy some of the winter sports as these things do so live in the memory [...]

I was greatly surprised to hear about Francis. This cat and mouse treatment is awful, but there may be a bright side to it. It may be a means of giving him his discharge from the army. When I think of our position I positively laugh at government administration. Here are we, just a mere handful of men, who if scattered throughout the community in the ordinary role of citizens would be an insignificant unit capable of doing no harm whatever to the Govt, even if we so desired, which we don't, and no-one would give us a moment's serious thought. Yet by keeping us in prison and repeatedly punishing us for the same <u>illegal offence</u>, they bring us before the public and make us the subject for discussion and dissention everywhere, causing themselves an awful lot of work and care, which I should have thought in the interest of smoothness of administration etc it would have been well to avoid [...]

Your extract from the MG was excellent and reads like an ILP tract. I trust it may enlighten Katie but I am afraid she has never yet asked herself 'What am I doing for the race to which I belong' or decided to what class she does belong. She is still in the (man property) stage and the domestic circle, where I suppose you ought to be but I am glad to say that in thought you left it years and years ago. I hope you will not infer from this that I think you as old as Methuselah.

You speak of a visit and I leave it to you to decide whether you come or not, as you reply so will I act.

I hear that our question is coming up in the House this week so <u>perhaps</u> something may happen [...] I am well and full of hope for the bright future which is coming.

All my love F

5. 'THESE LAST DAYS ARE THE MOST TRYING'

32 North Avenue, Letchworth, Herts
February 18th 1919

My dear Frank

Glad to know that you are still well and can sleep warm. Like you I thought we had finished with the snow after the rain. This morning the girls (who sleep in the front bedroom) called to me that it was snowing and lay on the ground quite thick; I was very much surprised. Of course they all went to school and are quite well. Chrissie had to stay home yesterday because her boots were wet and she had not a second pair like the others. I went this morning and bought her a pair so she was able to change at dinner time. They also took shoes to school, so should take no harm. I am more careful because I do not want them ill again.

We went to Mrs Williams's on Sunday soon after dinner and was glad she had invited us as I had no coal or coke and it was raining so not pleasant to sit fireless. I had some brought on Monday morning, but 1 cwt does not go far you know, but one of coke too helps out. Do you know why they are both the same price now, 2/3 cwt, isn't it high?

[...] I asked you about the visit just as you like. I have no news that I cannot write. Of course I should like to see you but if you would rather wait another month I don't mind. (Perhaps you will be home. As your time will be up in April, what date?) perhaps next month would be best.

Of course I have not moved yet, nor got a house. I find all the Glebe Rd houses occupied by the Belgians are taken up by Vickers. Mr Ladd tells me he has nothing to let or likely to have Returned soldiers come first and they have 200 applications for 50 houses. I asked for one on the 'Antwerp Colony'[147] and went up there this morning in snow and slush to see if he had left any message with Miss Hoge, but he told her what I have already mentioned and could not fix me up. It is my opinion they will not, so I shall not ask again, just wait, like Macawber, but I want to start gardening as soon as we get some decent weather and even if I

---

147 '... new houses were built for the refugees in the Westbury area [of Letchworth] which was nicknamed 'Little Antwerp'. http://www.hertsatwar.co.uk/belgian-refugees accessed 9 February 2018.

am safe from being turned out till next winter there will no doubt be the same trouble then and all being unsettled and an annoyance to Marshall's [...]

I did not go to see the Belgians off. The *Citizen* only briefly mentioned the going: 1,360 in two special trains which went straight to Tilbury docks so each person was allowed 300 lb of luggage. There still remains between 400 and 500 which will make their own arrangements for return but Mrs W's lodger told me they were mostly waiting for an Ostend boat. They planted a tree with a tablet in Howard Park to commemorate their stay in Letchworth. Some of the houses they have left are filthy dirty and they have been so crowded with lodgers.

I went to a meeting last Wed eve which should have been in Howard Hall, but it was not ready as the Belgians had been camping there, cooking, sleeping and living. So it was in the Wesleyan School Room. It was a 'Fight the Famine' meeting arranged by the Friends Service Committee. Some dreadful facts were mentioned of the state of the devastated countries and terrible starvation. In Poland there are no children living under 15; in Cologne 760 thousand people have died of starvation and what babies there are are mere skeletons with no milk or rubber for teats. The Friends got permission from the government to send a large number out to them. Austria and Russia of course is as bad. Food controller Mr Hoover[148] says whatever we may do to help there is bound to be about 10,000 people die of starvation in North Russia.

The object of the meeting was chiefly to urge the raising of the blockade which of course is affecting us as well as the enemy (I see we have 3

---

148   Herbert Hoover, a Quaker and American engineer, established the Commission for Relief in Belgium at the beginning of the war to import food aid to the starving populations of German-occupied countries while the USA was still a neutral state. He was commemorated after the war as a humanitarian, and later served as the 31st President of the United States.

5. 'THESE LAST DAYS ARE THE MOST TRYING'

million workless).[149] People of all countries want to be allowed to work and they will be able to get food for themselves. The pity of it is while so many are starving we can now get what Margarine we want without Coupons, and more meat is being allowed, bacon and pork without Coupons and an extra ¼ lb of sugar per head. The difficulty seems to be transport, but if it was troops or guns, that would be got over. Mr Pease has left the National Labour Press and is working for the Friends Service Com [...]

Miss Wilding found the Palmers quite settled down at Guildford. He seems quite satisfied with the place and evidently hopes for great things from it presently. In the meantime of course it means all outgoing and nothing coming in but they seem to have the capital to work on so that is alright. They pay out £20 weekly in wages. I believe he is still wanting you, but there are no houses to be had there. He seems to be still looking out for one for us. I daresay he wants to be rid of this. I still send my rent to him. Isn't silly, when I could pay it direct myself. I think I must suggest it again.

Our new neighbours are very quiet elderly people, no children but they do smile and speak to ours sometimes. I wonder what he has retired on! They have got some rabbits so will not mind my chickens.

Now I must stop, finishing this on Wed morning. Morris just come in and going to post it for me, then they will all be in for dinner.

We all send lots of love to dear Daddy. You are always in our thoughts and we so often talk about you at meals or evenings.

Your loving wife Lucy

Dora will ask about Esperanto book tonight.

---

149 The Allies maintained a naval blockade of Germany from 1914 to restrict its food and materials supplies. It was maintained after the Armistice until Germany signed the Treaty of Versailles in June 1919.

THE CONSCIENTIOUS OBJECTOR'S WIFE

32 North Avenue, Letchworth
February 24th 1919

My dear Frank

I hope the lines on this paper will not bother you. My father sent some for the children and I am using it as paper is so dear to buy.

I am so pleased Mr Cubbon was able to see you yesterday. He called in about tea-time and told me all about you. It was as nice as having two letters in one day and I feel sure you would enjoy his visit. He [is] so real, you know what I mean. He will have told you more news than I could have written in a week and he would give you a touch of the outside world. I was going to say the real life, but sometimes it seems to me quite unreal, all the terrible confusion everywhere, strikes, riots, assassinations, revolution and starving people after the peaceful years we have lived, makes one's head reel and wonder is this really living on this beautiful earth, or is it a taste of hell, or are we dreaming of ancient history. Well we can only sit back and hold tight; whatever it is we shall come alright presently. The worst of it is I feel inclined to be swamped and overwhelmed with it all instead of keeping awake and alert, ready for whatever may happen.

I am sorry I did not tell you more about the CO week in the [*Labour Leader*] but it was just the same (to us): demand for release, a good article by E D Morel on prison life which made it all more vivid to me than it already was, if possible. Such people urging release as Jerome K Jerome, Dr John Clifford, A Maude Royden, Israel Zangwill, Bertrand Russell.[150] No Poem.

---

150 Jerome K Jerome was a famous author of the day; Dr John Clifford was the former leader of the Baptist Church and a prominent anti-war campaigner, social reformer and advocate of passive resistance; Agnes Maude Royden was a leading figure in the Fellowship of Reconciliation and the Women's International League for Peace and Freedom; Israel Zangwill was a leading Jewish author, playwright, feminist and pacifist; Bertrand Russell was a philosopher and anti-war activist with powerful social connections.

I should like to write to you about the meeting of the International at Berne by Mrs Philip Snowden but you would need to read it all and I don't know what to pick out for you. The Belgians and the Swiss did not attend but the Swiss allowed them to meet in their Volkhaus, which is the Socialist and Labour headquarters at Berne [...] Each speech was delivered in three languages, English, German and French, and in the early part speeches were too long, some an hour. The British delegation has won admiration for the brevity of its speeches. We have a British way of coming to the point, much appreciated by weary delegates and translators and on the whole I think we have succeeded in saying all we intended to say and quite enough to make our meaning clear to all the delegates ... The least feeling person in England could scarcely have failed to be moved by the physical appearance of the German and Austrian delegates. The effect of short rations upon them was obvious, not only in their sunken cheeks but in the way their clothes hung upon them. The stories told under pressure of the food conditions in the cities of Germany and Austria was enough to move a heart of stone. Five hundred Austrians came into Berne by train to be fed for a time and sent home to make way for another lot. So these kindly Swiss are doing a little, so much less than they would like to keep these innocent mites alive. It hurts one's self-respect that the victors in this world conflict should continue against the innocent in a time of peace, when no danger from the enemy threatens, the methods of barbarism committed in time of war. Everywhere in this city, from people in all classes, there is put forward a plea for the raising of the blockade, so that normal economic relations be established between the countries as speedily as possible.

There has been a great meeting of women workers in the Albert Hall. The *Herald* has it: 'Rope workers, rag pickers and jam makers from the East End joined hands with the most highly skilled workers in engineering and women clerks from every government dept in proclaiming a constructive policy in a series of resolutions which comprise the Women's Charter. The following resolutions were passed with enthusiasm. The right to work. The right to life. The right to leisure, 40 hours a week 8 hours a day. Women have no doubt worked hard (and suffered) during war time and they intend to be properly treated in return.'

I am afraid I can quote no more. You have enough to think about for a week after Cubbon's visit.

Now you will be glad to know that we are all well. I agree that probably my presentiment of something happening is the air of spring. I always do get it. I had forgotten of course the something nice for you would be the same for us, the very nicest thing would be your return home but I am not going to worry any more about that, put it on one side like the house question. I have had these things so much on my mind that I have not slept well lately and I know that will not do.

Katie talks of coming down soon for a day. She is better again, she says, but my father has a bad cold and is very sad just now; naturally she will only stay for a day but it will be a change for her. I hope she is lucky enough to have a nice day. Things are already beginning to look spring-like and when the sun shines and the birds are chirping it all is very different to London, that most dreary place at the best of times, at least to me.

I have been talking today to a man who knew you at Brinsmeads,[151] Raymond of Common View Square. He was also a member of the Sons of Phenix[152] and was talking about the Lyndhurst Hall concerts, Dr Rayner and the Minstrel Troupe, Harry Gooding, and George Baker.

---

151   It is possible that Frank had worked for the prominent British piano firm John Brinsmead & Son as a cabinet maker.

152   It seems that Frank and possibly also Lucy had been members of this temperance society in their youth: 'The South London Unity of Total Abstinence Brothers and Sisters of the Phoenix Friendly Society seems to have started through the merger of local societies in the Southwark area. By the late 1880s its headquarters was in Clapham. Its supporters established a coffee house in Nine Elms at the beginning of 1887 with a large room capable of holding some 400 persons for meetings of Phoenix Lodges and other gatherings. They took part with their banners and regalia in the 1889 Dock Strike demonstrations.' Editorial, *Friendly Societies Research Group Newsletter* 16 (July 2008), http://www.historyofalcoholanddrugs.typepad.com/alcohol_and_drugs_history/2008/07/original-grand.html accessed 10 April 2018.

How all this takes our mind back many years and makes us remember more experiences. I want to persuade all our children to be good Templars (am I right?). Don't you think it would help to keep them safe if they were ever tempted.

If fine on Sunday morning I am taking them all to Howgills Meeting. I do feel we all ought to go somewhere for worship on Sundays. Perhaps it is silly of me to feel this. Somehow we have got beyond the ordinary church or chapel and I want something really sincere, an atmosphere of good if you can understand me. There has been a week of Theosophy at Howard Hall. I went on Sunday afternoon with Mrs Tickle. There was nothing new said to you or myself and it seemed rather up in the clouds; with so much going on industrially we cannot feel there is the brotherhood among the various religious people while they allow war and imprisonment to go on.

I had a committee meeting of the Adult School on Monday; a good number came. We arranged [the] programme for a month and Mrs Mallon got it typed for me, and then on Tuesday no one came again. It really is disappointing. Of course this is a special week at the Church Hall. Baily is trying to raise £500 to have a social club always going at the cottage next to Mrs Lack. He is full of good intentions and would almost tempt me to join if only to help in the work. It ought to be the ILP doing it all. Of course it is to draw people into the church and keep them in subjection, Vicar, Church and King.

On Sat March 22nd the Adult School are having a play from one of Tolstoy's at the girls club. Mr Fulworth is coming to take chief part. Mr Garside and Mr Wiltshire is in it and they want myself and Mrs Vandyke. I have not promised yet. I have not read the play yet […]

Miss Perkins, Dora's teacher, has now got a sketch club in class. Those who belong, of course Dora does, had to do something each week from a list of subjects and the others give marks by voting I believe. It is splendid practice for them; they have every advantage. They had a nature walk yesterday and Chrissie did one on Monday. How they do enjoy them and makes them more keenly alive to see things. Just contrast this sort of teaching with ours. If schooling goes on improving, it will be almost worth being reincarnated for, to be a child again […] My chickens are now laying 4 eggs a day, not bad from 7 and they mount up at 5½ each.

I saw Francis on Sunday; he is off to Salters in Kent this week. He told me that no more COs were to be employed on the HO scheme after 31st March and the Dr has stopped him from going back to Dartmoor as he was ordered. I am sending you the little book *In Praise of Freedom*. Have you had the Esperanto ones I sent you last Thursday? I will try to get you some more next week and will keep the list for reference.

I hope this letter will not exceed the limit and it will happen to fit your mood but I suppose they change even as they used to.

We are very glad the days are lengthening so nicely, but the children play out after school and then cannot understand the evening being so short and bedtime coming so quickly. I am glad too it is light in the morning earlier and not so cold to turn out, but this morning we had a little snow and turned very cold. Well summer is coming soon, so we cheer ourselves.

Now I must stop. Hope you keep well. Love from all the children and myself to dear daddy, still cherishing the hope to see you soon,

Your loving wife

Lucy

Bedford Prison
Feb 24th 1919

Mia Amata Edzinon

I feel the touch of spring of spring in the air and I must say it makes me feel restless. [...] I should imagine your feelings of expectancy is due to the springtide coming and do not suppose anything *nice* will happen as far as I am concerned, but I heartedly wish and hope that your presentiment may be fulfilled for your and the children. The nicest thing which could happen for me would be to get my release but this *not* to be yet and I can see no light on the subject at all.

5. 'THESE LAST DAYS ARE THE MOST TRYING'

[…] I have looked through the handbook and here is a list of the books I should like you to get if you can but please remember that I do not want to put you to any expense you feel you ought not to incur. I will place them in order of importance and perhaps one of the Adult School men could get them for you.

Seebohm's *Spirit of Christianity* 1/-

Bees in Amber 1/-

What Labour wants from Education 1d

Browning (a second hand copy) *Our Beloved Dead* 4d

Florence Nightingale 3d

Jesus Christ and the World Religion 7d

Fellowship Hymn Book & its use 1d

Popular History of Methodism 1d

God, Nature and Human Freedom 2½ d

Also try and borrow *Personality of Fellowship*, Glover's *Jesus of History* from Dr Crowley. I also want you to get Walt Whitman, and Ed[ward] Carpenter *Toward Democracy* but the latter is 3/6 I think, for the cheapest, so it can wait. There is a copy of Whittier's *Poems of the Inner Life* at home which you might like to look at perhaps. See also if you can borrow a *Life of Tolstoy* but as these latter came on later in the year there is no hurry. You can consult the handbook for all these books. What a list of wants and yet I could add more to them. For instance I want Bernard Shaw's *Doctor's Dilemma*, *Man and Superman*, John Bull's *Other Island*, published at 6d by Constable. Also *Francis Place* by Graham Wallace and *Human Nature in Politics* by the same author, these are cheap editions. Perhaps also you can borrow some of Shaw's or Wells' or Galsworthy's. Have a look round my own shelves and see what there is. I cannot remember any but No 7 John Stuart which you might send. I hope all this will not make your head reel, but you can look on it as a list for reference.

You ask me when my sentence expires. April 14th is the earliest date if I lose no marks.

Your facts about the awful devastation are appalling and if only the imagination of the people was great enough to grasp what it means I feel sure it would go a long way to prevent future wars. Unfortunately memory and imagination or rather power to visualize events is a gift so few people possess owing perhaps to the enforced self-centred lives we lead.

[...] Your doleful picture of being without a fire was not as poignant as it would have been three years ago. My advice is push the table back against the wall and skip or dance, both of which are good exercises and do not cost 9/s a cwt but invigorate the blood and if a sufficient supply of food is at hand to satisfy hunger nothing but good will result. You will think I am getting quite an anchorite, not so but am certainly anchored here for an indefinite period. You must try and enter into my moods as expressed in my letters and forgive me if anything I write seems harsh because I do not intend to convey that impression but the pen is a bad conveyencer of feeling as you know [...]

I do not want you to fill your letter with a reply to all the rubbish in this but just give me one of your excellent pen pictures of home. Your description of the fireside gathering cheered me immensely.

My love I send to you all

Vian Amata Edzo

Frank

❦

32 North Avenue Letchworth
March 3 1919

My dear Frank[153]

Please note it was the red lines down the paper I was apologising for. Sorry if this reaches you a little later than usual, but we in this world

---

153 This letter has a note on its margin: 'Dear Daddy would you like a picture next week love from Morris'.

are so busy just now, and we must all do our bit, you know. First I must tell you we are all well in spite of the weather which has rained without ceasing since Monday morning. Sunday was a glorious day, just like spring. We all went to Howgills in the morning. The children were very good and still. I think they were interested in the room, only two persons spoke, but I can feel thought, so it was a quiet time for them [...]

We had an Anti-Conscription meeting, but it was very poorly attended; these meetings were held all over the country last Sunday. After tea and a little read and talk together I went to Skittles leaving the children to put themselves to bed, Morris 7.30 Dora and Chrissie at 8. (How is this for home and domestic circle you mentioned a few weeks ago in connection with Katie). We had a stirring time on the 'Coming Revolution'. Miss Stevens the speaker said we must do all we could to prevent bloodshed, no need for anything of that sort. I told you about her some time ago, she spoke for our organisation of women's trade unions in Bermondsey. She had been at the Industrial Conference which was held last Thursday,[154] and I am afraid got nowhere with [it]. I suppose you have heard that Anderson has passed on, it seems we can ill spare such men in these days, he had great power and strength of purpose and now he [has] had his work cut short. This reminds me to tell you that I have been reading again the *Life* of Margaret MacDonald and I wondered if you would care to have it. Mrs Middleton has lent it to me and you are welcome to have it if you care to. The life of such people make me feel how very mean and nothing my own life seems to be and yet I do all it seems possible to accomplish, it must be brain power lacking, not will.

I think this week I must quote for you some Impressions by George

---

154 On 27 February 1919, 600 trade unionists and 300 employers met cabinet ministers and civil servants at a National Industrial Conference in London to begin work on proposals for reforms in British industry. Rodney Lowe, 'The failure of consensus in Britain: The National Industrial Conference, 1919–1921', *The Historical Journal* 21 (1978) 649–675, 649.

Lansbury:[155] he has been to Cologne and he says that multitudes of people are being led away by the ravings of the press thinking that the one thing left is to wreck vengeance on the German people, but he can honestly say he never heard a soldier or officer ask for vengeance on any one. In Cologne one feels how dreadful it is to be a defeated nation. When our soldiers poured over the Rhine into the city the people wondered what was going to happen to them, but they found that the British soldier was human first and a soldier afterwards, at least during the time of an armistice. All he met from officers to ordinary soldiers agreed that the people were doing all they could do [to] make the army comfortable. Some of our people think the people are too servile but German waiters, German Barbers, German merchants always were more obliging, naturally so, and surely it is better thus if for any length of time portions of their country are to be occupied by foreign troops. Then he goes on about the starvation and death rate and then says 'let there be no mistake there is shortage everywhere except in Great Britain. In addition there is terrible unemployment, 25,000 in Cologne, and every other industrial area in similar plight (4,000 women in Bermondsey). What is needed is that all barriers should be thrown down and raw materials and food poured in. If this is not speedily done, not merely will Mid Europe become stricken with violence and chaotic ruin, but we ourselves will inevitably suffer also. I would wish my countrymen and women to be big enough, generous enough to feed their enemies, to do good to any who have done evil, because I believe that by so doing we should be helping to build civilization. If we cannot respond to the call of humanity, we ought surely to respond to the call of self-interest. He finishes up by mention of the splendid Cathedral at Cologne with glorious towers and simple round pillars reaching a great height from floor to ceiling. [...] Mrs Philip Snowden has some more about Berne, but as it is Socialist Personalities, I need not quote from her. Casey has an article called 'Drudge and Drudgess all about the miners and the wives. You know quite well how he puts things for the women. Breakfasts, dinners, teas and suppers, bath tubs to be filled and emptied, babies to be nursed and got to sleep.

155 During the war George Lansbury was editor of the left-wing *Daily Herald*, and later became leader of the Labour Party.

5. 'THESE LAST DAYS ARE THE MOST TRYING'

You know of course that Mr Cubbon is running as candidate for County Council. I was at the Skittles last night (after Adult School) folding, about 20 people addressing envelopes and a lot of helpers generally. I have promised to go again tonight to address envelopes it is pouring with rain too. I was not home last night till ¼ to 11. [...]

11 oclock. Just home from Skittles: only a few turned up tonight, but we have got all the writing finished. Now delivering and canvassing has to be done in two days. Cubbon has a nice address with six points. Education, Health, Land Reform, Allotments, Small Holdings and Housing. Bond Holding has 14, one of which is Denouncers of shirkers, spurious pacifists and profiteers. None of these are very much to the point and as he is in America, Cubbon may stand a chance, anyway it is propaganda. Miss Bixby said tonight she wished you were home to be made Sec[retar]y in her place. We came home together again and it was such a dark wet night. I wished you were with me, but I will do all I can for your share in this work.

No news about a house. Mr Morris wants £100 more than he gave last summer and it will cost another £100 to put in repair so probably Mr Pease will not buy. That was my last hope. I shall have to take the Adult School rooms yet, they are available. Our old ladies next door have let their bungalow for six months, a young couple with a baby, they came to me for eggs, and they will have more to say to me than the other people. I must stop now, very tired, off to bed. I sent you some books on Monday, will try to get some more you asked for next week. Be sure and write Christine a letter and Morris says he hopes you will answer his. I think Dora really draws very well, she always has and Morris too. Am writing to your mother tomorrow it is her birthday this week.

We all send our very best love to you.

Your loving wife Lucy

THE CONSCIENTIOUS OBJECTOR'S WIFE

3. 3. 1919

My Dear Lucy,

I hope the lines on this paper will not bother you. I have my wants supplied in this respect and it is the best they can do for me. I should think your present of paper was a welcome gift, certainly I got a surprise when I received your letter.

I am delighted to receive part of [the] report you sent about Berne. I shared this pleasure with Inkerne W to whom I read it and at once we discussed the need for such places here in England. They are quite common in the large towns on the continent and when we go upon our tour we shall undoubtedly see and stay at some of them, so pick up Esperanto.

Cubbon's visit was a very pleasant surprise and I enjoyed it immensely. He is so breezy, like a March when the sun is shining just as [it] does whilst I write, making everything look brighter and creating a new flow of the life urge. You are mistaken about his budget of news as he told me nothing fresh except that the New Town book is just finished and will soon be published, for which many thanks.

Find out all you can about Jordans, also Ross Community. I think the future looks big with promise and it makes us all rejoice. Such a piece of news as the Albert Hall meeting is more fraught with consequences than all diplomatic meetings ever held, because it is the sign of the awakening of the long sleeping demos, upon whom all so-called civilization has been built. It is the demand for Life in the fullest sense which is coming to the front and will not be denied. Great men in all classes will go down before it if they try and prevent its fruition.

[...] I received Esperanto books and I want you to thank Miss Bartholomew for her generous help. I cannot say how great a boon the learning of Esperanto has been to me. I can read very well now, 'though I says it as shouldn't' and discovered in the BE[156] that the annual

---

156 Probably *La Brita Esperantisto*, the magazine of the Esperanto Association of Britain.

5. 'THESE LAST DAYS ARE THE MOST TRYING'

conference is to be held in June at Liverpool. Also that the London Esperanto Dramatic Soc held a conference at [the] Working Men's College at which the members of the Edco educational committee played an important part. It was good to read about old places so familiar as Morley College & the Maurice Hall etc.

[…] I heartily agree with your resolution to go to Howgills and take the children. They are now old enough to enjoy the atmosphere even if they do not understand all that is said. Like you I feel the need of spiritual fellowship with my fellows and we have endeavoured to get it amongst ourselves by discussing some point in the Adult School lessons.

[…] Your loving husband Frank

March 10th 1919

My dearest Lucy

I beg to inform you that it was the green lines to which I referred. I must say how much I enjoyed the matter of your letter. You certainly can write what I call a real newsy letter which always contains a breath of home in it. Sometimes you make little omissions, which of course I always put down to your being hurried and to your thought flowing faster than your pen can travel. I play at guessing completion with these but am compelled to ask for help in some of them, for instance what is the name of the play in which you are about to take part.

[…] Thank Friend Cubbon for books received which are very welcome to us. As I shall be changing my lodgings in a few weeks' time you need not send any more. I have quite a number now and do not want to have to hire a van to remove them in. Give my congratulations to Councillor Cubbon and wish him full power to his elbow. I hope Katie will enjoy good weather and that you all have a happy time together.

I am pleased to hear you have decided to take the Adult School rooms for I have thought they would suit as a makeshift home for us until we finally settle, but have not liked to say anything about it. I have arranged the rooms in my own mind and if you will but get rid of most of your large furniture I am sure you could be very comfortable [...]

My Best Love to you all your Loving Father and Hubby Frank

&

32 North Avenue, Letchworth, Herts
March 12th 1919

My dear Frank

I see you have our great news – Cubbons is in. I wonder how you learned it. I am afraid Bond Holding is surprised at the result. Now we are hoping to win a number of seats at the next poll; there is only about 3 weeks to work to as we are contesting all 15 seats. Nothing succeeds like success you know. I believe even Cubbons himself was surprised, anyway he was terribly excited. He came into the Whist Drive at Howard Hall where I was washing up (by myself) for 90 people. He told us the numbers: 1,100 polled (out of 5000) and he had 86 majority. He said now the wedge was in we must drive it home. It was 11.30 before I got home so was too tired to go out on Sunday till the evening when I went to the Skittles as usual. A Miss Green was speaking on 'German Democracy'. We had a very interesting discussion by Cubbon, Moss, Dr Booth, Miss Kidd, Judge and Brunt.

Katie came on Monday 1 o'clock. The children came home a little earlier, had dinner and went to the station to meet her, then went on to school. She looks much better than she did, not so worried looking and a little fatter, she admits herself she is more contented. She has her duty and Dad appreciates it and she is very fond of Jack and he of her so they are happy together. Of course you are not discussed. I enjoyed her visit, it was quite nice to have her to talk to me after the children had gone to bed and they were pleased to have her here. I told her not to come for Easter; perhaps they will have a weekend for the May Day, it will be better weather then. It will be at the end of the month. She knows however this is an arrangement subject to what happens to you and where I may be.

The Adult School rooms have been taken by a couple about to get married, so that is off. My luck is dead out in house-hunting. I am afraid now I shall have to make up my mind to stay here till turned out. I believe the time has now been extended, the Rent Act,[157] only I am not sure whether my rent cannot be raised and that is quite enough to pay, more than I can afford without letting. However I shall struggle through somehow, but am getting about fed up. I do <u>hope</u> you will soon be home. It is not easy to write what one wishes to say, the pen is a poor substitute for words, one often conveys quite a wrong impression by using a word in a wrong way or by omitting stops (as I do). Sorry I often puzzle you but I never read over my letter to you and just write it as I think. I do not often hurry over it but take an awful long time. Another thing makes it more difficult, I often think you already know my scraps of news I do write. Well perhaps we shall soon be able to talk to each other as we want.

Agitation is still going on to gain the release of COs. I heard today that several strong letters have been written in the *Daily News*,[158] even Hugh Cecil is taking it up. It was stated on Saturday that the Home Sec says it can't be done till the soldiers are all demobilised. I met Mrs Williams and she told me and we were both very upset about it, it makes the duration more indefinite. However Judge thinks it is quite hopeful. Labour was waiting for a definite statement like that. Who knows what will happen?

Perhaps you do not know that Labour has gained 10 additional seats in London County Council Elections and all over the place gains too. Katie knew nothing about this, had no interest she said, neither Dad or Jack, that seems so much the attitude; such a pity I think, and that apathy accounts for much that happens.

---

157 The 1915 Rent and Mortgage Restriction Act prevented rents from being raised for the duration of the war.

158 The Liberal newspaper *The Daily News*, whose first editor had been Charles Dickens, was owned by the Quaker George Cadbury during the war, and was thus sympathetic to COs.

[...] I had a letter yesterday from your mother (Lill wrote it). She sends her love to you and is pretty well, hopes you will be home soon. Alf has had lumbago and the children whooping cough. No other news. Beanna's husband is home now, she is going to tea with Katie on Thursday. They are very friendly. Katie is seeing her a lot at Stead's shop.

[...] Now I must stop. All loving thoughts to you my dear husband, your ever loving Lucy

We are all well hope you are too

17.3.1919

Mia Amata Edzinon,

It was with mixed feelings that I read your letter, as it contains so much of human feeling. I am glad to know you all keep well and as I have neglected to say anything about myself in my last two letters, I will mention that I also am well. It was pleasing to hear you had an enjoyable time with our sister but I must say it is not altogether pleasant to realize that one is the skeleton in the cupboard. I presume by the number you mention that the Whist Drives are a success.

I easily pictured Friend Cubbon's dramatic entrance and the enthusiasm which prevailed. The victory will put increased vigour into the local movement and also draw fresh people to it. After the black time through which we have been passing, to see the sun always brings us back to the foundation of our faith [...]

As to my arriving at the election result, it was quite a simple example of deduction. From the result of the last election it was easily seen that there is a large section in Letchworth and Stevenage favourable to Labour. The Labour vote is not a weather cock and it would therefore be steady next time, result a victory: easy isn't it. The tide is setting our way already.

5. 'THESE LAST DAYS ARE THE MOST TRYING'

You know of course that Newbold is in. Fancy a CO elected to Parliament.[159] This is a time of opposites. The Allies insisting on the army of Germany being no more than 100,000 and recruited on a voluntary basis is really funny when one remembers that England has conscription and intends to keep it in force for some time to come, whilst the Socialists who are and can be the only ruling power now in Germany have always placed the demand for the abolition of conscription and the reduction of armaments first upon their programme. It seems like a scene in *Alice in Wonderland*, if one can forget for an instant the awful price we are all called upon to pay for all this folly.

I really wish you could get a more equitable frame of mind regarding our release, for nothing is more distressing than uncertainty. Put away all thought of it as an immediate affair and go about your work quietly resting on the thought that time brings all things if we only wait long enough. After all, what is another year or two to anyone with a philosophic mind and a knowledge of governments.

[...] Your remarks about the children lead me to think that perhaps my absence has led to a certain false value of myself in their eyes and I hope that when I do come back they will not feel that I am very different from what, in their innocence of reality, they imagined me to be, thus be disappointed. This may also apply to yourself, as undoubtedly time and circumstance has played its part with both of us. Spring is in the air and the birds are giving us much pleasure now.

[...] I send you all my love and eagerly await your reply.

Frank

---

159   John Turner Walton Newbold had been a CO and active in ILP politics. He was elected to Parliament as one of the first four Communist Party MPs, but not until the 1922 general election, so it seems that Frank may have been mistaken.

THE CONSCIENTIOUS OBJECTOR'S WIFE

32 North Avenue, Letchworth, Herts
March 19th 1919

My dear Frank

I did not receive your letter till afternoon instead of morning post as I usually do, so was more than glad to read you are well. I noticed of course that you had omitted to say lately, but I always try not to worry or if I do let it not be apparent. I really do go about my work quietly as usual and only have inward disturbance at being anxious for your release. Natural, isn't it, and another year or two makes all the difference to you and I and the children, be as philosophic as we will. You suggest too that when you do come back you will be different from what we imagine you are. My dear, you are not an imaginary father and husband but very real and the children remember you so well it will be as yesterday you left home; this I am sure of. As for myself, what is an absence of two years after companionship of 21? I think we know each other very well. Of course we have both altered, time and circumstance has played its part, not to lessen the value of ourselves to each other I hope.

I am sorry I do not appear to notice your jokes. You know my serious mind of old. I am just the same, perhaps more so. [...] We in the real world feel the seriousness of the time we live in, so please do not blame me. I am quite happy and cheerful but not content. I regret having put a hasty 'fed up' expression in your letter of last week. It was only momentary really, and I am quite strong enough to continue the struggle.

When I said you were not discussed with Katie I meant our position not argued against as formerly. In fact I think before long they will begin to see the sense of it: they must come to see it eventually. Of course you know they have not moved along our lines and Katie is about where I was 12 years ago. She said some surprising things, for her, which I did not remark [on], only quite agreed with. I believe she thought it original but it is our past conversations and the [*Manchester Guardian*] article going home. One thing was why should the few have fortunes and the many nothing? We are getting on. I shall send an [*Labour Leader*] presently when anything specially good comes along. We don't want a frost to nip the little bud!

Have you heard that we are to have a *Daily Herald* from the 31st March?

Our Play is off for Sat. also our Adult School is to be suspended; no one turns up. I shall go to the one Mrs Burlingham holds at Hillshott on Friday afternoons. The lessons are too good to miss and Adult School work too good to give up […]

Herbert Morrison is coming very much to the front. He has worked very hard in the Elections for [County Council] as Sec of London Labour Party. There is an interview with him in the *Labour Leader*. He mention J. Myles who he saw in Pentonville a short while ago. He is very pleased with the result of course. The new members are very varied in trade and type. He says 'we have now to go forward for the Boards of Guardians in April and Borough Councils in Nov. and be ready for a Parliamentary fight at any time. The fight of our opponents will be harder than ever now that we have got a foothold.'

I do not think we shall go away this year. It would not be fair for the children to lose school. Dora is again thinking of a scholarship; her teacher asked her this morning. She was not <u>very</u> keen because we may be going to New Town soon, she said, then asked if Daddy would like her to go in for it. I answered, you would as you very much wish them all to be as well educated as possible and if she did not win, she would be learning more, so she consented. I fancy this is her last chance as they do not sit for exams after 13. She has a good chance I think.

You will have the New Town book by now, hope you will enjoy it as much as I did and give you hope for the glorious future not only for ourselves but our children. Now I must stop. Love from us all

Your loving wife

Lucy

March 24th 1919

Mia Amata Edginon

Your cheerful and loving letter was a real treat. I think you have what is called the knack of putting your thoughts into concrete expressions which 'tell' [...]

Am glad to hear you have decided to attend at Hillshott as like you I think the lessons too good to be lost. We had an interesting discussion on Sunday morning upon the pacifist attitude towards the great strike.[160] It arose out of the question of the possibility of people being starved to death through inability to get food. We came to no definite conclusion except that a man has the right to withhold his labour if arguments and facts fail to arouse the sense of injustice in the community and to bring the employer to act rightly, but even then we are faced with the result of such a possibility.

[...] I am not sending the visiting order as I do not think it worthwhile your coming over for such a short time, but I suggest that as I am changing my quarters on April 14th that you come over by the first train from Hitchin, 7.20. I think it gets here about 8 o'clock and meet me, when perhaps we can have a longer time together.

Thanks for New Town: it is splendid and I sincerely hope it will meet with a large and quick response from the progressive forces in the country so that someone can got giving. Our going there will not be for at least another year, probably more so, Dora need not build too much upon it. Am pleased with the way you have expressed my desires to her. Tell her I shall not be disappointed if the [scholarship] does not get through as I know she will have done her best. Thank Morris for his picture which is just fine. I recognised the Letchworth tree but not the man or the birdie. It shows the spirit of the future for instead of a

---

160 There were many strikes in the UK throughout 1919, a consequence of unsettled conditions after the war, economic uncertainty, and a new sense of the possibilities of freedom through revolution. See note above about the Glasgow strike of January 1919.

5. 'THESE LAST DAYS ARE THE MOST TRYING'

gun as would have been expressed by the song 'He had a little gun' etc, he is giving crumbs to the birds. I take it that Morris chose the subject himself. I think the best part of my letters are the quotations in them but my own space is limited.

Lots of love to you all and looking forward to a return home some day.

Yours ever Frank

---

32 North Avenue Letchworth
March 25th 1919

My dear Frank

The best part of your letter is to know you are looking forward to return home some day and next best to know you enjoyed my last letter. I <u>had</u> intended to try and meet you on April 14th but even then I may miss you as Mr Ogilvie did his boys: of course I'll try not to you may be sure. What about all your books? I thought of bringing them back when I came to visit.

We are all well, only feeling the cold very much, it seems sharper than in the winter, in spite of the bright sun. The children were in the garden this evening until nearly seven o'clock, it is nice we are getting light evenings.

Miss Wilding's time is getting short now, she leaves Letchworth next Monday. Ray is not released yet from Dartmoor, although his time expired last week. I had news of Fritton through Brenda Jones, his sister had written to her. He evidently started work too soon and then had an illness which he is now recovering from at Dr Salter's home with Francis. It seems strange; they worked together, and were in prison together, and have now come together again. Will Fritton, who was rearrested having been at liberty for some time like Francis I suppose, is at Oxford, is cheerful and quite hopeful of release for all at the end of March!! Today was to be a special question a settling about COs in the House. I have not heard the result yet.

We have not got the great strike yet. I had not thought of it from a pacifist point of view, and I have been thinking it over during the day.

I could say a lot about it but find it difficult to write. One thing if it does come it will be short and sharp and soon over. I am quite sure it could not go on for long as all industry would soon be paralysed and money would cease to make more, consequently the demands will be given into before starvation is possible. I should like to discuss this with you. I think the conclusion you came to was quite right, a man is quite right to withhold his labour (in the market) in the cause of justice and if there is only unity there would not be but very little, if any suffering. It is quite impossible for me to write more to you on this subject though I can see lots of ways and means. I really believe that most people realize the workers are not out for merely more money but better conditions generally, something will certainly have to be done if not the condition of life will get worse than before the war. Everything is so costly the profiteers cannot have it all their own way; for instance coal is 45/- ton and the miners get 4/- to dig it: where does the rest of the money go? People are beginning to wonder, and things are being shown up, how the miner lives and how many are killed annually and so on.

[...] Pixmore School is not joining in the Maypole festival this year, so they are going to have a field up this end of the town for Norton, only on May 24th. Of course our three will all be dancing. Morris is very graceful. I like his bow. He calls it to 'honour his partner'. He is going into the second standard at Easter, still with Miss Bracey. He has no trouble with sums. Chrissie does not like them and pities the boys having to do arithmetic while the girls sew, she likes that and will be a useful little woman before long but she enjoys a game too. I do not feel I have any news for you so will stop now and finish in the morning. Goodnight.

I have no more news now than I had last night, somehow I feel that the next few days are very important, such a lot of things are awaiting decision and such a lot happening.

5. 'THESE LAST DAYS ARE THE MOST TRYING'

You know how in a meeting when there is silence I can always feel the thoughts. I feel now and the air full of the same when one knows that there is trouble all over the world, is it any wonder. Famine and sickness and death in Central Europe and all this Industrial trouble here and amid all this distraction the framing of peace in Paris. Arthur Ponsonby says in the [*Labour Leader*] 'Keep your eye on Paris'.[161]

I cannot write any more, hope you will keep well and as strong as possible to face the future whatever may happen. All our love is with you and kind and happy thoughts of many people. Almost every day I meet someone who asks about you. Mrs Matthews is back to pack up. They have sold Manor Farm. I saw her yesterday.

Ever your loving wife

Lucy

32 North Avenue, Letchworth
April 2nd 1919

My dear Frank

Quite a lot of questions in your letter. I will tell you first who are the candidates for the Urban Election, Labour ones I suppose you mean. We are trying for all the 15 seats. I have 175 Polling cards to address tomorrow. We are all very busy I can tell you. The names are Clapham Lander, Miss Bartholomew, Mr Brunt, Mr Coates, Mr Crossley, Mr Cubbon, Mr Furnston, Percy Jones. Mr Kennett, Mrs Kidd, Mr Kidd, Miss Lees, Mr Moss. Mr Purdom, Mr Tickle. There are 20 others not our side.

The apple trees I have pruned myself, also the Loganberry. Have got the raspberries and strawberries in order, also the rhubarb, am getting

---

161 Ponsonby was a Liberal MP and a member of the Union of Democratic Control, an anti-war organisation. The negotiations that would bring about the Versailles Peace Treaty were underway in Paris at this time.

Broad Beans and Shallots in on Sat. DVWP. I am doing the garden all by myself this year. Of course Morris has got his little bit but he wants some of everything to go in.

[...] I wrote on Monday to the Home Sec[retar]y asking for your release at the expiration of this sentence. Have had no reply yet. I have been asked to let you know that Henry Wash 3 Palmerston Rd Bedford is willing to give hospitality which may be necessary and any other assistance to men on their release; this is from Mrs Ogilvie through Mrs Bowry to me. Anything might happen, one never knows.

You did not tell me about the books you have. I have got your bicycle home from Palmer's shop. I think it is alright. I am selling the piano. Shall you be satisfied if I get £8 for it? I offered it to Miss Last and now Mrs Cleeton says you once offered it to her. They both have the money ready and both are willing to pay this. I haven't decided yet who shall have it. It is rather amusing, I believe they would bid one against another but honestly I don't consider it worth more and I think Lasts have first claim, although they have had a fortnight to decide and Tom Cleeton came with the money on Tues evening, and I had received no deposit or any word about it from Last since they decided to have it on Saturday, so you see I am in rather a difficult position, and I told them they could have it for £6 as 2 of the wires are broken and ivories off and a hammer broken. What a thing it is to have a conscience [...]

The *Daily Herald* has survived its birth. I have one from Mrs Middleton each day but I really haven't had time to read it. I see someone is advocating a 40 hour week for wives and can see it quite possible with Cooperation and labour-saving devices. This must be for New Town. I do hope that scheme will be set going soon, I mean New Town. I think the majority of wives expect to keep working all their waking moments and half the nights with babies. I have been glancing through a book, *The Awakening of Women*, and it is most interesting.[162] It shows you how from the long past ages women have always worked the hardest. She

---

162   This may have been *The Awakening of Women* by Frances Swiney (William Reeves 1905, 2nd edition), reprinted in a third, revised edition in 1908.

did the inventing too, things for her own use which her lord and master was able to perfect in his leisure time which she never had. The author thinks women the superior and in time to come human beings will be sexless or all women. They are considerably in the majority now, 5 to 1 I believe, but for the present I must say I prefer a man about the house, as Mrs Tickle says she does not like a hen party as an objection to the adult school. I have not been able to go to Hillshott yet.

Miss Laws is playing mother to a small nephew (I hope I have not told you this before). He is aged 4 and his father, Miss Law's brother, was drowned. His mother died of flue and he was brought from his home in Canada to his grandmother in London. Miss L went and fetched him and intends to keep him if possible, she says she is young, more like his mother and a more suitable guardian for him, you know her way of saying this. She is finding him a tie and is never free in the evenings till about 10, staying with him when she puts him to bed etc.

[...] No more news.

  Lots of love from us all. Your loving children and wife Lucy

                April 7th 1919

Dear Wife

Many thanks for your letter, the news of which is so varied that I hardly know what to reply to first. The glimpses you give me of the gardening which you together with the other members of the family are carrying on fills me with a desire to be able to add my quota to the general stock. The things you mention having sown I had almost forgotten [...]

Thanks for the list of Labour candidates. It is quite a family party. Miss Lees is pushing to the front very quickly, isn't she. Miss Lawes is a very fortunate young woman to be able to get a family ready-made upon which to pour her mother love, and I am sure she will be the better for the attempt. The pity of the present and the future is the fact of so many unmarried girls whose hearts are big for service and love but who will never get the chance to become even foster mothers [...]

I hope your reply from the Home Sec will be a satisfactory one, though why you should need to worry the poor man I can't think.

By the way is the spring air affecting you all at Letchworth, that telegrams must be sent with rumours of release in them? These things disturb the usual calm of our monastic life and give rise to all sorts of strange thoughts. As to the piano problem I can only say that it would surpass Solomon, for to cut it in half would not decide the question.

Yes this my last letter from Bedford for this sentence and I hope you will enjoy reading it as I can assure you my ingenuity is taxed to fill all these yards and yards of lines with thoughts that will bear the light of day.

You are to be congratulated upon your success as a poultry keeper in a small way but I'm inclined to think that the high prices may have helped perhaps.

What you say about *Woman* is not new to me and if you refer to my letters you will find I mention some of the things you have quoted. As to the male becoming extinct I do not think that is likely, but certainly there is already a neuter race coming into being and they are to be found amongst both sexes. Havelock Ellis and Carpenter have both written on this subject. These neuters are called Uranians and can be distinguished by their characteristics, broadly speaking the mannish woman and the womanish man, but most of them are women and the age in which we live is certainly aiding in their development, but given a different environment in which greater freedom for the development of the moral and social side of mankind is allowed, the sex differences, which are so magnified today will disappear and dominance of men together with servitude of women will be replaced with comradelyness and service [will] be the keynote of all.[163] Eugenics is an interesting

---

163 Frank has been reading the writing of the influential doctor Havelock Ellis, who was the first to publish serious studies of homosexuality, and offered theories of transgender psychology and human sexuality later adopted in psychoanalysis. Edward Carpenter, author, social reformer and philosopher, lived openly as a homosexual man, despite the punitive laws against male homosexuality at the time.

subject but if placed apart from all other great subjects it leads to unsupportable postulates and absurd theories. Just as the earth is a circle and is bound in the cycle of the universe, so are all human activities, whether in the realm of thought or action, and one deflected from its proper relationship with the rest puts the whole out of gear.

You ask about my books. Well, I have not yet decided whether to contract with the Midland [Railway] for a special rate or to charter a boat and send them home by the Ouse. Or do you mean what am I reading? At present I'm interested in travel and am reading Belt's *Naturalist in Nicaragua*. It is full of interesting stuff such as ant life, bees, beetles, bugs and fleas, birds and butterflies etc also gold-mining, gardening, cattle, whirlwinds and rivers, sculpture and ancient customs, glacial periods and theories of all kinds. I turned my nose up at this book some months ago but spring plays strange tricks with us and what appeared dull and uninteresting in winter comes forth with a different aspect when the birds call and the sap is running. Our chestnut trees are pushing out their leaves and the Hyacinths and Daffodils are coming into bloom. As our release seems very probable I leave it to you to decide whether it is worthwhile your coming over next Monday.

I hope I have not left anything unsaid in my letter. On reading it through I find myself much in evidence in it which is rather unusual is it not. You will be pleased to hear that my health is greatly improved.

I send you all my love and look forward to a speedy reunion

Mia Amata Edzino

Frank

8. Noel Palmer, Katie, Morris, Dora, Frank, Chrissie and Lucy, Letchworth 1919.

Index

Page numbers in *italics* refer to illustrations.

A

Admiralty   6n
adoption   301
Adult Schools   63, 183, 191, 208, 282
   Hillshot   295, 296
   Letchworth   xiv, xvi, 6n, 28, 28n, 50, 84, 121, 211, 227, 256, 258, 273, 295; committee   89–90, 92, 145, 281; handbook   102, 250, 261; potential home for Sunderlands   237, 287, 289–90, 291; talks   46, 85–6, 121
   Summer School   58, 63
air raids   xvii, 44–5, 69, 83, 84, 89, 98, 125, 126–7, 128, 161, 180
aircraft   xvii, 44–5, 83, 83n, 161–2, 220, 223
alcohol   xiv, 116–17, 116n, 158, 280–1, 280n
Alder, Percy   121–2
Allen, Clifford   51, 51n, 142
Alpha Union   69, 69n
alternative service   xii, xiii, 33, 42, 42n, 165, 165n, 237
amateur dramatics   221, 281
Amor, Miss   144, 180
Anderson, William Crawford   285
Armistice   xvi, 226, 229, 232, 277n
Army, British *see* British Army
Arnold, Matthew   113
Artists Rifles Regiment   152

B

Baldock   17, 27, 63
   Letchworth and Baldock Citizen (newspaper)   104, 104n, 121
Ball, Mr   140
Barker, Leslie   271
Barker, Mrs   219
Barnstaple   xvii–xviii, 143, 144, 146–8, 150–1, 152–3, 154, 155, 164, 185–6
Bartholemew, Miss   68, 142, 207, 211, 212, 232, 249, 262, 299
Bedford   xv, 125, 218
   Bedford Barracks   1–7, 9–10, 12–16, 19–21, 22–4, 26, 28–9, 34–41, 57–60, 62–7, 70–2
   Bedford Prison   xvii, 51, 76–7, 81

Bedford, Mrs   9
Bedford House   250
Bedfordshire Regiment   26
bees/beekeeping   30, 115, 123, 129
Belgium   219, 233, 267, 276n
Belt, Thomas, *The Naturalist in Nicaragua*   303
Bentham, Ethel   222, 222n
Berne Conference (1919)   279, 288
Beveridge, Bruce   18
Bible   35, 40, 131, 210
Bible of Nature, The (book)   114
bicycles   69, 77, 79, 125, 133, 149, 208, 300
birdsong   52, 108, 119, 281, 293
Birlingham, Mrs   295
Bixley, Miss   261, 287
Blackburn, Miss   211
Blackmore, R D, *Lorna Doone*   155
black-out   255
Bland, Mrs   208
Booth, Dr   290
Borrow, George
   The Bible in Spain   133, 138, 141
   Life of the Gypsies   81
Bowry, Mr   31, 80, 151, 225
Bowry, Mrs   82, 99, 300
Bradley, Mrs   17
Brayshaw, Mr   215
Briant, Nellie   225, 250, 266
Britannia Insurance   xv–xvi, 11, 78, 86
British Army   26, 37, 37n, 67, 152
   Calais Mutiny   267, 267n
   medical examinations   3–4, 7, 19, 59–60, 60n, 64–5, 70, 180
   physical fitness categories   7, 60n, 64
   and strikes   267, 267n, 269–70
   treatment of conscientious objectors   4, 5, 7
   uniforms   *xii*, 4, 4n, 6, 8, 26, 37, 59, 71
Brockway, Fenner   xii, 70n, 114, 114n
Brockway, Mrs   51
brotherhood, universal   xii, 44, 50, 77, 148n
Brown, Kemp   17, 19, 80, 176
Browning, Robert
  'Evelyn Hope'   201
   Our Beloved Dead   283

Brunt, Donald (D D)   19, 50, 57, 68, 79, 104, 183–4, 245, 265, 290, 299
Brunt, Mrs   30
Buchan, John, *Mr Standfast*   xiv
Buckingham, Carl   160, 165
Buckingham, Claudia   144, 148, 152, 158, 160–1, 189
Buckingham, Mr   152, 183
Bulwer-Lytton, Edward, *The Last Days of Pompeii*   79, 79n
Bulwer-Lytton, Lady Constance Georgina   239
Bungalow, The   55, 55n, 90, 90n, 143, *304*
   drainage problems   105–6, 107, 108
   sublet by Lucy   127, 128–9, 130, 138, 144, 146, 165
Burgess, Mr   23
Butler, Harriette   221, 221n

C

Cadbury, George   291n
Calais Mutiny   267, 267n
Campbell, R J, *The New Theology*   216
caravans   66, 66n, 132, 195–6, 237, 263
Carlyle, Thomas, *Sartor Resartus*   133, 159
Carpenter, Edward   170, 302, 302n
   Civilization: Its Cause and Cure   113
   England's Ideal   113
   Towards Democracy   133, 138, 283
Casey, Mr (friend)   16, 231
Casey, Mr (political writer)   286
Catholicism   147, 149, 152, 157–8, 160
Cecil, Hugh   291
Cecil, Lord Robert   61, 61n, 235–6
censorship   xii–xiii, 5, 5n, 210
Chesterton, G K, *Essays on All Things*   65
chickens   xvi, 47, 49–50, 51, 79, 90, 118, 121, 129, 138, 198, 208, 212, 244, 282, 302
Christian World (newspaper)   272
Christianity   35, 38, 40, 49–50, 100, 256, 283 *see also* Bible; Catholicism; Church of England; nonconformist religion; preaching; prison: chaplains; Quakers
Christmas   87, 95–9, 101, 245
Church of England   158, 162
cinema   5, 205–6, 248
Clapham, Dr   134
Clarke, Mr   2–3, 244

307

Clarke, Mrs   241
Clifford, Dr John   278, 278n
Clifton, E J   xv, 48, 56, 98, 120, 121, 127–8, 131, 147, 180, 193, 206, 225, 249, 254, 290, 291
   and death of wife   129, 130
   Lucy visits   197–8
   opposition to conscientious objectors   44–5
   relationship with Frank   129, 130
   visits Lucy   203, 205, 207
Clifton, Katie   xv, xvii, 18, 23, 27, 45, 48, 54, 56, 89, 120, 127–8, 130–1, 145, 147, 148, 161, 180, 197–8, 240, 244, 248, 271–2, 273, 274, 280, *304*
   health and illness   188, 209, 249, 253
   opposition to conscientious objectors   290, 292, 294
   political views   291, 294
   relationship with Jack Parker   69, 83–4, 115, 193, 193n, 206, 209, 210, 225, 254, 255, 290, 291
   visits Lucy   75, 78, 79, 203, 205, 207, 289, 290
Clifton, Mrs (Lucy's mother)   xvii, 27, 48, 51, 56, 79, 81, 83, 114, 115, 120–1, 142
   illness and death   45, 126–8, 131, 132
   opposition to conscientious objectors   11, 62, 78
clothing   4, 4n, 7, 14, 16, 30, 47, 67, 105, 160
coal   69, 213–16
   prices   213–14, 275, 298
   rationing   190, 213–14
   shortages   144, 149, 215–16, 262, 264, 267, 271–2
Coates, Mr   299
Cobbold, Mr   113, 210, 212
Code, Mr   177–8, 179, 183, 186
Commission for Relief in Belgium   276n
Commonwealth Community (Ross-on-Wye)   255, 256, 258, 258n, 288
communal living   69, 86, 206, 300
Congregational Church   158, 162
conscientious objectors   ix, x–xi, xix–xx, 3, 3n, 70, 71–2, 139, 140, 215 *see also* alternative service; courts-martial; tribunals
   'absolutist'   xii, xv, xxiii, 6n, 64, 103, 111
   agricultural work   6, 6n, 40, 42n, 59, 165, 165n
   Army treatment of   4, 5, 7
   and cowardice   17, 62, 64
   medical examinations   3–4, 7, 19, 59–60, 60n, 64–5, 70, 180
   opposition to   xi, xv, 11, 17, 44–5, 54, 62, 290, 292, 294
   post-war treatment of   258, 259–60, 261, 265, 265n, 266, 269, 271, 272, 273, 274, 291
   press coverage of   272, 278, 278n, 291, 291n

in prison   31, 33, 72, 114, 114n, 185, 185n, 209, 297; privileges   93–4, 210; release   274, 282, 283, 291, 293, 296; release and re-internment   151, 151n, 297; sentences   3–4, 23–4, 39, 51, 51n, 80, 180, 255
   refusal to wear uniform   6, 8, 26, 37, 59, 71
   support for   xiv, xxv, 11, 17–18, 28, 30, 31–2, 35, 66, 142, 143, 300
   work camps for   xv, xxiv, 80n
Conscientious Objectors Information Bureau   254
conscription   x–xi, 139, 139n, 140, 196, 272, 272n, 274, 285 *see also* alternative service; conscientious objectors; No Conscription Fellowship (NCF)
cooking   69, 115, 117, 121 *see also* food
Co-operative Movement   82, 89, 91n, 235
council elections *see* elections
courts-martial   xv, 3–4, 6, 19, 20, 28, 35, 35n, 36, 37, 59–60, 64, 70–1
cowardice   17, 62, 64
Cree, Mr   202, 208, 212, 257
Cree, Ray   99, 114, 232, 237, 244, 260–1, 297
Crees, Miss   84
Crossley, Mr   299
Crowle Smith, Reverend   131, 132, 139
Crowley, Dr   46, 80, 114–15, 126
Crowley, Mrs   213, 241
Cubbon, Mr   9, 38, 219, 245, 278, 287, 288, 289, 290, 292, 299
Cuppuck, Mr   14
Curzon, Lord   111

D

Daily Herald (newspaper)   83, 83n, 286, 286n, 295, 300
Daily News (newspaper)   291, 291n
dancing   48, 85, 173, 173n, 234, 298
Dartmoor Prison   xxiv, 185, 185n, 244, 255
Darwin, Charles, *Voyage of the Beagle*   113
death   127–8, 129, 130, 131, 132, 230, 231
Defence of the Realm Acts   xxiv, 90
demobilisation
  military   265, 266, 267n, 291
  war workers   213, 216, 232, 240
  women   213, 216, 279
Dessin, Eva E E   282
Devon   xvii–xviii, 127, 148, 154, 160, 161–2, 164, 166, 172–3, 177–8
  Barnstaple   xvii–xviii, 143, 144, 146–8, 150–1, 152–3, 154, 155, 164, 185–6
  Dartmoor   184, 185
  Dartmoor Prison   xxiv, 185, 185n, 244, 255

Newbridge   153, 183–4, 187–8, 192, 196
Dickens, Charles   291n
   Dombey and Son   242, 265
   Martin Chuzzlewit   77
   Nicholas Nickleby   140
   Oliver Twist   152
   Pickwick Papers   150, 154
   A Tale of Two Cities   108
divorce   67, 89
doctors   14, 59–60, 60n, 64–5, 70, 91, 110, 127, 134, 261, 265, 265n, 297
Donnelly, Mr   105
Drummond, Henry   256

E

Eastman, Mr   18, 18n, 78, 89, 112, 165, 166, 168, 235, 254
education   85–6, 281 *see also* Adult Schools; schools
   of Sunderland children   95, 147, 149, 151, 154, 155, 157–8, 160, 162, 192, 197, 298
Education Act 1918   85, 85n
elections   215
   county council elections (1919)   287, 290, 292
   general election (1918)   xvi, 230, 231, 233, 235, 237, 241, 244, 248, 248n, 252, 254, 258–9, 273
   general election (1922)   293n
   urban council elections (1919)   291, 299, 301
Ellis, Havelock   302, 302n
environment *see* nature and environment
Esperanto   112, 112n, 115, 116, 117, 226, 259, 261, 282, 288–9
   books   211, 212
   Dora learns   138, 144, 166, 207, 220, 245
   Frank learns   133, 143, 167, 179, 185, 191, 212, 220, 246, 247, 252
   La Brita Esperantisto (magazine)   288, 288n
   Lucy learns   149–50, 166, 169
eugenics   114, 302–3
Exmoor   184

F

Fabian Society   xxv
famine (in Europe)   276–7, 279, 284, 286
fatherhood   209, 251, 252, 253, 294, 301
feminism   67, 69, 84, 84n, 134–5, 183, 186, 212–13, 216, 260, 279, 300–1, 302, 302n *see also* women's suffrage

Fiennes, Arthur   265
Fineburg, Mr   108
Fisher, H A L   85n
Fisher, Lettice   85–6, 85n
flowers   131, 146, 148–9, 168
food   5, 10, 13, 24, 46, 69, 157, 158, 178, 226 *see also* cooking; housekeeping; vegetarianism
   apples   2, 3, 14, 29, 52, 79, 82, 87, 88, 89, 98, 178, 193, 196, 198
   in Bedford Barracks   3, 15, 24, 40, 59, 61–2, 64, 65
   bread   3, 9, 13, 15, 24, 40, 59, 61, 63, 65, 82, 87, 175, 178, 243
   butter   9, 13, 24, 82, 147, 250
   cakes   87, 157, 184
   cheese   13, 15, 82, 157, 189, 226
   at Christmas   98, 250
   eggs   xvi, 10, 14, 49–50, 51, 79, 90, 118, 121, 177, 198, 244, 282
   famine (in Europe)   276–7, 279, 284, 286
   fats   104, 108, 189
   foraging   184, 226
   fruit   177–8, 226, 250
   honey   30, 123
   margarine   15, 59, 91, 104, 118, 147, 189, 226, 250, 277
   Marmite   87, 109, 147, 157
   meat   59, 110, 115, 118, 121, 189
   milk   110, 157, 188
   nuts and nut butter   69, 82, 87, 87n, 88, 98, 104, 147, 226, 250
   oats   82, 87
   parcels   xvi, 10, 14, 29, 30, 32, 34, 40
   potatoes   42, 52, 68, 78–9, 157, 159, 175, 208
   prices   xvi, 82, 90, 95, 98, 148, 177–8, 180, 188, 193, 198, 243, 244, 282, 302
   in prison   47–8, 62
   rationing   68, 68n, 89, 104, 109–10, 118, 121, 123–4, 147–8
   Robeline   188
   shortages   42, 68, 80, 89, 91–2, 91n, 104, 108, 109–10, 115, 141, 157, 180, 193, 250, 279
   sugar   68, 89, 118
   tea   10, 15, 59, 61, 89, 91, 98, 99, 141, 189
Food Vigilance Committee   110
Fox, George   100, 100n
   Journal   108–9
Fox, Mr   152, 155, 183, 184, 196, 249
Foyles Booksellers   170, 210
Francis, Arthur   44, 134, 266, 297
freedom   149, 168, 259–60
Friend, The (magazine)   121–2, 121n

311

Fritton, Charles   193, 195, 212, 266, 297
Fritton, Will   297
Fulworth, Mr   281
Furmston, Mr   117, 122, 299
Furnster, Mr   68

G

Galsworthy, John   283
Galton, Francis, *Inquiries into Human Faculty*   114
games and toys   10, 14, 16, 36, 48, *53*, 97–8, 202, 206, 248, 250, 251, 262, 290, 292
Garden City movement   ix, xiii–xiv, xvi, 38, 46–7, 61, 114, 121–2, 122n, 193, 198, 202, 213, 214, 224, 255, 272 *see also* Welwyn Garden City ("New Town")
gardens/gardening   42, 46, 51, 78–9, 121, 131, 152–3, 177–8, 208, 275–6, 299–300
Gardner, Mrs   126, 127, 130, 131, 134, 135, 142, 165
Gardner, Reg   29, 80, 131
Garside, Mr   104, 281
Gay, Miss   132, 134, 211
gender and gender roles   186, 212–13, 216, 231, 302, 302n
general elections *see* elections
German (language)   143
German citizens, internment of   102, 102n
Germany   224, 234, 276–7, 277n, 279, 286, 290, 293
Gillett, Joseph Rowntree   2, 2n, 23, 30, 255, 257
Gillman, F J, *The Fellowship hymn book and its right use in adult schools*   283
Glasier, Katherine   70n
Glover, T R, *The Jesus of History*   283
goats   xvi, 197
Gomersal, Mr   250
Goodall, Mr   33, 42, 42n, 48, 50
Goodall, Mrs   33, 42, 42n, 47, 50
Gospel Oak (London)   198
gossip   218, 258
Green, Miss   290
Gregory, Miss   51
Gregory, Mr   38, 51, 180, 184–5
Gregory, Mrs   83, 250, 271
Gregory, Nellie   101
Guildford   xvi, xx, 225, 227, 229, 232–3, 234–5, 241, 255, 257–8, 260–1, 265, 277
Guys, Miss   196

H

Hall Jones, Mr   119, 209, 261
Hancox, Mr   xv–xvi, 3, 3n, 4, 5, 7, 8, 11, 18, 19, 22
Hardie, Keir   248
Harding, Mrs   1, 14, 50, 85
Hardy, Mrs   258
Hardy, Thomas   208, 215
   The Mayor of Casterbridge   261
Harris, Joseph Theodore   121
Harris, Mr   165, 165n
Harris, Mrs   165
Harrison, Mrs   139, 139n
Heads without Heart (book)   112
health and illness   xvi–xvii, 33, 45, 51, 64, 66, 103, 126–7, 157, 163, 209, 241, 250, 266, 268, 292
   Army physical fitness categories   7, 60n, 64
   colds   25, 27, 29, 30, 113, 218, 219, 230, 233, 261, 264
   dental problems   68, 125, 130, 134, 138, 145, 149
   exhaustion   46, 138
   headaches   27, 33–4
   holiday, benefits of   157, 161, 165, 173, 189, 196
   indigestion   42, 47–8
   influenza epidemic   xvii, 180, 188, 218, 222, 225, 230, 261
   neuralgia   222, 223, 249
   rheumatism   253, 256
   scarlet fever   75, 78–80, 81–2
   skin complaints   211, 215
   tonsilectomy   73–4, 86–7, 88–9, 91, 92, 106–7
Henderson, Arthur   68n, 248, 248n
Hendon Aerodrome   223
Henlow Aerodrome (RAF Henlow)   109, 109n
heredity   113–14
Heydeman, Lucy   xxi
Heydeman, Tom   xxi
Hibbert, Gerald K, *God, Nature and Human Freedom*   283
Hill, Mr   105–6
Hitchin   xv, 1–2, 57, 229
Hoare, John   5n
Hobson, J A   219
Hoge, Miss   275
Holding, Bond   115, 140, 287, 290
Home Office   xv, xxiv, 6n, 24n, 31, 36, 42n, 80, 80n, 237

homosexuality   302, 302n
Hoover, Herbert   276, 276n
Horsley, Sir Victor, *Alcohol and the Human Body*   116, 116n
House of Commons   274, 297
housekeeping   69, 87, 146-7, 226, 255, 264-5, 300 *see also* cooking; food; shops/shopping
housing   61, 122, 219, 226, 228, 276 *see also* Garden City movement; Sunderland, Lucy: housing
Howard, Ebenezer   xiii, 50, 51n, 61, 61n
Howard, Mr   35, 38
Howard Hall (Letchworth)   85, 139, 208, 218, 223, 230, 234, 267, 276, 290
Howard Park (Letchworth)   276
Howgills (Quaker Meeting House, Letchworth)   61, 61n, 63, 65, 255, 281, 285, 289
humour   66n, 69, 113, 115, 118, 124, 125, 129-30, 159, 163, 175-6, 185, 210, 212, 259, 263
Hunter, Hariette   221, 221n
Hunter, Jonny   57
Hunter, Mrs   272

I

illness *see* health and illness
ILP *see* Independent Labour Party (ILP)
In Praise of Freedom (book)   282
Independent Labour Party (ILP)   xiv, 50, 61, 83, 99, 145, 235, 248, 261
    in Barnstaple   154
    and elections   233, 287, 291, 295, 299, 301
    meetings   85, 208, 215
    membership numbers   213
    opposition to conscription   51n, 285
    socials   230, 250, 258, 260, 281
    women members   219, 258-9
    Women's Conference   221, 226
industrial action   265, 267, 267n, 269-70, 271-2, 273, 296, 298
influenza epidemic   xvii, 180, 188, 218, 222, 225, 230, 261
Ingoldsby, Thomas (Richard Barham), *The Ingoldsby Legends*   260
Inkerne, W   288
insurance (business)   ix, xv-xvi, 11, 78, 86, 183, 186, 188, 228 *see also* Sunderland, Lucy: work
Internationale (song)   226
internationalism   17-18, 220
Ironside, Mrs   98
isolation   7, 62, 124, 151, 181-2, 260, 267, 268-9 *see also* loneliness

J

Jacques, Mrs   47
Jefferies, Miss   28, 48, 80, 84, 161, 170, 174, 175–6, 178, 179, 180, 198, 230, 255
Jerome, Jerome K   278, 278n
John Brindsmead & Son   280, 280n
Johnson, Mr   11, 16
Jones, Percy   299
Jones, Rufus, *The Inner Life*   48, 48n
Jordans (Buckinghamshire)   100, 122, 122n, 126, 159, 288
Judge, Mr   290, 291

K

Kays, Mr   78
Kearney, Mrs   92
Kennett, Mr   299
Kidd, Miss   290
Kidd, Mrs   299

L

Labour Choir   250
Labour Leader (newspaper)   70, 70n, 83, 254, 272, 294–5, 299
Labour Party *see* Independent Labour Party (ILP)
Ladd, Mr   232, 258, 275
Lander, Clapham   17, 19, 180, 299
landscape   150–1, 152–3, 168, 184, 187–8
Lansbury, George   285–6, 286n
Latman, Mr   72
Lawes, Miss   19, 83, 99, 145, 149, 208, 226, 250, 301
Lees, Miss   218, 220, 226, 299, 301
Leonie (Belgian lodger)   219, 222, 225, 226, 230
Letchworth   xiii–xiv, 82, 109–10, 219, 299 *see also* Adult Schools: Letchworth; elections; Independent Labour Party (ILP)
   Belgian refugees   110, 110n, 171, 229, 249, 261, 267, 272, 275, 275n, 276
   The Bungalow   55, 55n, 90, 90n, 105–6, 143, *304*
   Howard Hall   85, 139, 208, 230, 276
   Howard Park   276
   Howgills (Quaker Meeting House)   61, 61n, 63, 65, 255, 281, 285, 289
   influenza epidemic   xvii, 180, 188
   Little Antwerp   275, 275n
   Mission Hall   49–50
   munitions industry   110, 110n, 218, 219, 220, 223

   Pixmore school   298
   Quaker community   ix, xiii–xiv, xiv
   shops   40, 40n, 80, 82, 89, 89n, 91, 104, 115, 162, 179, 226, 259, 281
   Skittles Temperance inn   xiv, 6n, 33, 50, 51, 61, 120, 208, 215
   Spirella Hall   235
   Wesleyan School Room   276
Letchworth and Baldock Citizen (newspaper)   104, 104n, 121
letters
   as history   xix–xx
   importance of   32, 101–2, 140, 156, 180, 206
   prison regulations   *43*, 116, 117, 156, 161, 162, 210
libraries   48
lighting   255
Lindsay, Mr   4, 265
Little Antwerp (Letchworth)   275, 275n
Lloyd, Mr   8, 9, 13
Lloyd George, David   68, 68n, 231, 248n
London   188, 191, 197–8, 225, 272, 291
London, Jack, *The Valley of the Moon*   35, 35n, 37, 74, 123, 205, 206
loneliness   7, 11, 51, 81, 83, 98, 135, 142, 245, 248 *see also* isolation
Longfellow, Henry Wadsworth   48
  'Hiawatha'   54
  'Miles Standish'   137
Lovel, Mr   235
Lugden, Mr   177
Lytton, Constance (Lady Constance Georgina Bulwer-Lytton)   239

M

Macarthur, Mary   222, 222n
Macaulay, Lord, *Historical Essays*   113
MacDonald, Margaret Ethel   84, 84n, 285
MacDonald, Ramsay   248, 248n, 254
   Margaret Ethel MacDonald (book)   84, 84n, 285
Macfadyen, Dr   91, 127
Machin, Mr   100
Mactavish, J M, *What Labour Wants from Education*   283
Mallon, Mrs   281
Manchester Guardian (newspaper)   273, 274, 294
Markievicz, Constance   248–9, 248n
Marshall, Catherine   111, 111n
Marshall, Mr   105, 105n, 130, 212, 232, 243, 261, 276
Martin, G Currie   282

Matthews, Mr   19, 47, 133, 137
Matthews, Mrs   19, 46–7, 92, 118, 121, 137
Matthews, Sheila   211
Mazzini, Giuseppe, *Duties of Man*   113, 133, 159
Middleton, Mrs K J   76, 77, 78, 79, 83, 98, 134, 142, 159, 161, 165, 176–7, 178, 193, 196, 198, 203, 216, 217, 235, 241, 255, 273, 285, 300
   gives books to Frank   209, 210
   letter to Frank   75
   support of Lucy   87, 97, 264
Military Service Acts   x–xi, xv, 139, 139n
Milton, Mr   225, 229, 232–3, 255
Minns, Mr   166
Mission Hall (Letchworth)   49–50, 49n
missionaries   221
money   xvi, 64, 264, 291, 298
   Sunderland family income   xvi, 30, 64, 69, 78, 87, 138, 165, 166, 167, 235, 255, 264, 291
   wages   214, 216, 233–4
Morel, E D   51, 51n, 278
Morgan, Mrs   183, 184, 187, 188, 191–2, 196
Morris, Mr   254
Morris, William   21n, 126, 133, 138, 141, 142
Morrison, Herbert   295
Morrison, Mr   104
Moss, Mr   83, 290, 299
Moss, Mrs   83
motherhood   49, 85–6, 117, 131, 134–5, 148, 174, 264–5, 271, 301
munitions industry   108, 110, 110n, 218, 219, 220, 223, 227, 233–4
Munro, Anna   139, 139n
music   14, 117, 245, 246, 249, 250, 300
Myles, Mr   31, 80, 111, 117
Myles, Mrs   46, 63, 92, 104, 115, 121, 177, 211
Myles, Peter   50, 55, 69, 99
  arrest   177
  and conscription   140, 162
  imprisonment   180, 211, 295

N

National Industrial Conference 1919   285, 285n
nature and environment   67, 73, 125, 174, 281
   birdsong   52, 108, 119, 281, 293
   flowers   131, 146, 148–9, 168

landscape   150-1, 152-3, 168, 184, 187-8
   sea   92-3, 146, 160-1
   walking   101, 184
NCF *see* No Conscription Fellowship (NCF)
"New Town" *see* Welwyn Garden City ("New Town")
Newbold, John Turner Watson   293, 293n
Newbridge (Devon)   153, 183-4, 187-8, 192, 196
Nickels, Mr   99
Nightingale, Florence   283
No Conscription Fellowship (NCF)   xi, xii, 35, 35n, 38, 51n, 68, 111, 111n, 162
Non-Combatant Corps   xi, xii
nonconformist religion   35, 66, 131, 158, 162, 256
Normandy (Surrey)   xvi, xx, 225, 229, 232-3, 234-5, 241, 255, 257-8, 260-1, 265, 277
Northampton   xv, 35, 36

O

O'Brien Harris, Dr Mary   121
Ogilvie, Mr   272
Ogilvie, Mrs   300
Old Moore's Almanac   187, 187n
Open Brethren   35
Osborn, Mr   9, 13, 16, 19, 50, 56
Osborne, Mrs   208
Ostend   219
Oxenham, John, *Bees in Amber*   283

P

pacifism   ix, xiii-xiv, 61, 90, 91, 114, 114n, 137, 139, 139n, 296, 298 *see also* conscientious objectors
pageants   221
Palmer, Dora *see* Sunderland, Dora
Palmer, Mrs Noel   50, 257, 265
Palmer, Mrs Sydney   17, 28, 30, 138, 196
Palmer, Noel   xviii, xx, 9, 16, 16n, 50, 140, 193, 198, 202, 205, 208, 213, 215, 219, 222, 223, 243, 261, 265, 277, *304*
   lodges with Sunderlands   195, 197, 233, 247
   offers work to Frank   225, 225n, 227-8, 229, 231, 232
   starts fruit farm   225, 227, 235, 240, 257
Palmer, Sydney   xxi, 30, 32n, 35, 82, 89, 92, 105, 128, 133, 196, 232
   letter to Frank   31-2
   visits Frank   19, 51, 54

318

Palmer, William   xxi
Pankhurst, Sylvia   17, 17n, 18
Parker, Jack   69, 193, 193n, 198, 206, 209, 210, 225, 254, 255, 290, 291
Parsons, Mr   265
Pass, Bradley   255
Pass, Miss   22, 141–2, 143
peace settlement   232, 234, 237, 299, 299n
Pearce, Mr   80, 104, 262
Pearsal, Mr   258, 259
Pease, Mr   208, 277, 287
Perkins, Miss   281
Perry, Mr   214–16
Philips, Maria   222
photographs   42, 53, 54, 55, 76, 99, 132, 134, 142, 150, 156
Plasticine   98, 262
Poland   276
Ponsonby, Arthur   299, 299n
postal system   117, 141
poultry-keeping   xvi, 14, 47, 49–50, 51, 79, 90, 118, 121, 129, 138, 198, 208, 212, 241, 244, 282, 302
Pound, Mr   128
Poynting, Miss   47
preaching   66, 69, 72–3, 131
Presbyterian Church   256
Prescott, Julia   xi, xxi
Price, Mrs   2, 134, 144
prison   25, 48, 58, 67
   Bedford   xvii, 51, 76–7, 81
   chaplains   44, 55, 100, 100n
   Dartmoor   xxiv, 185, 185n, 244, 255
   food   47–8, 62
   German citizens, internment of   102, 102n
   letter-writing regulations   *43*, 116, 117, 161, 162, 210
   sentences   3–4, 23–4, 39, 51, 80, 180, 255
   St Albans prison   36
   treatment of conscientious objectors   58, 72, 185n
   visiting   44, 116, 124, 130, 136, 161–2, 163, 166
   Wandsworth   31, 33, 41, 42–3, *43*, 47–8, 54–8, 58
   Wormwood Scrubs   xv, xxiv, 7, 16, 23, 24, 25, 31, 72, 114, 180
Prisoners (Temporary Discharge for Ill-Health) Act, 1913   151, 151n
prostitution   222, 222n
Punch (magazine)   259, 259n, 260
Purdom, Mr   299

Q

Quakers   xvi, 48, 63, 121–2, 121n, 137, 137n, 255, 285, 289
   Cadbury, George   291n
   concerns   161, 161n
   Fox, George   100, 100n, 108–9
   Friends' Ambulance Unit   xv
   Friends Service Committee   276, 277
   and Garden City movement   xiii–xiv, 122, 122n
   Howgills (Meeting House, Letchworth)   61, 61n, 63, 65, 255, 281, 285, 289
   Jordans (Buckinghamshire)   100, 100n, 122n, 288
   in Letchworth   ix, xiii–xiv
   opposition to conscription   xi, 285
   prison chaplains   44, 100, 100n
   simplicity   169–70, 169n
   Whittier, John Greenleaf   137, 137n
   Woolman, John   137, 137n

R

Randolph, Mr   1
rationing   118, 123, 189–90
   coal   190, 213–14
   food   68, 68n, 89, 104, 109–10, 118, 121, 123–4, 147–8
Raven, Maud   18
Ray, Mr   50
reading
   children   85, 153, 216, 261–2
   Sunderland, Frank   48, 74, 77, 108–9, 113–14, 115–16, 123, 126, 133, 138, 142, 150, 155, 159, 166, 169–70, 176, 205, 210, 224, 242, 247, 256–7, 282, 283, 289, 303
   Sunderland, Lucy   123, 169, 170–1, 201, 216, 265, 285
Reconstruction, the   90, 90n, 118
refugees   250, 250n, 276, 279
   antipathy to   171, 219, 220, 222
   Belgian   110, 219, 224, 225, 249
   leaving Letchworth   229, 261, 267, 272, 276
   in munitions industry   110n, 223
   Serbian   218, 220, 223
religious tolerance   157–8, 160
Rent and Mortgage Restriction Act (1915)   291, 291n
Representation of the People Act 1918   106n
Reynolds, Miss   17, 80, 89, 105, 184, 185, 207

Reynolds, Miss Amy   117, 177
Rhondda, Lord (D A Thomas)   68, 68n
Rix, Mrs   219
Ross-on-Wye   255, 256, 258, 258n, 288
Royden, Agnes Maude   278, 278n
rumours   142, 143, 258, 259, 271, 291, 300
Ruskin, John   205
Russell, Bertrand   xii, 114, 114n, 278, 278n

S

Salter, Ada   265n
Salter, Dr Alfred   265, 265n, 297
schools   147, 149, 155, 157–8 *see also* Adult Schools; education
Seebohm, Frederic, *The Spirit of Christianity*   283
Selfridges   225
separation allowance   64
Sepiros family   95
Serbian refugees   218, 220, 223
Seventh Day Adventists   35, 40
sewing   ix, 22, 105, 121, 148, 211, 213
sexuality   302, 302n
Shaw, George Bernard   xx, xxv, 283
Shelley, Percy Bysshe   247, 249, 257
shops/shopping   xiii, 40, 40n, 80, 82, 89, 89n, 91, 104, 115, 140, 162, 179, 223, 225, 226, 259, 281, 292 *see also* food; rationing
Shortt, Edward (Home Secretary 1919-22)   291, 300, 301
Simmonds, Mr   83
simplicity   169–70, 169n
Sinn Féin   248–9
Skittles Temperance inn (Letchworth)   xiv, 6, 6n, 33, 50, 51, 61, 120, 208, 215, 218, 221, 222, 226, 285, 287, 290
Smith, Harvey   236
Smith, Mr   106
Snowden, Ethel   222, 222n, 279, 286
Snowden, Philip   248, 248n, 254
socialism   ix, xiii–xiv, xxv, 17–18, 38, 50, 70, 70n, 72, 77, 113–14, 231, 259–60, 270, 298 *see also* Independent Labour Party (ILP)
Society of Friends *see* Quakers
South London Unity of Total Abstinence Brothers and Sisters of the Phoenix Friendly Society   280, 280n
Spirella Hall (Letchworth)   235
Spon's Workshop Receipts (book)   129

St Albans prison   36
St Paul   77
St Quintin, Captain   10
Stacey, Mrs   85, 165, 180
Stamp, Reggie   99
Stevens, Miss   213, 285
Stone, George   78, 79
strikes   265, 267, 267n, 269–70, 271–2, 273, 296, 298
Sturge, Mary D, *Alcohol and the Human Body*   116, 116n
submarines   44–5
Summer School   58, 63
Sunderland, Alf   15–16, 25, 52, 52n, 133, 244, 292
   letter to Frank   7–8
Sunderland, Carrie   52, 52n, 79, 134, 244, 249
Sunderland, Chrissie   x, xv, 14, *53*, 75, 78, 81, 97–8, 101, 117, 135, 160–1, 196, 271, *304*
   appearance   55, 136, 137, 192, 217
   birthday   247, 250
   birthplace   198
   education   95, 157–8, 192, 298
   gardens/gardening   121, 153–4
   health and illness   xvi–xvii, 27, 29, 30, 51, 66, 73, 188, 261, 264
   letter from Frank   21
   reading   261–2
   relationship with Frank   9, 252, 253
   religion   157–8, 160
   visits Frank   133, 136, 217
   visits Katie in London   248, 253
Sunderland, Dora   x, xi, xv, xxi, 29, 30, 37, 47, *53*, 84, 87, 97–8, 101, 104, 145, 160, 169, 187, 196, 211, 245, 271, *304*
   appearance   165, 192
   birthday   87–8, 94–5
   cooking   69
   education   95, 157, 162, 165, 192, 197, 208, 233, 281
   gardens/gardening   121, 153–4
   health and illness   27, 75, 78–80, 81, 261, 264
   learns Esperanto   112, 116, 117, 138, 143, 166, 207, 220, 226–7, 245
   letter from Frank   20
   letters to Frank   12, 41, 61
   marriage   xxi, 51n
   music practice   14, 20
   reading   85, 153, 216
   relationship with Frank   9, 54, 123, 190, 252, 253
   scholarship examination   122, 144, 295, 296

visits Frank   133, 136, 209
 visits Katie in London   244, 248, 253
Sunderland, Frank   xi–xii, *xii*, xvi, xx–xxi, *304*
 absent without leave   57, 57n, 59, 69, 69n
 Army service   xi, *xii*
 arrested   ix, xv, 1
 character   xi, 119–20, 194, 247, 268
 children, relationship with   9, 54, 123, 190, 202, 252, 253, 293, 294
 and conscientious objection   ix; 'absolutist'   xv, xix–xx, 6n, 7, 26, 34, 34n, 103; family opposition to   11, 290
 courts-martial   xv, 6, 19, 20, 28, 35, 35n, 36, 64, 70–1
 depression/sadness   28, 34, 59, 151, 155, 200–1, 202, 245
 education   xi, 143
 and education of Sunderland children   149, 151, 155, 160
 Esperanto, learning   116, 133, 143, 149–50, 167, 170, 179, 181, 185, 191, 203, 212, 220, 246, 247, 252, 282
 and feminism   67, 186, 212–13, 260, 302
 and freedom   200–1, 242, 243
 and Garden City movement   126, 129
 health and illness   42, 47–8, 64, 103, 113, 124, 163, 241, 256, 268; dental problems   125, 149; fitness categorised as C3   7, 60n; neuralgia   222, 223
 humour   66n, 113, 124, 125, 129–30, 159, 163, 175–6, 185, 210, 212, 259, 263
 isolation, feelings of   7, 62, 124, 151, 181–2, 260, 267, 268–9
 in-laws, relationship with   48, 129, 130, 132, 290
 Lucy, relationship with   xi, 42, 55, 113, 128–30, 136, 143, 210, 251; concern for Lucy   39, 128–30; letters, importance of   140; psychic connection   9, 23, 24, 39; separation, effect of   14, 23, 161–2, 163, 181–2, 200–1, 251, 268–9; wedding anniversary   169, 170
 medical examinations   3, 7, 19, 70
 nature and environment, importance of   52, 67, 73, 125, 150–1
 optimism   42, 124, 167, 203, 223
 plans for future   32, 52–3, 55, 72–3, 137, 149–50, 167, 169–70, 175, 186, 204, 205, 214, 228, 236–7, 245
 politics   ix, 74, 214, 231, 245, 259–60, 270, 274, 288
 in prison: coping strategies   92–3; granted special privileges for good conduct   93–4; legal position   31–2; Wormwood Scrubs   xv, xxiv, 5, 5n, 31
 prison sentences   xv, xix–xx, 23–4, 39, 40
 reading   48, 74, 77, 108–9, 113–14, 115–16, 123, 126, 133, 138, 142, 150, 155, 159, 166, 169–70, 176, 205, 210, 224, 242, 247, 256–7, 282, 283, 289, 303
 release date   282, 283, 289, 293, 294, 296, 302
 religious faith and beliefs   xi–xii, 39, 40, 48, 55–6, 72–3, 100, 160, 223, 252
 support from Letchworth community   28, 30, 31–2, 35, 142, 143
 tribunals   xii, 8, 20, 116, 121, 122–3
 vegetarianism   2n, 3, 3n

visitors   9, 92–3, 161–2, 166, 187, 190–1, 217; Chrissie   136, 138, 217; Cubbon, Mr   278, 288; Dora   136, 138, 209; Jefferies, Miss   161, 174, 175–6; Lucy   36, 37, 46, 51, 55, 101, 103, 108, 113, 116, 124, 130, 132, 136, 138, 201, 209, 217, 243, 274; Middleton, Mrs K J   217; Morris   125, 128, 209; Myles, Peter   55; Palmer, Sydney   19, 51, 54; Tickle, Mr   180, 187, 190–1; Tickle, Mrs   187, 190–1

visits Lucy at home   27, 57n, 69

work   xi, xx–xxi, 92–3, 210, 227–8, 235, 236–7, 263, 280, 280n

Sunderland, Lucy   x, xii, xiv–xix, xx–xxi, 53, 135, 152, 304

and Adult School   xvi, 28, 46–7, 63, 85, 113, 183, 208, 211, 215; committee member   80, 89–90; Secretary   92, 145

appearance   217

Belgians, dislike of   219, 220, 222

and communal living   69, 86, 206, 300

and conscientious objection   ix, 91; family opposition to   xv, 54, 78; support for Frank   xiv, 11, 17–18, 31; writes to Home Secretary   300

cooking   115, 117, 121

death of mother   127–32

depression/sadness   47, 152, 219

and education of Sunderland children   95, 147, 154, 157–8, 192, 298

Esperanto, study of   166, 169

and feminism   x, 88, 183, 188–9, 216, 286, 300–1

Frank, relationship with   xi, 69–70, 126, 167, 169, 170, 253; concern for Frank   25, 101, 117–18, 243; letters, importance of   32, 101–2, 156, 180, 206; psychic connection   11, 50, 157, 183; separation, effect of   11–12, 17–18, 46, 47, 73, 83, 112, 126, 131, 141, 152, 156–7, 164, 168–9, 180, 182–3, 195–6, 201, 230, 232, 251, 267

Frank, visit from   27

Frank, visits to   32, 33, 37, 51, 55, 56, 77, 99, 101, 102, 108, 109, 113, 116, 120, 124, 125, 132, 136, 196, 198, 201, 209, 217, 239, 243, 274, 275

and gardening   51, 68, 78–9, 82, 121, 129, 275–6, 299–300

health and illness   xvi, 75, 76, 77, 78, 187–8, 249; colds   25, 218, 219, 230, 233; dental problems   68, 74, 125, 130, 134, 138, 145; exhaustion   46, 138; headaches   27, 33–4; holiday, benefits of   157, 161, 165, 173, 189, 196; rheumatism   253, 256; skin complaints   211, 215

holidays: in Barnstaple   xvii–xviii, 127, 128, 130, 132, 135, 143, 146, 152–3, 160–1; in London   188, 191, 193, 197–8, 225, 249; in Newbridge   183–4, 187–8, 191–4, 195–7

housekeeping   88, 105–6, 107, 108, 144, 146–7, 264–5

housing   xvi, xxi, 196, 234, 249, 254, 257, 258, 262, 275–6, 287, 291; eviction, threat of   232–3, 236, 243, 261, 265; sublets The Bungalow   127, 128–9, 130, 135, 138, 144, 146, 165

humour   69, 115, 118

lodgers   xviii, 6, 6n, 30, 40, 42, 42n, 69, 83, 86, 197, 207, 219, 221, 222, 230

loneliness   11, 81, 83, 98, 142, 245, 248
and money   56, 168, 193, 195, 235, 255, 264, 291; family income   30, 64, 69, 78, 87, 138, 165, 166, 167, 235, 255, 264, 291
and motherhood   49, 85–6, 117, 131, 134–5, 148, 174, 264–5, 271
nature and environment, importance of   168, 174, 184, 187–8
optimism   195–6, 202, 256
plans for future   32, 45, 56, 69, 152, 169, 171–2, 177, 183, 188, 201, 202, 206
politics   ix, xvi, 17, 50, 182–3, 241, 244, 287, 298
poultry-keeping   xvi, 14, 47, 49–50, 51, 79, 90, 118, 121, 129, 198, 208, 212, 241, 244, 282, 302
reading   123, 169, 170–1, 201, 216, 265, 285
religious faith and beliefs   xvi, 49, 50, 63, 131, 157–8, 162, 253–4, 281, 285, 289
strength   138, 188–9, 267
support from Letchworth community   xiv, xvi, 46, 47, 82
work   212, 216; as insurance agent   ix, xv–xvi, 7, 8, 11, 17, 22, 23, 63, 78, 92, 112, 128, 130, 165, 166, 168, 183, 186, 188, 205, 228, 235, 254; sewing   ix, 22, 79–80, 89, 105, 121, 148, 204, 211, 213, 215
Sunderland, Morris   x, xv–xvi, xx, xxi, 14, 48, 49–50, 51, *53*, 54, 87, 88, 97–8, 117, 134–5, 146, 155, 160–1, 162, 196, 198, 205, 211, 248, 249, 250, 262, 284n, 296–7, 298, *304*
appearance   156
birthday   32, 33, 35, 102, 103, 112
education   94, 101, 158, 160, 298
Frank, letter from   21
Frank, relationship with   252, 253
Frank, visits to   120, 124–5, 128, 209
Frank, writes to   104
gardens/gardening   121, 152–3
health and illness   xvi–xvii, 27, 29, 30, 73–4, 75, 77, 78–80, 81–2, 86–7, 88–9, 91, 92, 106–7, 157, 261, 266
Sunderland, Mrs (Frank's mother)   8, 48, 50–1, 79, 95, 108, 133, 229, 235, 244, 245, 247, 287, 292
Sunderland, Robert   xi, xx–xxi
Swiney, Frances, *The Awakening of Women*   300–1
Symonds, Miss   192
Symonds, Mr   19

T

Tait, Mrs   60, 61, 65
Taw (river)   147, 148, 168
Taylor, Mrs   2, 24

Telford, John, *The Popular History of Methodism*   283
Temperance movement   xiv, 116–17, 116n, 280–1, 280n
Templars (children's Temperance movement)   117
Thackeray, William Makepeace
    Pendennis   81
    Vanity Fair   77
theatre   221, 281
Theosophical Society   148, 148n, 153, 281
Thomas, D A, 1st Viscount Rhondda   68, 68n
Thomas, George   80, 157, 205, 244, 261
Thomas, Johnny   157
Thomas, Mr   30, 255
Thomas, Mrs   56, 69, 78, 82, 115, 157, 201, 204, 244
Thoreau, Henry David   xvii, 170
    Walden   133, 159, 171, 174
Tickle, Mr   40, 40n, 82, 89, 115, 162, 179, 180, 187, 190–1, 259, 281, 299
Tickle, Mrs   17, 82, 83, 85, 98, 145, 162, 187, 190–1, 301
time   256, 259
Tolstoy, Leo   216, 281, 283
town criers   147, 192–3
toys *see* games and toys
trade unions   213, 285, 285n *see also* industrial action
train travel   24, 57, 147, 154, 160–1, 161n, 197, 235, 248, 272, 276, 296
Treaty of Versailles   277n, 299n
tribunals   xi, xii, xxiii, 8, 20, 37, 111, 116, 117, 121, 122–3, 215
typewriters   195, 197, 210

U

unemployment   286
Upward, Allen, *The Divine Mystery*   257

V

Vandyke, Mrs   273
vegetarianism   xvi, 2, 2n, 13, 15, 115, 192
Veloce, Mr   11
Vickers   275
Virol   188

W

W H Smith (company)   xiii, 97, 110, 129, 133, 223
wages   214, 216, 233–4
Wale, Miss   102
Wales, Miss   250
Walkden, Miss   17, 202, 204
walking   101, 184
Wallace, Graham   283
Walworth, London   83
Wandsworth Prison   31, 33, 41, 42–3, *43*, 47–8, 54–8, 58
War Office   6, 6n, 24, 24n, 31, 36, 40
war profiteers   122–3
war workers   xvi, 110n, 213, 216, 218, 219, 220, 223, 232, 233–4, 240, 279
Wash, Henry   300
Webb, Beatrice   xx, xxv
Webb, Sydney   xx, xxv
Webster, Jean
   Daddy Longlegs   136, 136n
   Dear Enemy   136, 136n
Webster, Mr   29, 57
Webster, Mrs   6, 6n, 30, 40
Weinsteen, Mr   151
Wells, Bertha   99, 108
Wells, H G   283
   A Soul of A Bishop   100, 100n
Welwyn Garden City ("New Town")   xvi, 46–7, 46n, 55, 77, 114, 118, 121–2, 126, 132, 174, 179, 193, 213, 214, 224, 229, 230, 233, 241, 255, 257, 295, 296, 300
Wesleyan School Room (Letchworth)   276
Wesleyanism   131
Whale, Miss   254
Whiteing, Richard, *No 5 John Street*   79, 79n
Whitman, Walt   129, 166, 169, 170, 283
Whittier, John Greenleaf   137n
   Poems of the Inner Life   283
   'Snowbound'   137
Wilder, Miss   257
Wilding, Miss   202, 205, 248, 277, 297
Williams, Aneurin   221, 221n
Williams, Mr   225
Williams, Mrs   82, 114, 202, 243, 249, 272, 275, 291
Wilson, Dr   261
Wiltshire, Mr   31, 33, 137, 165, 178, 244, 248, 255, 258, 281

Wiltshire, Mrs   17, 33, 90, 121, 255
Winestein, Mrs   138
Wittimore, Mr   244
Women's Freedom League   139, 139n
women's suffrage   106, 106n, 139, 139n, 186, 244, 273
Woolman, John   137, 137n
Workers' Educational Association   184–5, 185n
Wormwood Scrubs prison   xv, xxiv, 7, 16, 23, 24, 25, 31, 72, 114, 180
Worsley, Mrs   89
Wright, Mr   37, 38, 40

Y

Young, Arthur, *Travels in France and Italy*   170

Z

Zangwill, Israel   278, 278n
Zeppelin raids   xvii, 44–5, 83, 83n
Zimmon, Mr   91

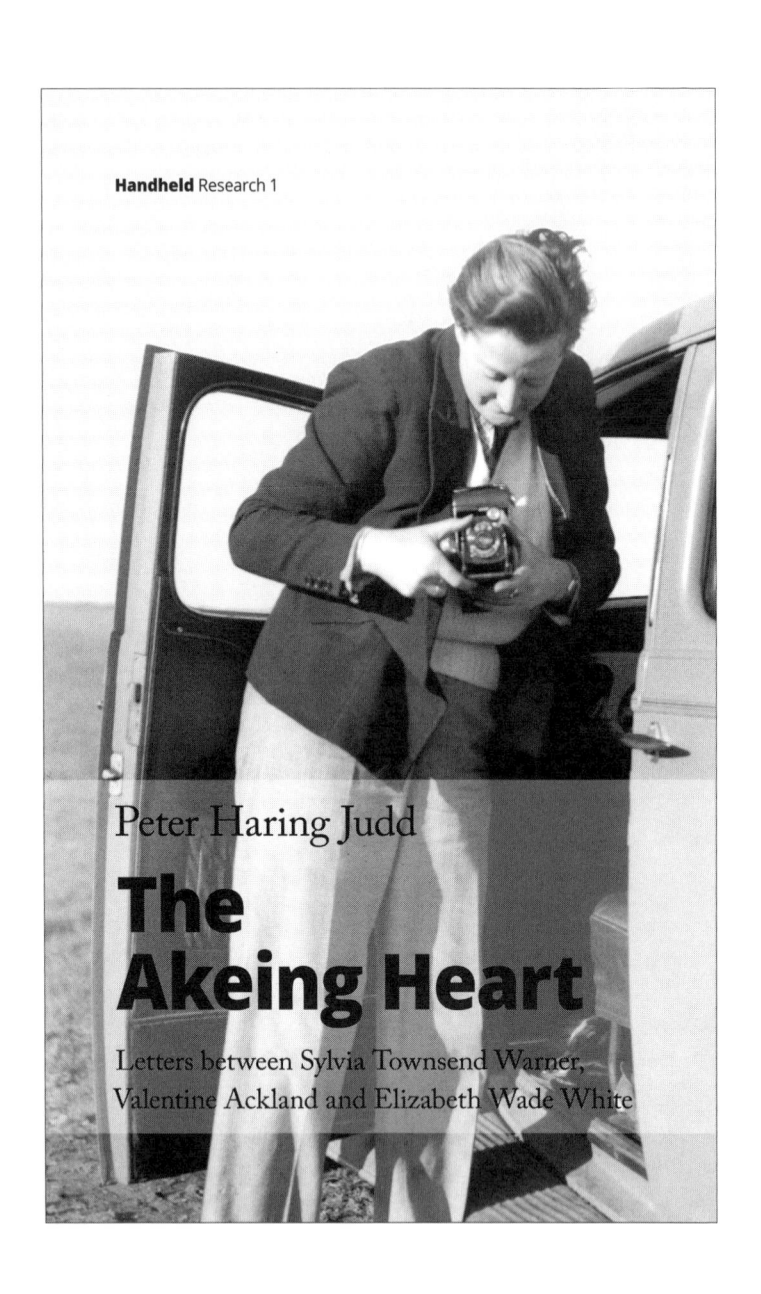

Handheld Research 1

Peter Haring Judd

The Akeing Heart

Letters between Sylvia Townsend Warner, Valentine Ackland and Elizabeth Wade White

Handheld Press 2018, £24.99
ISBN 9781999828035 hardback, also available as an ebook

The Akeing Heart

Letters between Sylvia Townsend Warner, Valentine Ackland and Elizabeth Wade White
by Peter Haring Judd (Handheld Research 1)

The Akeing Heart is the story of the tormented relationships between the British novelist and poet Sylvia Townsend Warner; her life partner the poet Valentine Ackland; the American ingénue who invaded their happiness, Elizabeth Wade White; and Elizabeth's neglected companion Evelyn Holahan. Valentine was the serial seducer, and Elizabeth the demanding lover claiming her sexuality for the first time. Sylvia kept faith in anger and despair, while Evelyn offered Elizabeth devoted fidelity to balance Valentine's romanticism.

This revised edition of correspondence over twenty years between the four women makes this book one of the finest collections of twentieth-century literary letters about love and its betrayals.

Review for this edition: 'Peter Haring Judd has curated the most thrilling, romantic and heartbreaking accounts of a major 20th century literary love story. Covering the period of the Spanish Civil War and the Second World War, in 1930s New York and Connecticut and in 1950s Dorset, this is an intense and beautifully written exploration of two decades in the lives of four women.' — *DIVA* magazine

Reviews for the 2013 edition: 'This long-hidden treasure-trove of letters, with its many wonderful new photographs and illustrations, is a revelation. The "other woman's" voice is heard, and the shape of the Warner-Ackland-White love-triangle changes subtly. *The Akeing Heart* is the most important and startling addition in decades to what we know about these perennially fascinating writers.' — Claire Harman, author of *Sylvia Townsend Warner. A Biography and The Diaries of Sylvia Townsend Warner*

'Judd's story is an engrossing one, and the best of the Warner letters evince her characteristic joy in language and observation. Most moving are her efforts to retain Elizabeth's friendship while allowing the affair to take its course.' — Michael Caines, *The Times Literary Supplement*